Reilly

Corey

SO-ADY-824

Lyndsay

Tara

Kristin Murphy

Jake

Nate Schu

Ashlee Altenbach

Justin Jorgenson

Dwyne Smith

Elinor Burkett is an award-winning journalist and the author of five previous books on topics as wide-ranging as AIDS and child sexual abuse. A former reporter for the *Miami Herald*, she has written for the *New York Times Sunday Magazine*, the *Atlantic Monthly*, *Rolling Stone*, *Mirabella*, *Metropolitan Home*, and *Elle*. Before turning to writing, she spent thirteen years as a college professor. She and her husband make their home in the Catskill Mountains of New York.

Praise for Elinor Burkett

The Right Women

"An exceptionally intelligent, humane book."
New Yorker

The Gravest Show on Earth

"Impassioned . . . takes up where *And the Band Played On* left off. . . .
Burkett writes with enormous energy and genuine outrage."
Michiko Kakutani, *New York Times*

"Searing. . . . It will likely leave you feeling satisfied or vindicated
one moment, provoked or stunned the next."
Esther Kaplan, *Nation*

"The fierceness of Burkett's mind and the fury of her reporting
are a welcome clarion call."
Peter Jaret, *San Jose Mercury News*

"Here she has written the unsaid—brilliantly."
Harper's Bazaar

The Baby Boon

"Just as a fish can't describe water, humans can't see the biases, mores,
and conventions of their own little worlds. Elinor Burkett is one of the
rare flying fish who can discern the prejudices of our own era and
describe them in colorful, often hilarious detail."
Ann Coulter

Another Planet

Also by Elinor Burkett

The Baby Boon

The Right Women

Consumer Terrorism (with Frank Bruni)

The Gravest Show on Earth

A Gospel of Shame (with Frank Bruni)

Another Planet

A Year in the Life of a Suburban High School

Elinor Burkett

HarperCollins*Publishers*

HarperCollins books may be purchased for educational, business, or sales promotional use. For information, please write: Special Markets Department, HarperCollins Publishers Inc., 10 East 53rd Street, New York, NY 10022.

FIRST EDITION

Designed by The Book Design Group

Printed on acid-free paper

Library of Congress Cataloging-in-Publication Data is available upon request.

ISBN 0-06-621148-4

01 02 03 04 05 ❖/RRD 10 9 8 7 6 5 4 3 2

For Ivan Bernstein,
Fair Lawn High School, Class of 1973

Ain't no sunshine when you're gone

Cast of Characters

ASHLEE ALTENBACH: *bouncy and garrulous senior*

JAKE ANDERSON: *musician and member of the gifted-and-talented program*

BEN BASTYR: *sophomore class clown and school videographer*

ANNA BICAN: *singer, actress and girlfriend of Nick Olson*

MATT BROWN: *cocaptain of the football team*

NICK BUSSE: *angry young man, on a special study program at a local community college*

MARISSA CLAUSEN: *leading Goth*

KATIE COOK: *varsity soccer goalie, former team cocaptain*

TINA FARRELL: *queen of the miniskirt*

JAYNE GARRISON: *linchpin of the "alternative" crowd*

LISA GILBERT: *aspring actress and member of the gifted-and-talented program*

CHRISTY GOLD: *daughter of the youth pastor at Friendship Church*

JUSTIN JORGENSON: *member of the gifted-and-talented program and the pep band*

KATIE KEOUGH: *member of the gifted-and-talented program, a modern-day hippie*

RYAN LANGHORST: *quiet Focus student*

REILLY LIEBHARD: *the school genius and a member of the pep band*

TONY LORENZ: *cocaptain of the basketball team, best friend of Eric Prchal*

TOM MAUST: *president of the student council*

SHANNON MCGINNIS: *vice president of the student council, Miss Teen Minneapolis*

ZACH MOSES: *cocaptain of the football team*

KRISTIN MURPHY: *senior living on her own, in drug recovery*
ROGER MURPHY: *only black male student in the school until midyear*
NICK OLSON: *president of the chess club, a friend of Roger Murphy*
ANDY OTTOSON: *student theatrical lighting designer, son of an English teacher*
ERIC PRCHAL: *cocaptain of the basketball team, best friend of Tony Lorenz*
LYNDSAY SCHUMACHER: *cheerleader, student council member*
NATE SCHWEICH: *Special Education student, manager of the football team*
DWYNE SMITH: *midyear transfer student from inner-city Minneapolis*
SCOTT VIG: *Native American student, a social leader of the school*
PETE WILLIAMS: *Roger Murphy's closest friend*

Staff

JOHN BENNETT: *football coach and guidance counselor*
BILL BOND: *staff development specialist, former English teacher*
LORI BOYNTON: *assistant principal*
MARA COREY: *first-year English teacher*
MIKE CARR: *first-year Social Studies teacher*
PAULA GAFFNEY: *Social Studies teacher and girls' soccer coach*
DUANE "GOLDY" GOLDHAMMER: *campus police officer*
JOE GORACKE: *veteran Social Studies teacher*
KATIE HALLBERG: *director of the gifted-and-talented program*
TOM HASSIG: *choir director*
MARY HAUGEN: *director of activities and athletics*
JEFF HOEG: *young English teacher*
RON LACHELT: *veteran Biology teacher*
CRAIG OLSON: *principal*
RICK SOHLER: *senior guidance counselor*
LES SONNABEND: *superintendent of schools*
SARA STREGE: *English teacher, the "bad girl" of the faculty*
MARY WENNER: *attendance secretary*

Noon, Monday,
August 2, 1999

More than three months had passed since the bullets ricocheted off the walls of the library at Columbine High School, striking terror into the nation, and since Littleton, Colorado entered the pantheon of public horrors—alongside the World Trade Center, the *Challenger* disaster, and the Sixteenth Street Baptist Church in Birmingham, Alabama. Americans staggered in confusion at the latest assault on their innocence.

Scores of journalists had descended on the once complacent suburb, holding out the tantalizing prospect of healing insight. They emerged with details about . . . trenchcoats. Pundits had transmogrified old-fashioned schoolyard bullies into well-scrubbed parodies of the Crips and the Bloods and converted Goth, the latest teen fashion statement, into a satanic cult. When they decamped for a fresher story, they left us hanging with shards of half-truths about music and style and adolescent angst.

You didn't have to be a seventeen-year-old to know that that cruel parody of high school life was an empty promise. But perhaps you had to be a seventeen-year-old to make sense out of those jumbled images.

I wasn't seventeen years old, and I was under no illusions that I could unravel the unfathomable, that I could divine a single crisp explanation to a seemingly inexplicable reality. Obsession, however, is the occupational hazard of journalists, so that afternoon I flew to Minneapolis to go back to high school, to linger for a year in the halls and malls where America's Dylan Klebolds and Eric Harrises spend their days.

A member of the national chorus that was speaking in a single, almost desperate voice, I was driven by a single question: "What's going on in our suburban high schools?"

Inside the walls of Prior Lake High School—a typical suburban high school remarkably like Columbine—I hoped to glean at least the beginnings of an answer.

6:45 a.m., Thursday, September 2, 1999

Perhaps it was the utter stillness of the old building, broken only by the echoes of a handful of teachers tacking up posters to try to mask the reality of cold concrete block walls. Or the fact that the floors, usually dulled by a patina of dried splashes of Dr. Pepper, ground-in chewing gum, doughnut crumbs, and the scuff marks of 2,000 shoes, gleamed from their summer waxing. Or that the tread of the teachers arriving in ones and twos was a lively staccato, rather than a lugubrious beat.

But at that hour—before Katie Couric beamed her first smile of the day at the nation, even before all the newspapers had been flung onto suburban lawns—Prior Lake High School felt suffused with possibility.

Or maybe that was simply Ron Lachelt's romantic view of what it meant to return to school—to start out fresh, to look out over shining young faces and . . . hope. Hope that the alert-looking girl in the back row wouldn't start dating some jerk and blow off her homework. Hope that the boy who seemed so excited about his Biology class wouldn't spend the trimester sleeping because he would decide to work nights to save up for a new car. Hope that the district would receive a financial windfall so he could thumb through the equipment catalogues that had stacked up all summer without feeling like a fool. Hope that a bunch of politicians would stop telling him how to teach. Mostly, hope that at least some of his students would find the dignity and promise he had found in learning.

The emptiness of a school building on the first day of school is vast enough to accommodate endless illusions.

Ron Lachelt was an unlikely teacher-philosopher. As he lumbered into his Biology classroom—his arms bulging, his back perfectly straight—there was nothing about him to suggest Deep Thinker. He looked more like a Green Beret, a weight lifter or a deer hunter, all of which, in fact, he also was. And dressed carefully, intentionally, in a tie and jacket, he also bore little resemblance to the image of the teen idol he had become over eighteen years of teaching. At the age of fifty, he was way too old, and way too fond of forcing kids to dissect cats, of all messy and horrible tasks, to be worshipped by high school students.

But Lachelt *ruled*, at least that was the word at Prior Lake High School. Alternately, Mr. Lachelt was *God*.

In those last moments of quiescence before all hell would break loose with a thousand students careening through the hallways, yelling out the news about Shannon and Jon, slamming their lockers and tossing plastic water bottles across the corridors, God planted himself firmly at the door of his Biology room and let his energy build. In another hour, he would usher in twenty-six impressionable young sophomores who had been advised, lectured and warned that high school would not be like middle school. No more coddling. No more kids' stuff. You're moving into the "real world," and now everything you do actually counts. Lachelt beamed confidently. He would provide lesson number one.

Across the corridor, Mara Corey was fighting to maintain her composure, to project even a modicum of Lachelt's easy air to camouflage her anxiety. She had already written her name on the blackboard, and erased it, three times. Mrs. Corey. Mara Corey. Ms. Corey. She had rehearsed her opening lines, rechecked the course standards sheets stacked on her desk, read over her seating chart—and she was still sweating. If she fooled her students, it would only be because they were incapable of considering the possibility that a grown-up could be terrified of them.

Corey, who could have been a queen-size model—creamy skin, lustrous hair, and a cherubic face—was an oddball among high school teachers, who tend to cherish memories of their own days as students, as the athletes or student council members who ruled their schools, as science nerds who had been inspired by Physics teachers. Corey harbored not an iota of such nostalgia. "To say that I was bored in high school is to ignore the fact that I didn't give a crap," she said bluntly. "And I was not inspired by any teachers. I hoped they would inspire me, but they did not."

Intent on becoming the teacher she had never had, Corey, 28, had taken a $4,000 pay cut from her job as a waitress to join the English faculty at Prior Lake. Her nervousness that morning was not simple first-year teacher jitters, nor was it fear that she would prove unable to teach kids to construct college-level term papers or extract the symbolism from Ernest Hemingway. She was on the lookout for the young Mara Coreys who needed her help; she was terrified that she would let them down.

Mike Carr, the other new teacher in her part of the building, offered little comfort. Where Corey was all the sharp edges of internal struggle, Carr was entirely smooth. Blond and wiry, he was easy with, and on, himself. His arms swung loosely, his moods flowed comfortably, and he spent not a moment of the day in self-flagellation.

High school had been the high point of Carr's life, and he couldn't imagine a better place to remain. Never much of a student, he had been tethered to Bloomington-Jefferson High School by the camaraderie and excitement of school sports. An Eagle Scout and basketball player, he had managed to get through Bloomington without puffing on a single cigarette, allowing a drop of liquor to pass his throat, or trying even the mildest drug. In his senior year, he had attended every school athletic competition, whether at home or away. "That was the thing to do," he said, almost charmingly oblivious to the reality that most of his classmates had had somewhat different notions of their social obligations.

On that first morning of classes at Prior Lake, Carr had breezed into work, his carefully calculated outfit—a white long-sleeved Polo shirt, black suit pants, Greg Norman shoes, and an expensive tie his mother had bought him for the occasion—the only evidence that he viewed the day as anything other than normal. "I want to look sharp," he said, bouncing slightly on the balls of his feet at the thought of the coming pep fest. "I'm not nervous. Why be nervous on the first day of school?"

At the far end of the corridor, Jeff Hoeg, the sort of postfeminist young man who has no trouble discussing his feelings, was having butterflies of his own. It wasn't that Hoeg had never faced a room full of judgmental teenagers before. At the age of thirty-one, he was a five-year veteran. But, scheduled to teach Honors students, he was worried that they would know more than he did.

The night before, he had barely slept, lying in bed rehearsing his opening speech again and again. When he awoke at 5:30 A.M., the tape was still running. He had dressed carefully in the new khaki pants and Tommy shirt he had bought for the occasion at the Mall of America. The name on the shirt was no accident. "Kids love brand names," he said. "When I wear Polo, or Tommy, or Abercrombie, they always notice. Many students focus more on my clothes than my classes."

That morning, he had pulled into the faculty parking lot just after the cochair of the English department, whose 6:30 A.M. arrival was a benchmark for the teachers. His first stop was his classroom—to throw away the dregs of the last Diet Coke of the previous afternoon. His second stop was the teachers' lounge—to buy his first Diet Coke of the new morning. All that remained was to check his class lists for students he might remember from the year before, or students about whom he had been forewarned.

Suddenly, the din filtered into the building, starting as a low rumble, as if a Mack truck had veered too close to the school. Then it built, in pitch and intensity. Hoeg smiled. It was time. Tacking a note to his door, a reminder that homeroom had been canceled in favor of the traditional Welcome Back pep fest, he glanced back at his classroom before joining the festivities in the gym.

High schools aren't exactly cozy places, warm environments that invite contemplation and discussion. The lighting is harsh, the combination desk/chairs cramped and unyielding. When you add the bells and the hall monitors, you have sent a pretty clear message: No one in his right mind would be there if he did not *have* to be. So teachers spend hours decorating—*humanizing*—their rooms. Corey had plastered hers with *The Simpsons* cartoons. Lynn Lally, whose English classroom sat between Corey's and Hoeg's, had converted her space into a shrine to Elvis: a life-size cardboard King sat in the corner, a green ELVIS PRESLEY BLVD. street sign hung over her blackboard, and her walls were swathed with Elvis photographs, posters and the classic Elvis on black velvet. Ron Lachelt kept his space low-key, an array of animal skulls and a poster reading, "She Who Throws Mud Loses Ground" suggesting his priorities.

Hoeg had designed a bulletin board that matched famous authors with their works and spent hours rearranging the furniture in the small space. But nothing could hide the reality of three white walls and one glaring orange one without a single window—or the orange industrial carpet that no one would dare touch with a bare foot. Then his gloomy expression shifted into an upbeat smirk, as if a personal pep talk had just jolted through his body.

"To be a great teacher, you have to capture all your students on the first day, the first minute, the first second," he said, steaming down the stairs. "Those first impressions I give are as important as the first impressions the students give to me."

Chapter One

7:40 A.M., **Thursday,**
September 2, 1999

Most adult residents of Prior Lake, Minnesota, were still sweating through their early morning jogs along the mist-covered lake, their offices in downtown Minneapolis still dark. But when Roger Murphy and Nick Olson tooled into the parking lot at Prior Lake High School on an already-stifling fall morning, they were late—willfully, proudly, almost gleefully, so. Showing up five minutes after the bell on the first day of school might not be much by the standards of youthful rebels of other generations. But in a world in which the most minor of sins—the whiff of cigarette smoke on a jacket, the display of a Playboy Bunny symbol on the back pocket of your jeans—provokes the secular equivalent of hellfire and damnation, there's not much room left for penny-ante insubordination.

As the radio blared yet another debate about Jesse Ventura, Minnesota's new governor, the two boys trolled the parking lot in Rosebud, Nick's 1979

Volare, looking for mooring in a crowded and chaotic harbor: Ford Explorers dusty from racing the back roads, sparkling new trucks with cellular phones, bruised economy cars with prom garters dangling from the mirrors and older sedans—Delta 88s, Chrysler New Yorkers, Oldsmobile Cutlasses—that were obviously recycled family cars.

Roger and Nick, both seniors, had been friends since their freshman year, when they'd met in Physical Science class. Even in those days, Nick, who bore a passing resemblance to Alfred E. Neuman and whose humor was a postmodern version of MAD magazine, was a serious chess nerd. Roger was that scary kid who'd just transferred back to Prior Lake after eight years in the inner city. Their friendship had been cemented the day Nick spilled rubbing alcohol on a lab counter and set it on fire. The teacher assumed that Roger—Roger Mohammed Murphy—the only black male student in the school, was the culprit. Roger, who favored dreadlocks, dark shades and an ever-changing collection of the punk version of baubles and bangles designed to mock bourgeois jewelry, was always the culprit, although he was never sure whether that assumption was provoked by his race or the fact that he was a serious Metalhead.

Roger and Nick had spent much of the summer weaving Odyllic Forces and following the Road of the Beast to the Path of Power and the Inner Voice—which means they'd been playing White Wolf role-playing games. The first day of school could hardly compete with their efforts to strengthen the Gauntlet in order to protect Earth from the other Realms. They knew they were *supposed* to be thrilled, to be fired up with Rah, Rah, Go Lakers, and isn't it great that the first football game was on Friday. They'd heard all the hype and seen all the movies. To them, that stereotype was just another indication of the utter stupidity of adults. "Pep fests are the Jock-capades," said Nick. "And look at us. Nobody would ever confuse us with Jocks."

Once a sleepy town, Prior Lake had been transformed with the construction of the massive Bloomington Ferry Bridge in 1995 that opened up the empty land south of the Minnesota River to the sprawl of the Twin Cities. Where the 1,600-acre pristine lake that wound through the center of town had been dotted with cottages, its shores were now lined with cavernous custom contemporaries with soaring ceilings, sweeping lawns and a minimum of three living rooms each. Suburbanites charmed by Prior Lake's small-town atmosphere were decimating it by razing corn fields and old frame farmhouses to make way for $300,000 McMansions. On warm summer afternoons, the lake itself resembled a parking lot during a boat show. The median house price in town had risen to $170,000, $50,000 above the national average. The median household income, $75,000, was almost twice the national figure.

The local economy was booming: students delivering pizzas earned $13 an hour, and Burger King was offering signing bonuses to would-be assistant managers. Minnesota's state coffers were so full that Ventura had just defied governmental gravity by sending money *down* to the taxpayers.

So, few sixteen-year-old students were forced to survive without their own cars, and on the first day of classes, they had parked their vehicles in the designated student area, in the teachers' lot, the visitors' spaces, on the grass, and in front of concrete blocks holding up the streetlights. A 1989 Ford Tempo, its stickers saucily declaring its owner a "White Trash Princess" and a "Skinny Little Bitch," hogged two spaces. And a filthy Pathfinder, with Tinky Winky, the recently outed gay Teletubby hanging in a noose from his mirror, a rubber duckie biting his crotch, adorned the lawn dividing the lot from the street. Only the four official handicapped spaces were empty, but even Nick and Roger wouldn't have crossed that line.

The two finally found an unattended swath of sod and sauntered through the heavy glass doors of the cafeteria onto the ground floor of their school. That's when the racket hit. "Fuck, a pep fest," Roger growled. Reeling from a hangover, he was in no condition to endure a pep rally. Then again, Roger was *never* in any condition to endure a pep rally. "Think about it," he said, his tone caustic as usual. Roger's fierce intellect was ladened with the darkest of humor, but inevitably delivered with a gentle smile. "Mandatory pep. And the educational value of this is. . . . what?"

As he and Nick made their way through the cafeteria and into Jerabek Hall, also known as the Gold Gym, ignoring a solid wall of showcases filled with the school's athletic trophies, they passed two boys moving in the opposite direction, sneaking out to escape the Banditos, the mini pep band that had just finished off the school song ("We are the sons and daughters true of our Prior Lake High") and was moving into their version of "Wild Thing."

The Banditos' rendition of "Wild Thing" was one of those traditions that had no relationship to any known reality, past or present. Yet no one seemed to find it peculiar that in 1999, sixteen white Anglo kids swathed in serapes and sombreros chased each other around while playing a song performed in 1965 by the Troggs, a band few had ever heard of.

Roger and Nick followed the blare of the horns and saxophones through the double doors into the gym and headed up the shaky bleacher aisles toward the aerie that was the domain of their clan. Their belated journey to the cheap seats drew frank stares and bemused gazes from the Abercrombie & Fitch loyalists whose waters parted as they made that long trek. The crowd rippled with a complicated emotional tug between envy of their courage and disdain for Roger and Nick's alienness. Huddled together on the sidelines, the teachers were too caught up in their own faded but golden memories of high school to pay much attention.

Rising above them on three sides, stands of bleachers shuddered under the force of kilotons of adolescent gravity, of the ordinary shifting and trading of seats, of the kicking and stomping essential to any successful pep event. Even without sight or sound, the gym would have been a dead giveaway. It reeked of a high school horde, exuding the odor of three decades of bygone athletes, redolent of a sweaty energy peculiar to the young. The gym's concrete walls and towering ceiling seemed designed to amplify the roar of a thousand teenagers struggling to hear the latest gossip over the squealing of microphones, the clatter and chatter and amplified cheers.

Roger and Nick had just shoved past the resident Deadhead, who sat reading Ken Kesey's *Sometimes a Great Notion*, when the cheerleaders began leading the students, class by class, through the ritual response cheer, an exercise in interclass rivalry. "Zero, Zero," the seniors erupted just as Roger and Nick reached their destination.

Their friends, swathed in a dozen varieties of mall punk, smiled in frank admiration at their tardiness. Jayne Garrison signaled her solidarity by heaping more insults on the young women leading the juniors in their deafening, "Zero One, Zero One." Jayne knew full well what the next line was, but before the sophomores could utter a peep, she glanced at her boyfriend and bellowed, "Go, cheerleaders," at the top of her lungs. The teachers gathered at the edge of the bleachers shot her the types of disapproving glances adults deem sufficient to control teenagers. In Jayne's case, they were not. With hair that changed color and shape almost daily and thirty-nine-inch bell-bottoms, Jayne tried to strike the pose of a bad girl, but it was clearly an effort, a thin patina removable with the gentlest of scraping. The cheerleaders, however, were her symbol of everything that was wrong about modern America.

Lanky Pete Williams, who'd managed to cut every pep fest the year before, shot Nick and Roger a stoned smile of approval. Roger's closest friend, Pete was a member of the Special Education program—his "disability" one of the latest adolescent diagnoses, ODD, oppositional defiance disorder. "Oppositional and defiant, isn't that the definition of a teenager?" he asked, his voice dripping with sarcasm. "But I belong in Special Ed. I was born without the 'playing the game' gene."

The "alternative" kids, a tiny clique of loners and druggies, Goths and Metalheads, toted heavy chips on their shoulders. Their numbers had shrunk with the graduation of most of Prior Lake's punks two years earlier. And the final months of the previous year, the months after the slaughter at Columbine, had been a nightmare. The *Minneapolis Star-Tribune* had run dozens of stories warning adults to beware of students who spiked their hair, or painted their fingernails with black polish. The assistant principal had told them to forget the shades because teachers needed to be able to see their eyes. The school cop didn't even try to pretend that he wasn't them around the building. They'd heard the message loud and clear: You look like potential Dylan Klebolds.

For most of their classmates, the massacre at the Colorado high school had receded into the realm of ancient history. But Pete, who admitted that he would clearly have won any "The Student Most Likely to Blow Up the School" competition, wondered if the teachers and administrators would still watch him as if convinced he were hiding a weapon. Would they measure his pocket chains, which were to be no more than six inches long, or hassle him about the spikes on his jacket? Would he and his friends survive another year at PLHS?

The bleachers below him were a classic lesson in social geography, and a virtual marketing map. Students on the top tiers—musicians and drama kids, for the most part—wore Murderers or Misfits T-shirts, not Jansport, and used Manic Panic on their hair instead of mousse. The rows in front of them belonged to the hip-hoppers, boys sporting new FUBU sweatshirts and baggies with size stickers still on the legs. Their attitude was as ghetto as boys who'd never been near the ghetto could possibly conjure. They spilled over into the Asian gang, a coterie of eight or ten Cambodians and Hmong, most members of the school's break-dancing troupe, The Flying Noodles.

Off to one side, a knot of active Christian kids, stalwarts of Friendship Church, an evangelical bulwark on the outskirts of town, clustered around the youth minister's daughter. Like most suburbs, Prior Lake liked to think of itself as a traditional community where families played together and neighbors spent Sunday morning in prayer. But that was a reassuring illusion. One-third of the students were lucky to sit down to dinner with their families even one night a week. And while almost all professed a belief in God, fewer than 15 percent of the students attended church regularly, most only because their parents forced them to do so. The handful of teenagers firmly embedded in their family's faith tried to integrate themselves into the student body, but the Bibles they carried in their backpacks, in the pockets where their classmates stashed cigarettes, rolling papers, or the latest copy of *Playboy*, were a heavy stigma.

Tommy Hilfiger, Polo, Eddie Bauer and Billabong dominated the makeshift podium and the lower seats, the preferred brands of the school elite, which wore its confidence as naturally as its Nikes: preppies and partiers and preppy partiers across the whole spectrum of cool, from would-be frat boys to the prim president of the senior class. A sea of vivid blue, green and yellow tie-dye glared unnaturally in the midst of those muted tones, the shirts of the girls' soccer team, declaring "Champions Unite." The soccer girls radiated the same pride of ownership, with much the same bravado, over their school as the football or basketball players.

Eric Prchal and Tony Lorenz sprawled on the front bleachers, Tony's eyes fixed on Lyndsay Schumacher, a tiny blond cheerleader who'd just caught his interest. Loose and handsome, Eric and Tony seemed to have all the "right stuff" to rule the school. Tony played football, Eric had a seat on the student council, and they were cocaptains of the basketball team. But those credentials, mediated by adults, actually reduced their panache. The real upper crust, Prior Lake's own Brahmins, refused to play the game. Students like Scott Vig and Tina Farrell, who wouldn't have been caught dead seeking the approval of grown-ups, or confining their lives to their petty rules, were the arbiters of social superiority.

The most telling visual divide was not between social groups—between Jocks and Wiggers, Preps, Punks, Burnouts, Rednecks, Sluts and Goths. It was between the sexes. The girls, who had devoted their middle-school years to the eradication of split ends and whiteheads, had graduated to antifashion. Buff was in, but few flaunted new clothes or freshly styled hair. The boys had become the peacocks, sporting earrings, bleached hair, designer hair gel, and perfectly crafted outfits. No self-respecting male teenager of their fathers' generation would have spent the last week of August shopping for new clothes, or the morning before school preening in front of a mirror. But times had changed, as boys learned from gangsta rappers, Latin lovers and boy toys the prowess of the male sex symbol.

When the final notes of "Wild Thing" faded, the cheerleaders erected their classic pyramids, undulating geometric formations of girls garbed in flared blue-and-gold microskirts that would have been right in style in 1957. Lyndsay Schumacher, the 1999 SnoBall princess, tossed her ponytail with the braggadocio of decades of cheerleaders, her excitement unmistakable, her pep not quite infectious. It was only the first day of her senior year, but she was already suffering from premature nostalgia at the prospect of its passing. "I know I'm not going to want it to end," she said breathlessly.

Lyndsay had been at school for almost an hour by the time Roger and Nick showed up, although she was not a regular early riser. At the end of her junior year, however, she'd panicked at the thought of missing out on something—anything—in high school and had run for student council, tried out for cheerleading and applied to be a student peer counselor. She faced a marathon schedule of meetings, practices, games and classes that left few holes for obligations like homework.

That morning, Lyndsay had been due at a student council meeting at 7 A.M. sharp, and she knew that such expectations were flouted at students' peril. Mary Haugen, the student council advisor and the school's athletic and activities director, was a stickler about tardies, and no one—student or faculty—willingly risked Haugen's wrath.

Haugen—for whom an evening "out" usually meant attending a school dance, overseeing a football game or leading a student workshop—was an adult version of perky Tracy Flick, Reese Witherspoon's character in the movie *Election*, and was equally serious about school spirit. She was Prior Lake's "other principal," the virtual dean of the extracurricular facets of the school, although woe unto those who used the word "extracurricular." "Cocurricular," she corrected them, unwilling to concede that, say, geometry, or history, might be more central to a school's mission than student council.

By the time Lyndsay arrived for the early-morning meeting, the air in the room was already crackling with tension. Haugen had instructed all student council members to wear their yellow council T-shirts for the first day of school. A cocaptain of the girls' soccer team had appeared instead in her soccer shirt, a reminder that the girls were playing Rochester that evening. "You're ruining the unity of this group," Haugen had berated her. The three dozen other students in the room had dug into their papers or fixed their eyes on the walls. Nobody had dared argue.

Over the summer, the student council executive board members had worked feverishly to prepare for the new year. Shannon McGinnis, the vice president, had spent at least one day each week organizing the group's first summer meeting, ordering food for a barbecue for new students, leading sophomores on a tour of the building, and helping plan the first assembly. By August, student council had become her full-time job, as the executive board ironed out the final details of the perfect kick-off to the new year. Their plans had been ambitious: The entire school would assemble on the football field, where the Banditos and the cheerleaders would whip some school spirit. The year-long theme, "The Sky's the Limit," emblazoned on an enormous banner, would be launched with élan in the final moments of the pep fest. The students from each class would line up to spell out their graduation years, and a hot-air balloon would loft the principal into the sky.

The day had turned out to be too windy for hot-air balloons, even for outdoor assemblies. Most of the students were too busy talking or slurping back Mountain Dew to pay much attention to the cheerleaders. And when the student council president opened the ceremonies by announcing the year's theme and proclaiming, "There are no such things as problems; there are only opportunities," the applause fell far short of deafening.

The half-hour rally wound up being more informational than inspirational, to the surprise of virtually no one under the age of twenty. Craig Olson, the bearded and soft-spoken principal, introduced the new teachers, then moved on to the predictable housekeeping matters: how to deal with problem schedules and broken lockers; admonitions about parking, safety, and the other myriad regulations that govern high school life. By the time the student president rose again with a final motivational message about achieving unimagined heights, the students were already lined up in the aisles, fighting to escape to class.

The Banditos fired up their horns and saxophones once more, and the crush at the doors became a parody of the entrance to a Backstreet Boys concert. The school, opened in 1969, was a long, low tan structure that blended almost seamlessly into the flat, tan landscape of the northern plains. Originally designed with an interior courtyard to serve as a student gathering place, the building had lost that amenity to one of a series of additions that had been tacked on to accommodate a skyrocketing student body. Everyone knew that only a demographic catastrophe could stifle the need for a new school. The year before, the freshman class had been exiled to the middle school. Still, gridlock choked the narrow passageways.

Prior Lake Police Officer Duane Goldhammer—Goldy to the students—stood to one side of the gym entrance, watching his new charges file out, his roguish grin balancing the gun in his fanny pack and the shield on his belt. Goldy had been drafted by the New England Patriots straight out of college but had joined the police force when he realized he was suffering from what he called a "serious lack of talent." His assignment was to patrol the halls of the high school and middle school. At the other exit, the chemical health counselor sternly scanned the deluge for students whose pupils looked suspiciously dilated, whose gait a tad unsure.

Teachers who had not scurried off to their rooms for the first period herded the students along. Most moved in slow motion, which was hardly surprising, given the hour. Dozens of studies had proven that American teenagers don't get enough sleep, and that a later school start time would improve their ability to learn. But schools aren't ruled by educational logic. "Beans, buses and balls"—food service, transportation and athletics—control them, and the buses that had dropped off the high school students were already picking up their second load for the elementary schools.

Untangling themselves from their serapes, Reilly Liebhard and Justin Jorgenson headed for the back stairs, hoping to hand in their Banditos uniforms before the first class bell. Their choice of steps wasn't random, or even a quick assessment of the relative congestion of the two stairways. In high school, *everything* has meaning, and, at Prior Lake, the front stairs—adorned with a poster reading "JUST IMAGINE—What It Would Be Like If We Replaced All of Our Put-downs and Teasing with Compliments and Smiles"—were the domain of the confident. Someone had already scrawled a graffiti response to the cheery message: "Then we'd be bored!"

The back staircase, leading to the band and choir rooms, was the turf of arty kids, Nerds and Outcasts trying to avoid being jostled by the Jocks. Reilly raced up it at his normal pace, which would have put most New Yorkers to shame. Justin dawdled, even on a day that was supposed to be the turning of his new leaf. A member of Synergy, the school's program for gifted kids, he had slacked off for almost two years. However, he'd vowed that he'd end his high school career by dazzling his teachers with brilliant, insightful work—to the dubious stares of his friends.

Even as Reilly sprinted past his fellow Bandito, his mind and mouth kept pace as he offered up a running commentary on the pep fest, which he likened to a Fascist Party rally. "Why was everyone shouting?" he asked. "Because they're Lakers. Lakerness—what a good reason to allow yourself to be manipulated. We're the best, just because we say so. What the hell is a 'Laker' anyway? Just a convenient way of making people into little interchangeable building blocks for a more easily controlled society." He finally took a breath, utterly unaware that his political analysis sounded entirely out of place coming out of the mouth of a seventeen-year-old with a seventeen-inch neck and a forty-four-inch chest, or that no one around him could keep up with his verbal barrage.

His classmates had given up trying to keep up with Reilly years earlier, when he ambled into his first-grade classroom at Westwood Elementary School already able to read, write, and recite the names of the presidents and all the state capitals.

When the other kids raced outside for recess, Reilly stayed inside, reading. In second grade, the school organized the children to collect the metal rings from pop cans to raise money for Ronald McDonald House. "So, Reilly, how many tabs do you think we've collected?" the principal asked Reilly casually one morning, as the boy emptied his offerings into the collective barrel.

"Let me think about it," he responded earnestly, not understanding the concept of a rhetorical question. That afternoon, he began weighing small quantities of tabs and persuaded a maintenance worker to heft the entire barrel onto a scale. At home, he performed his calculations and, the next morning, proudly provided the startled principal with an answer to his question.

"Mommy, Mommy, something's the matter with me," he grumbled to his mother, Joy. The other kids hated him. He was too young to understand what the word "genius" meant.

When Reilly caught sight of another THE SKY IS THE LIMIT banner, he was off and running again. "Last year's theme was 'Dynamite Comes in Small Packages,' an unfortunate choice given what happened at Columbine," he continued, noting an irony that had escaped every other member of the school community. "So I have to wonder, this year, what disaster might fall out of the heavens."

For most of the seniors, being back in school was disaster enough, a return to adolescence after months of adulthood. Teenagers, after all, are the engine that drives the suburban economy, and most of the upper classmen had just spent their summer vacations managing retail clothing stores, driving heavy equipment, caring for children in local daycare centers, stocking supermarkets and running all-nite quick marts. They'd earned serious paychecks and been treated as responsible human beings by their bosses. Few did more than sleep at home. They woke themselves up, grabbed doughnuts on their way to work, ate dinner with their friends after work and then hung out—at the movies, along the lake or at bonfires in the country.

The instant they set foot on school grounds, however, they were catapulted back into childhood: their every movement, every article of clothing, every odor was scrutinized and judged according to somebody else's rules. They could be disciplined for carrying CD players in their backpacks, for wearing too-short skirts or forgetting to turn off their beepers. If a teacher caught what she believed was a whiff of marijuana on their clothing, they could be sent to the campus cop. Their movement through the school—from class to class, activity to activity, lunch to the library— was tracked, hour by hour. Administrators intervened in their personal arguments, their lives were ruled by bells. Ultimately, they were powerless to do anything but whine.

Dashing to change out of her cheerleading outfit and into her student council T-shirt, Lyndsay Schumacher wasn't thrown off-stride by that trade-off for a nanosecond. "This is MY year," she gushed, the pride of having reached the pinnacle of Prior Lake society vibrant in her voice. "I'm a senior. I don't have to bow to anyone. I can walk in front of the lunch line if I want to."

As a student leader, a ruler rather than a lowly serf, Shannon McGinnis, Miss Teen Minneapolis as well as vice president of the student council, strode through Prior Lake High School with that same sense of satisfaction. The All-American girl, with a Yankee bearing that cried out for loafers with tassels, Shannon kept her back straight, her head up. Her confidence was so strong that she felt no need to wear even a hint of makeup or coif her hair. "I can go anywhere and teachers don't question me," she said warmly. "They know I'm a leader in the school. I can feel their respect."

Tom Maust, the president of the student council, was more cocky still about his position, swaggering with the swelled chest of a young man convinced he had earned the respect of his peers. His election had carried no such message, although Tom, who was stubby and still hadn't outgrown his acne, seemed either indifferent or oblivious to that reality. How did he capture the political pinnacle of student power? "Through hard work, determination, weaseling, experience, knowledge, weaseling, kindness, compassion, weaseling and just a little bit of luck," another senior summed it up succinctly, reflecting a widespread sentiment.

Beneath the easy self-assurance of the student leaders—indeed, of many of the seniors—roiled a quiet anxiety. For the first time in their short lives, time was running out. In a few months, an era would close and, with it, the attendant possibilities and promises. Had they had enough fun during their final years of childhood? Accomplished enough? Had they made a decisive enough mark to launch themselves into the future? All over school, the phrase "This is my last chance" was on seniors' minds, if not on their lips. The fear of regret was palpable.

"This is it, my last best shot," said Eric Prchal, the 6'7" basketball cocaptain, as he headed to the class of the new Social Studies teacher, Mike Carr. All that stood between Eric and a Division I basketball scholarship were some great moves on the court, and he knew that if there were a moment to shine, it better be coming up.

For other seniors, however, regret of a different sort was already tangible, regret that they were on the verge of yet another year in the confined and restrictive environment of high school. "It's a waste of a good year doing nothing I care about," said Katie Keough, a latter-day hippie whose soft, girlish voice matched her bell-bottoms, kelly-green shirt and hair ribbons. For three years, Katie had bucked student custom by taking a full load of classes and not a single study hall. She was about to pay for that dedication. Just five credits shy of graduation, she would have to spend the entire year at Prior Lake, since three of those credits were required courses that she could not take simultaneously. She would have happily loaded up her schedule with art classes, but that department's offerings were meager, especially in comparison to those of the Physical Education department. Since state law prohibited students from enrolling part-time, she'd signed up for "whatever," as she dubbed it. "I just want it over and done with quickly," she said.

Nick Olson had tried to find a way out of Katie's dilemma. He wasn't done with learning, not by a long stretch. But he wanted to study Latin, and Prior Lake's Language department offered only Spanish and German.

He was fascinated by philosophy, but Philosophy courses weren't even on the school's dream list. And while he was always ripe for more science, the Science department taught only six, mostly basic, classes. The spring before, he'd queried his counselor about alternatives, but the only option to a high school schedule of Theater, Journalism, Stress Management and study hall was PSEO, the Post-Secondary Education Option, which, under Minnesota law, gave students at the upper academic end of their classes the right to attend college instead of high school on the school board's dime— if they could get in. Nick might have made the grade, but he lacked reliable transportation. "So I was, basically, S.O.L.," he said. Shit out of luck.

The sophomores, the new kids on the block in a grades 10–12 high school, buzzed with a different cacophony of emotions, somewhere between excitement and panic at the journey they'd taken from HOMS, Hidden Oaks Middle School, across the street. Looking tiny and babyish compared with the seniors, they were easy to spot as they made their way through the unfamiliar terrain —searching out their lockers, confusing the 400 and 500 corridors, clustering in gaggles of nervous laughter, trying almost desperately to look cool.

Ben Bastyr sported a carefully planned effect of bleached hair and a small goatee, and covered his anxiety by wielding a video camera he called BenCam and interviewing everyone in sight. Ben was desperate to fit in. Although his test scores had earned him a slot in the gifted-and-talented program, he had refused to participate, preferring the more socially acceptable role of class clown. But that first day, like most of the sophomores who'd relished their middle school years, he was making no jokes. "All these guys look so big, so quick to judge," he said, handing BenCam over to a friend to film his comments. "Will they be stuck up? Will I be beaten up like I was at first at the middle school? Will they ruin my year?" He looked anything but sanguine at the prospect of such a fate.

The outsiders from HOMS—a typical middle school that's a merry-go-round of vicious teasing and fierce pressure to conform, of fighting, bullying and social scapegoating—looked out the window across at the alma mater of their nightmares and faced high school with higher hopes. "It's Communist China over there," quipped one sophomore active in the band and theater programs. "I'm finally out of that hell."

In her Renaissance headdresses, lacy gloves and net veil, Marissa Clausen muttered quietly: "Nothing could be worse than HOMS." For years convinced that Marissa's Gothic clothing revealed a practicing witch, the middle school boys had quietly tormented the fifteen-year-old, whom they openly feared. "It HAS to be better than it was over there," she said, trying hard to smile. "Anything would be better than being yelled at, mocked and pelted with pop cans."

Nick Busse drove past his old school that morning, glanced at the marquee that read, in wobbly letters, WELCOME BACK! S TUDENTS AND STAFF, and smiled, a full, no-holds-barred grin that lit up his face. Nick, who bore an uncanny resemblance to James Dean, hadn't smiled much during his years at Prior Lake. A gifted writer and one of the school's real academic talents, he'd fallen out of synch with his schoolmates while he was still in elementary school. He'd tried to fit in. He'd worn the right clothes, worked for perfect grades and thrown himself into cross-country skiing and track. But he still felt like a stranger. When he plunged into overt moroseness, his teachers and counselors had urged him away from alienation. Join more activities, get more involved, they'd advised him. The more they urged, the further he fell. "That's right, the solution to hating it here is to spend more time here," he said.

At the end of his junior year, comfortable with his old blue Chevy Blazer, he'd seized on the alternative Nick Olson had rejected and signed up for the PSEO program with relief. "I spent twelve years with most of these kids, but I have no idea who most of them are and they have no idea who I am," explained Nick, who had just received word that he was a National Merit Commendee. "And what did I learn there? Frankly, I can't think of a single thing."

The week before Prior Lake High School began its 1999–2000 academic year, Nick had begun classes at Normandale Community College in nearby Bloomington. As he rounded the corner to drive past Prior Lake High School that morning on his way to Normandale, Nick wondered, for an instant, how it would feel to see the overflowing lot, to imagine the bells ringing inside.

"Those poor bastards," Nick said. "They still have to ask permission for everything. I can eat when I'm hungry, choose which classes to skip and never have to answer to hall monitors, guidance counselors or any other dickhead telling me that if I want to do something I need to ask nicely.

"I'll miss my friends, the people I would hang around with at school. But Prior Lake never felt like an education. We never learned about the great philosophers, about political movements, or anything that demanded any depth. It felt like we were just going through the motions—filling out worksheets, going to class, holding class discussions. But the worksheets were inane, the classes were boring and the discussions were meaningless.

"It was like they wanted to run a school but were afraid to teach us anything."

Chapter Two

8:10 A.M., **Thursday,**
September 2, 1999

The windowless corridor that was home to Corey, Carr, Hoeg and God was a pedestrian snarl. Think Times Square with half of Midtown Manhattan rushing to the subway simultaneously, or the Dorothy Chandler Pavilion on Oscar night—in miniature. The seniors were too cool, too self-important to rush, or to cede way to the sophomores, who wandered semiaimlessly, searching for rooms that were inevitably on the other side of the building. The intersections between the passages turned into power struggles between the entitled and the meek. And punctuating the pandemonium, the teachers lined up next to their doorways like guards at Buckingham Palace overseeing the commoners.

Jeff Hoeg was squirming, shuffling his feet as he leaned against the wall by his classroom. He longed to be inside, welcoming his students, rather than positioned outside like a traffic cop. But administrative decrees designed to safeguard the students trumped the best-laid educational plans. "Welcome back, glad to see you again," he hailed his students by name, having brushed up on them before the pep fest.

Hoeg, who had a penchant for living in and commenting on the moment simultaneously, interrupted fond greetings, a steady flow of pats on the shoulder. He was shaking his head, his earring catching the fluorescent light. "Pep fests at the beginning of the school year are not the best idea. The kids want to get started, and so do the teachers. It throws off our rhythm and wastes our time just so the student council can show what they have been doing all summer long."

As his room filled up, Hoeg tried for some personal touch even with the new kids, the ones he knew only by reputation, no matter how negative. "Hey, Marissa, nice to see you." Hoeg beamed. With her long, black skirt and lace mantilla, Marissa carried a certain degree of notoriety even among the staff. She expresses herself in a dark way, Hoeg thought, but I bet she's smart. Somebody different. Good. Just what the other kids need.

The hall emptied out in the thirty seconds after the bell rang, and Hoeg peeked around the corner, checking for stragglers, then shut his classroom door, smiled at the nervous sophomores and flew through his canned opening lines. "I went to Denny's the other day and ordered a bowl of chili," he announced to openly befuddled students. Perfect, he thought, I have their attention. "When the waitress told me the guy next to me had just gotten the last bowl, I looked over, noticed it was still half-full and asked him if I could have the rest. 'Sure,' he said as he passed it to me. I started eating and, about halfway through, I hit something hard. I looked down and found a dead mouse in the bowl. 'That's about how far I got, too!' the guy next to me said."

Confusion and puzzlement stifled the laughter of his Honors 10 English students, who sat glued to their seats. Before they could begin to figure out what the young teacher with the bleached hair was talking about, Hoeg moved on to more serious matters, like the course standards, the required readings, exams, worksheets and quizzes. But as he ran through the predictable litany of expectations, Hoeg was nonchalantly performing card tricks. What's this dude up to? students' furrowed brows suggested. Do they get my point, Hoeg wondered, that how they present themselves determines how successful they will be? Was his point really clear? In a sense, it was irrelevant to him. At least their eyes hadn't drooped before the first fifteen minutes had passed.

The air was stifling. The school was not air-conditioned, and teachers like Hoeg, with rooms in inner corridors, couldn't even hope for a breeze. It didn't help that odors from the bathrooms tended to waft directly to his door. "I like to describe myself as a woulda, shoulda, coulda teacher," Hoeg explained. "I share my experiences with them, 'I shoulda played basketball, coulda been in a play or woulda been in the top 10 percent.' It hits home with many of the kids I see today because so many are used to having everything handed to them without a bit of effort. My hope is that they can learn from my regrets."

Did it make his skin crawl to have to play the two-bit comedian in order to teach them that lesson? Not in the least. "Whatever it takes," he said gamely.

On his way to Journalism, Nick Olson stopped by Hoeg's door and peered inside enviously. He'd had Hoeg for two courses and had even learned from him to love Shakespeare, which he considered a remarkable feat. Over the summer, Nick and a friend had invited "The Hoeginator," as they called the young teacher, to go bowling, and Hoeg had spent one afternoon with them at the lanes. "It was good to know that there were teachers who actually treated teenagers like human beings," said Nick.

Down the hall, Mike Carr was in over his head, but blessedly ignorant of that reality—at least until a dozen students traipsed into his classroom with studied indifference. Fresh-faced and perfectly pressed, Carr, who assumed that his students would be pretty much identical to the person he'd been just six years earlier, found himself facing the surliest, most ill-behaved and out-of-control students in the school. Roger Murphy slunk low in his seat, his chains almost rattling on the floor, checking out the other animals in the zoo—at least that's what his affect proclaimed—while interjecting the occasional sarcastic comment. One boy looked like a more familiar type in a T-shirt and gold chain, but every time Carr turned around, he was yelling, or telling someone to fuck off. And Ashlee Altenbach, an energetic cheerleader, simply couldn't stop talking. "It's not my fault, I have ADHD," she announced giddily, a note of near pride lacing that assertion of her diagnosis with Attention Deficit Hyperactivity Disorder. A slinky blond Britney Spears wannabe glanced at her with envy and quipped, "I wish I had ADHD for an excuse, but I don't."

They weren't *bad* kids, not by any meaningful definition of the word "bad." They could be surly and uncooperative—the definition of bad in most suburban communities—but they didn't shoot up heroin in the bathroom, organize gangs or spraypaint graffiti on lakeside homes. They were just the Focus seniors, who specialized in eating new teachers for breakfast and spitting them back out before lunch. The previous year, they had ignited an ethanol fire in one classroom, programmed their watches to beep insistently and irregularly in another and brought Carr's predecessor to tears. They were also among the sweetest and brightest students in the school, but that fact wasn't easy to grasp when they were in full swing.

The Focus program was a school-within-a-school for kids who were too antsy, angry or alienated to hack it in a mainstream high school program. The mandate was clear: Help them graduate and keep them out of everyone else's hair. Like similar "alternative" schools around the country, the program was endowed with at least one element of every conceivable trend in pop psychology. Since a high percentage of Focus students were from "dysfunctional" homes, they were organized into school families as allegedly functional surrogates. Their birthdays were celebrated, they were taken on skiing trips or to amusement parks.

Deemed needy of personal attention, they were kept in small classes, a maximum of ten at a time. Considered incapable of long periods of concentration, they were taught on shortened schedules of thiry-three-minute classes. Tough love was carefully balanced against delicious rewards. Three unexcused absences, tardies or outbursts won them two weeks "on contract," the Focus euphemism for probation. But twenty days in school without a tardy, an absence or a conduct slip earned them a get-out-of-school-free card, good for one day. And when everyone behaved, they were even piled into school vans for group breakfasts at local restaurants.

Nonetheless, the conceit of the program was that Focus students were held to the same academic standards as mainstream kids, or at least that was the party line.

Jayne Garrison sat back and studied Carr, letting Ashlee and the boys probe his mettle while she played the shy waif. Students belched, farted and insisted they couldn't control themselves. They raced off to their lockers with a flip, "Oh, eh, I forgot my book," and were gone for fifteen minutes. Unfamiliar with the Focus contract system—which the students immediately misrepresented to him—Carr was helpless before a group of kids unwilling to be reasoned with or shamed into obedience.

By the time his two Focus hours were over and his first class of mainstream students burst in for American Government, Carr was already exhausted. This will be better, he reassured himself. These kids will be like I was. And as they filed into his classroom, they certainly looked more familiar. A comforting number wore the same clothes he had affected in high school; they actually sat at their desks and only rarely tossed papers across the room. So far, so good, Carr thought.

Carr hadn't gone off to Augustana College in Sioux Falls, South Dakota, dreaming of spending nine months of each year hectoring teenagers about the three branches of the federal government. At that stage in his life, his idea of career planning consisted of fantasizing about coaching a Big Ten basketball team. When he finally bowed to the reality that his chances of leading the Hoosiers to a championship were slim, he looked around for a backup plan and thought about how much fun his high school teachers seemed to have had, how much free time they had over the summer. And he figured he wouldn't even have to give up his coaching reverie; he could just scale it back to the thrill of a state high school championship.

Carr's parents were less than thrilled at his career decision. For the son of a Northwest Airlines pilot, teaching represented sharp downward economic mobility. And finding one of those poorly paid jobs didn't prove easy, despite the much-publicized teacher shortage. After graduation, Carr had spent a full year working as a long-term substitute and sweated most of the summer before Prior Lake called to offer him a position. On the opening day, he still hadn't gone beyond relief at finding steady work. A job. A salary. A relaxed administration that didn't require teachers to submit advance lesson plans. He tried not to think about the fact that the basketball coaching staff was firmly entrenched. Or that there weren't many other young, single people, or a group that departed school en masse on

Friday afternoons to down some "brewskies." At least he could pay the rent. At least *these* kids, the kids in his mainstream classes, looked normal.

As he introduced himself in a manner that seesawed between stern and boyish, thirty-four students looked Carr over, checking him out with practiced teen radar. He's trying way too hard to be cool, one boy concluded in that instantaneous analysis students perform on adults. He wants us to like him. That's a sure way to get trampled on. Kinda cute, the girls thought, but awfully cocky, maybe a little bit too loud. Eric Prchal didn't have to waste a minute in speculation. Trying to be friendly, Carr had mentioned that he'd heard about Eric's prowess on the basketball court. "Got him." Eric smiled.

At the other end of the corridor, dressed in a crisp gray pantsuit, Mara Corey handed out her course materials and ran down the list of requirements in her brisk, no-nonsense manner. No one dared trample on her. Even in her terror, she exuded too much authority. Anyway, the students in front of her had enrolled in College Prep Composition, which had a reputation for being a brutal course, the kind of course only students serious about college elected.

"I want you to take this course standards form home and have a parent or guardian sign it," she explained. "This is important because this is a tough class." Corey had heard too many pedagogical war stories, most involving parents of allegedly aggrieved students. She was not about to be broadsided by some mother who would actually *believe* her daughter when she insisted that the teacher had never mentioned anything about a required research paper.

You're expected to be at your desk when the bell rings, she continued. If you're late, you will make the time up after school. If you show up in class without a pencil and paper, you'll lose participation points. If you plagiarize a paper, it will win you an *F*. If you plagiarize the research paper, you'll get an *F* in the course. And don't think I won't catch you, she said, explaining how sophisticated teachers had become at finding materials on the Internet.

Every pair of eyes in the room rolled in tandem, like the cherries on a slot machine. "Give us a break," they seemed to say. Corey knew better than to back off. Prior Lake had no schoolwide policies on tardies or plagiarism, and she couldn't risk leaving those matters unclear. If you're off on an extended vacation when a paper is due, that's your problem, not mine, she persisted. And if I assign you a five-page paper, don't give me twenty-four.

She'd finished her litany. It was time to lighten up.

Although Corey hid it well, she was disappointed that there was not a single Mohawk, not even one Dead Kennedys T-shirt, in the class. No young Mara Coreys here, she thought, remembering the shaved head and huge earrings she'd flaunted as a teenager. Unlike Carr, Corey had been a teen rebel who'd lived on the margins of high school life, preferring The Cure, a New-Wave version of the Velvet Underground that declared losers and geeks to be cool, to pep fests and basketball tournaments. Although she'd graduated with a 1.2 cumulative grade point average—close to a straight *D*—her youthful arrogance was bolstered by perfect scores on the ACT exams. Corey had consoled herself by fantasizing that the world would one day discover her intellect and shower her with success as an actress, a writer or great thinker whose books on the state of the world would be celebrated internationally. How the "world" would find her in suburban Minneapolis was vague. But that is the nature of a teenage chimera.

Pulling a bag of sugar, a plate and a funnel out of a paper sack, Corey asked for two student volunteers. When no hands popped up, she drafted a boy in raggedy blue jeans and Doc Marten boots and a girl sporting a soccer jersey for one of those standard "warm-up" exercises that university education professors love, and that students find both dreary and pointless.

"So, who's the funnel and what's the sugar?" she asked, instructing the boy to pour the sugar through the conical plastic in a steady stream and the girl to provide color commentary about what he was doing. His face reflecting utter disdain for the activity, the boy nonetheless complied dutifully. The girl stood there mute, too tongue-tied to utter a syllable. "What does it look like?" Corey gently pushed, hoping to pull the young woman out of her mortification. The shy senior's silence was deafening. Corey swiftly explained the funnel as a metaphor for traditional education.

This time, the eyes clouded rather than rolled. "We're almost eighteen years old, for chrissake."

As the long period ended and her prep hour began, Corey finally had a chance to take a breather. She'd been in high gear for days and hadn't begun to process her first impressions of Prior Lake. The principal was, well, clearly different. The day before, at the first faculty meeting of the year, Craig Olson had faced his troops dressed in a plaid shirt and shorts and quipped, "We need a motto for the new season, and, at first, I thought 'Just Cut Off Their Oxygen' might be a possibility." No one had seemed certain whether the line demanded laughter. Olson's humor was too dry for most of the teachers. He sure broke the staid high school principal mold, Corey thought, an antiestablishment persona running the establishment.

Olson was an unlikely principal, a "big picture" guy in a job heavy with the mundane. In fact, he was an unlikely educator, having gone to college to become a physician. But Olson had burned out on the narrowness of the science curriculum, the hypercompetitiveness and the rote memorization of the premed track at the University of Wisconsin. Late in his junior year, he had looked over his transcript to see where else his coursework might lead him and realized that he wasn't far from a degree in science education.

His student teaching experience in rural Wisconsin had done little to convince him that that last-minute major would lead to a viable career. In order to save money on salaries, the school he was assigned to routinely brought in one-semester "interns" like Olson, on whom the regular teachers merrily dumped all their "yahoos." He hadn't spent two minutes in a public school since his own graduation from one, and there he was, facing a classroom filled with uncontrollable adolescents, with a supervising teacher too busy to help him and a faculty advisor more than an hour away. "It was negligent in all respects," Olson said. "But that was the mid-1970s, and that's the way schools were. We're still paying the price for how bad schools got back then."

His first full-time teaching job hadn't made education seem a much more promising profession. As the ninth-grade physical science teacher in a blue-collar district in Milwaukee, in his "best term," Olson awarded *D*s or *F*s to 60 percent of the kids. He kept waiting for someone to chide him. No one ever did. By the end of the year, he'd been ready to move on.

A three-year stint in the Peace Corps in Kenya provided temporary relief, but when he arrived back in Wisconsin, Olson still needed a plan. He knew he didn't want to return to the classroom. "I am not a person who responds well to the routine of 'OK, well, the bell rings at 7:25, the teacher does the first class for forty-seven minutes, then the bell rings again and, five minutes later, he teaches the second-hour class and so on,'" he explained. "I'm no good at just looking at something and saying, 'this is a piece of crap,' and giving it a *D* or an *F* without reading the entire thing unless I figure out that the student basically plagiarized the whole thing and there was no point reading it."

Educational administration seemed a logical lateral move. "You can check off a list of things that I didn't particularly care for about being a teacher, and most of the stuff I did like—getting to work with kids, working with people who care about kids and working with folks in a pretty stimulating environment—I could do as a principal," he said. "I'd also get some stimulating challenges, problems to figure out that would tax my abilities." After completing a graduate program in administration, Olson took a job as principal of a rural school in northern Minnesota. Two years later, he moved to Prior Lake, first as the assistant principal of the high school, then as the principal of the middle school. He'd been running the high school since 1994.

For the first faculty meeting, the staff had gathered in what used to be called the Library, and today is the Media Center since books have been largely replaced by computers. The librarians did their best to keep some actual volumes on the shelves, but their budget was meager in a society convinced that technology was more important to education than tomes. Great, Corey thought, more research on the Internet, the great unwashed font of undifferentiated information.

As she settled in at the meeting, Corey had studied the faculty. A pony-tailed Physics teacher joked with the other Science teachers, but she'd already learned that he deigned to speak with few of his other colleagues. In fact, he bragged about having little to do with them, about never setting foot in the teachers' lounge. "I spend my time with students, not faculty," he'd told her haughtily, proud of his reverse snobbery.

As Olson handed the meeting over to Lori Boynton, his second in command, Sara Strege and Janean Schmidt—Schmidty to both students and teachers—whispered back and forth, commenting on the new male teachers and trading off-color comments. The two were a pair, the names Strege and Schmidty linked as inexorably as Simon and Garfunkel or Thelma and Louise. They were the faculty equivalent of Joan Rivers, and their ribald personae titillated their peers.

The teachers' geographical hierarchy was strikingly parallel to that of the students. Physical Education instructors in team sweats or shorts gathered around one of the long tables, leaning back in their chairs, while the three shop teachers—musketeers in blue-collar work clothes—isolated themselves by the windows, unsure of where, or whether, they fit in. Katie Hallberg, the Calculus maven perched next to Tom Hassig, the choir director, as far as possible from the other members of the Math department, with whom she was locked in a mutual-lack-of-admiration society. In the eyes of their colleagues, Hallberg and Hassig were the resident intellectual snobs.

The staff wouldn't have won any awards for diversity—racial, religious or regional. The new Art teacher, an Asian woman, was the only nonwhite member of a group that was entirely Christian, almost exclusively upper Midwestern and bereft of a single gay man or lesbian willing to take the risk of raising the rainbow flag.

Yet, professionally, the diversity was sharp. The choir conductor and the theatrical director were infamous for closing up the school night after night, while other teachers appeared entirely disengaged, arriving at school promptly at 7:00 but never lingering a minute past 3:00 P.M., the end of the work day. Lynn Lally, the Elvis aficionado, blabbered to her students about her multiple divorces and family traumas. Joe Goracke, one of the senior Social Studies teachers, was warm, but horrified at such a breach of a careful professional distance. The biologists never showed up in anything less than "professional" attire, crisp coats and ties, while one of the other Science instructors taught in jeans and torn T-shirts and one male Phy Ed teacher sported Lycra shorts year-round.

Corey had already been told that the divisions went deeper than attire or style and flared into open conflict whenever the staff was forced to engage an issue like the wisdom of establishing a schoolwide policy on tardiness or plagiarism. The previous fall they had locked horns over revamping the daily schedule to allow fewer but longer classes—so-called "block scheduling"—and a battle royal was roiling between the "Back to Basics" and the "Students need more electives so each can find something he's good at" partisans.

The only aspect of their jobs that fostered unanimity was their collective disgust with how much time they spent being anything but educators. Inside their classrooms, they weren't just teachers; they were the clothing-and-drug police, the lateness brigade and the parent hand-holders. And they were required to each spend at least one period of the day either patrolling the halls lest errant students wreak havoc outside of the classrooms, or as jailers instructed to impose total silence on students consigned to day-long detentions, as study hall monitors responsible for keeping the hullabaloo from spilling out of the door, or as lunchroom supervisors—positions that demanded they encroach upon the turf of janitors by bussing tables and picking trash off the floors.

"Unskilled laborers," scoffed Ron Lachelt. "That's what teachers have become."

Faculty meetings were never supposed to last more than one hour, or at least that's what administrators promised. But that first meeting had run on ad nauseam. Lori Boynton, the assistant principal, had tried to speed through the bureaucratic tedium, but she knew that teachers ignored the piles of notices and memoranda placed in their mailboxes every morning. She had to grab their attention while they were captive.

Teachers' every move had become someone's political football. They were supposed to bar students from class if their parents hadn't sent in proof that they'd received booster vaccinations against seven different diseases; to accept responsibility for what their students brought up on the school's Internet server; to ask parental permission to show movies considerably tamer than what kids watched on television; to as much as discuss a topic like AIDS; even to screen the film *Schindler's List*. The line shifted so swiftly, and unevenly, that they never knew when they were approaching a parental demarcation that might lead directly into a minefield. Boynton had to keep them up to date.

They don't look like happy campers, Corey thought as she watched them from her seat at the English table. That was hardly surprising. The teachers were locked in a tense union negotiation, cash for printing and new materials was woefully tight, local voters had just defeated a proposal to increase taxes to improve the school's technology, the building was bursting at the seams and they were all holding their breath, praying that the citizens of Prior Lake wouldn't reject the district's request for a special bond issue to build a new high school.

The touchy-feely member of the administrative team, Boynton had tried to lighten the mood. Calling on every lesson she'd ever learned about modern psychology, she'd struck an upbeat note with a cheery reprise of the previous year. "I feel so good about you," she said perkily. "The respect and good relationships you created got us through. You all deserve a round of applause."

Despite the budget crunch and the overcrowding, Boynton might have succeeded as the faculty cheerleader, but the state of Minnesota had just mandated new graduation requirements, due to kick in with the sophomore class, and teachers all across the state were horrified by the plan. Minnesota's legislators hadn't joined the national "higher standards" bandwagon by just instituting achievement testing. With their Profiles of Learning, they had reinvented the wheel, laying out what was, in essence, a new statewide curriculum and pointed instructions to teachers on how to deliver it.

Students would no longer earn high school diplomas by spending the requisite number of hours in classrooms, bringing home acceptable grades or passing achievement tests. They would also complete at least twenty-four out of possible forty-eight "performance" packages to demonstrate their proficiency in ten "learning areas," from "decision-making" to "resource management." Sounds confusing? Try being a teacher in Minnesota.

The conceit of the Profiles was that a high school education should consist of more than dry lectures, and that students should not be treated as passive vessels into which teachers poured information, which they then regurgitated back in papers and examinations. Rather, the politicians who designed the program insisted, young people should perform hands-on projects that would equip them with superior critical-thinking and problem-solving skills for the new century. But no one had much sense of how the new standards would work. What kind of project qualified as meeting the standard for "community interaction"? If the standard for analyzing algebraic patterns was woven into an Algebra course, what happened if a student flunked the project designed around that standard but passed the rest of the class? How should they deal with students transferring from other states, who would have completed few of those requirements? What could a school do if a transfer student from within the state had passed a course elsewhere that did not include a performance package which was included in that same course at Prior Lake?

The Commissioner of Education had been strikingly silent on these topics.

Veteran teachers had lived through dozens of revolutions, each promising to produce brighter, more discerning and engaged students, and they'd bought into almost all of them. This one, however, was different; it was an open affront to their professionalism. The latest educational fad wasn't just instructing teachers what to teach—detailed in long lists sent down from the state Department of Education—but how to judge students' mastery of the material. "They think that they need to tell me that Biology includes teaching heredity?" Ron Lachelt asked, spitting out the question with unvarnished disgust. Lachelt was the school's most consistently upbeat teacher, but on the subject of the Profiles of Learning he edged up on bitterness. He'd already pulled Corey aside and warned her of the insidiousness of the state's requirements.

"They don't think I know how to teach biology?" Lachelt continued. "Why don't they just give me a script, prepare my materials and give me a check-off sheet for grading? In fact, then they could just hire robots to replace us."

As Olson and Boynton outlined the school's progress in coming into compliance with the new regulations, a dark cloud descended over the room. "The grad standards are like a rope," Olson pleaded. "You can do neat things with rope, including making a noose out of it. It is up to you."

Ron Lachelt had glared, as if to say, "We don't need a lecture on rope weaving."

On break between classes that first morning, Corey watched dozens of students block the door to Lachelt's classroom as his sophomores made their way to their desks. Jayne Garrison and a gang of other seniors with spiked hair and studded jackets had lingered, trying to drag him into one of the conversations about religion and politics that she and her friends always had with him between classes and after school. It was 8:08 by the time all twenty-five sophomores settled down. Lachelt's recitation of the rules was perfunctory. Secure and confident in his knowledge, and his ability to teach it, he was more concerned with sending the students his core message: "You have no bigger cheerleader here than me."

"If your cat dies, your parents have a big fight, you get into it with your boyfriend, come see me. You don't have to pour your heart out to me. You don't have to tell me what's wrong. But if I know something's going on, I'll work with you. No late work is accepted, but don't sweat it if you miss an assignment. You'll have the chance for 850 to 900 points during the trimester, so, if you miss five, the world doesn't come to an end."

Lachelt's eyes roamed the room, landing on each student in turn. He wasn't trying to pick out the perpetual latecomer, or the kid who would be the class whiner. One by one, he was asking, longingly: Will he get it? Will she feel the spark that might ignite a passion for learning? Will any of them fall in love with ideas? With books? With the journey? Lachelt wasn't naive about the prospects, at least with any significant percentage of his kids. But he was no more immune than his fellow teachers to the quest for students who reminded him of himself—a tough commodity to find in a comfortable suburb at the end of the millennium.

The child of lumpen parents, Lachelt had grown up in the 1950s and 1960s in a small town in west central Minnesota. His mother had waitressed to help the family get by since his dad, who'd never really recovered from one hundred days–plus on the front lines during World War II, drew most of his comfort from a bottle. It was clear to the young boy that no one from his family was going anywhere fast. Other kids dated, played sports and threw themselves into school life; Lachelt fled to the woods, hunting deer and trapping muskrats alone. When he chanced on the house of a teacher while trick-or-treating one Halloween, he glimpsed a pile of books and a poster of France. "That's what I want," he told himself. "That's who I can be."

Books became his salvation, education his roadmap out. "Carl Sagan once said that if mankind is capable of magic, it has to be because of books," he said, his blue eyes actually twinkling in the glare of the fluorescent lights in his office.

But the shy outcast was still a boy in a hypermacho age, so his focus was divided. Lachelt read through the works of Mark Twain and graduated to historian Will Durant, but he also watched every war movie that appeared on television or the big screen of his local movie theater. While he dreamed of a life of books and ideas, he also longed to be part of the "big, bad tough brotherhood." His goal wasn't to kill gooks or save America from the Red Menace. He wanted to prove to himself that he could be the best, which, in that age and society, meant the U.S. Army's Special Forces.

Lachelt was convinced that the Vietnam War would always be there, so, with too much invested in the power of education to do anything foolish, like dropping out of school, he enrolled at the University of Minnesota at Morris, figuring that he could join up as soon as he flunked out. Except he didn't flunk out. Instead, he discovered philosophy, which provided richer answers to his questions than the Wordsworth poetry he'd plumbed before. "I read Sartre's classic lecture, 'Existentialism Is a Humanism.' It made my head hurt, and I loved it." In Albert Camus's "The Myth of Sisyphus," the tale of the mythical hero who paid for his passions with an unspeakable punishment, his whole being exerted toward the accomplishment of absolutely nothing, Lachelt found a metaphor for the lives of the adults around him, the life he was intent on avoiding.

After graduation in 1971, he took his shot at his other dream, joining the army and going through Officer Candidate School. Lachelt knew he didn't want to be an artillery "cannon cocker," so he volunteered for infantry, hoping that it would be his ticket into Special Forces. But that elite unit was downsizing in the twilight of the Vietnam War. Sitting in his room late on a rainy night, Lachelt decided that he had to break through into the dwindling unit. It was do or die. He threw himself on the mercy of a friendly colonel, and, a few days later, began the long training that would win him a green beret.

In the years after his military service, Lachelt searched for a mooring in the outside world, working as a naturalist and an elementary school teacher before winding up in the Science department at Prior Lake in 1987.

"I've been through three superintendents, nine principals, and I'm still here," he said. "He who attacks most, conquers."

Lachelt conquered regularly, and completely, despite a penchant for the type of corny jokes and hokey plays on words ("it's amino world!") that would sink most other instructors. "Congenial and encyclopedic," was Reilly Liebhard's assessment of the biologist. "He somehow manages to know all this amazing stuff, and better yet, he's actually able to share copious amounts of it with all different types of people without coming off as even the tiniest bit of a pompous know-it-all."

On that first school morning in 1999, with two dozen students looking at each other, passing notes and pretending not to nod off, it was unclear how much, or how many, he would conquer. "I like people who have opinions, so don't be shy," he said, goading them, trying not to intimidate them. "I might not always agree with them, but at least it shows that you're thinking."

The room was utterly quiet.

"I wasn't an A student in high school, so I understand if you don't get it. Come see me. I'll work with you. Remember the aphorism 'When the going gets tough'? Well, it should really say, 'When it's too tough for anybody else, it's just right for me.'"

No one said a word.

"Never underestimate the power of a sophomore."

Chapter Three

6:30 P.M., Friday,
September 10, 1999

On Laker Field, it was the beginning of the school year the way school years are supposed to begin in all those mythic tales about the energy of youth and a whole town coming together to celebrate its kids, about a pep band infusing energy into the twilight, hot dogs and families and the sun setting behind the water tower, and the flag waving in the breeze. The fairy tale is always about football, and Nate Schweich was getting ready for the first home game.

One minute the stocky fifteen-year-old sat on a bench in the dank locker room twisting his blue Lakers baseball cap from front to back, back to front. The next, he was dancing to Limp Bizkit, Matt Brown, the 6'2", 338-pound cocaptain of the football team, miming him from behind. Nate loved to dance, and Matt was a rap zealot.

John Bennett caught the restlessness out of the corner of his eye and grabbed Nate from behind in a bear hug. "Who's the boss?" he asked, jabbing the boy in the arm in a familiar, let's-all-be-guys together ritual. Bennett was fond of those kinds of rituals, and he was definitely a guy. He slapped backs, flirted with the gals and preened like a peacock. "That's right, remember, peacocks are all male," he said, as if 100 percent comfortable in his own vanity. He was not, which is why he kept quiet about the fact that in 1971 he'd represented his home town of St. Cloud in the Mr. Teenage Minnesota pageant. At the age of forty-seven, that was too much, even for John Bennett.

Nate shuffled in front of The Boss—Bennett loved to be called The Boss—and continued their well-worn dialogue. "You," he answered, smiling, without a trace of irony in his voice.

"Who's the assistant boss?" Bennett continued the interplay.

"ME." Nate smiled, pointing to himself awkwardly.

Surrounded by Bennett, who topped 6'5", and scores of oversized hulking forms adjusting their pads, pulling up their socks and retying their cleats, Nate, short and perpetually beaming, wasn't easy to spot. When the fifty-four members of the varsity squad of the Lakers football team had walked into the locker room in their shorts and T-shirts two hours earlier, they hadn't seemed to take up much space. By game time, they'd swelled up, almost bulging against the walls of the room.

Most of their uniforms would return to the locker room after the game as pristine as when they'd left, their players having spent the evening standing on the sidelines. Juniors and seniors willing to put in the time were guaranteed spots on the varsity squad, but that didn't mean they ever got to face the enemy on a Friday night when the stands were packed and the lights made players feel like rock stars. Instead, they were consigned to playing in the Junior Varsity games on Mondays, when no reporters showed up, no scouts studied them from the bleachers.

For some, having the right to wear a football jersey on the Friday of a big game, seeing a number beside their name in the program, was enough. They rarely stirred up any fuss about how little time they spent in the limelight. Their fathers were another story. "You have the kids who eat, sleep and drink football, but that's always a small group," Bennett explained. "But there are others who come out because their parents think it's the thing to do. They probably don't want to play, but their dads started coaching them in the eighth grade because they always wanted to play ball themselves. And those are the fathers who constantly complain when you don't give their sons more playing time."

In navy-blue sweatpants and warm-up shirt, Nate was the only kid in the locker room without a uniform. Suffering from Down's syndrome, he was not physically able to play football, but he could manage the team. At least that was the fiction John Bennett, the head coach, had created when he decided to try to integrate Nate into the school. He'd had to twist a few teenage arms, to chide his players about tolerance and generosity. But, although Nate was still ribbed for holding his fork in a fist, and for the lisp caused by the swollen tongue of people with Down's, the players had adopted him as something of a team mascot, including him in trips to the movies, evenings at the bowling alley, even adding him to the pit crew of a racing team. No more lunch at the Special Ed table for Nate. He sat proudly with the school's leading Jocks, and woe to the macho asshole who dared called him a "retard." At the end of the season before, the varsity squad had presented him with his own letter jacket.

Nate, whose wardrobe included every available article of blue-and-gold Lakers clothing, never missed a game or a practice, distributing balls during drills, delivering water bottles to red-faced players, running errands for the coaches. At the end of each scrimmage, his was the moment of glory, as he stood in the center of the field and clapped the team into a loose huddle. "Breakdown," he screamed. "Team," the players responded. "Breakdown," Nate repeated. "Team," the mantra continued three times. Then Nate counted down from three and a deep bass roar erupted from the pack, "Lakers."

Outside, Nate's father, Ted, sat in the stands, hemmed in by parents and grandparents studying the play list and comparing notes about the prowess of the Holy Angels, the opposing team, wishing he were somewhere else— like the locker room. That's where he'd belonged twenty-five years earlier, the cocaptain of the team the year the Lakers had an almost perfect season and emerged triumphant as the conference champions. The greatest team in the history of the school, Ted liked to brag. Ted had been no football star. But enough time had passed for reality to be varnished into legend.

The scene looked almost eerily familiar to Ted: the Lakers were playing in the same old stadium for the same proud middle class parents who hung on their kids' every achievement; the old rock in front of the school—the students' own billboard—was painted for the occasion; "Buff" Busselman was still calling plays; the cheerleaders were still waving the same blue-and-gold pom-poms. But that was obviously an illusion.

Prior Lake had "bumped into the city," as Ted put it. The town, as the country, had lost its innocence. In his day, players and their parents had revered their coaches. By 1999, they were just some guys screwing up the kids, or at least that was Buff's take on what parents thought. Teachers had bowed to adolescent sensibilities and, where Ted and his pals had slapped each other's nude bodies with towels after games and practices, terrorizing the body shy, the shower rooms were filled with cobwebs. School showers were anathema to the new generation. The Germs—the partiers of Ted's era—had skipped out of school at lunchtime to buy 25-cent scoops of beer at the B&D on Main Street, girls had taken quick cigarette breaks in the bathroom, and boys still had room to be boys, which meant that the coach had paid no attention if a good fight broke out during practice or at halftime.

"Remember, the opponents are our guests," the announcer abruptly reminded the spectators, a sign of the changing times. "Good sportsmanship is everybody's responsibility."

Inside, John Bennett gathered the team around him. The mood was solemn, the anxiety obvious. The Lakers had lost their season opener 13–6 to Hutchinson, the conference powerhouse who annually blocked their every attempt to emerge as a football contender in the state. It wasn't easy to beat the Hutchinson Tigers on their own turf. Theirs was a football-crazed town where spectators arrived four hours before games to ensure themselves seats on the fifty-yard line. If the Tigers won only seven of their annual ten games, the entire town bemoaned the poor season.

Standing in front of his players, Bennett had to mess with their minds so they wouldn't think themselves into defeat. They'd already been at school for more than an hour—for chalk talk, team calisthenics and drills. The assistant coaches had run the Mean Machine, the defensive line, against Holy Angels' favorite offensive plays, and reversed the drill. The final step was an exercise in attitude.

Bennett's players weren't quite sure what to make of their coach. During the season, he was their buddy. He played the goofball, dancing or telling stupid jokes, and they could never decide if he knew he wasn't really funny or was clinging to his high school days by acting like a silly kid. Out of season, he seemed distant, they said, as if he were indifferent to them once they became irrelevant.

Even in his twenty-fourth season of coaching, Bennett was dead serious about his job. He worked the crowd on the field and in the locker room, trying to pump up the kids who weren't getting the glory, remembering to say something—no matter how much of a stretch—to any kid who was trying. At the age of forty-seven, however, he was weary with the rest of his job. He burnt out after eleven years teaching Biology and had arrived at Prior Lake in 1987 in the Physical Education department. For more than a decade, he taught team sports in the fall trimester, winter recreation the second term and both team and individual sports in the spring. Two years earlier, he had found himself standing outside an ice hockey rink in the dead of a classic Minnesota winter teaching broom ball to four classes in a row. "Do I want to be doing this for twenty more years?" he asked himself. "I just couldn't see it." He'd moved over into the Guidance office, where the staff spent more time disciplining students for cutting class and showing up late than counseling them about their futures. In almost a quarter century of coaching, Bennett had led a team to only one conference championship. "Just once, just once I want to be at the state championship as something other than a spectator," he said wistfully.

As he stood in front of his players trying to summon up the words that might launch them to a victory, he didn't look all that optimistic. "We've been working hard for three weeks, twenty practices in three weeks in hot weather," he said quietly. Buff, the former head coach, now Bennett's assistant, was a yeller, which meant that no one listened when he raised his voice. Bennett saved his vocal cords for emergencies. That night, the tone needed to be soft, almost a whisper. "No one is in better condition than you are. You're prepared. You know what you need to do to win. Remember, at this point in the year, the best team wins in the fourth quarter. So go out and execute."

The young men paused for a moment of reflection. It used to be prayer, but Bennett knew that prayers had been declared verboten.

As the team raced out of the locker room, the twelve cheerleaders—eight of them blond, five sporting ponytails—flipped and clapped and tossed one another into the air. The Banditos segued from "Soul Man" into the Prior Lake fight song, and eight hundred fans broke into wild cheers.

One by one, the members of the squad sprinted through a phalanx of pom-poms and were introduced by the announcer to the blares of trumpets and the screeches of Reilly Liebhard's saxophone. Number 78, Matt Brown was the crowd pleaser. He'd ended his junior season as All-Conference, All-Metro, and All-State, and the *Minneapolis Star-Tribune* had chosen him as a player to watch, a "punishing straight-ahead blocker with surprising quickness." The whole town was convinced that Brownie, as everyone called him, was headed for the big time. Everyone but Bennett, that is.

Big, strong and quick on the field, off the field, Brownie was lumbering, as if he'd learned to play the dumb, happy Jock to such perfection that it had become his persona. The teachers, he said, never pushed him. "They figured I was the football kid, so what was the point?" And they rarely caught a glimpse of Brownie's streak of sweetness, or it was obliterated by a penchant for sass which was clever but, inevitably, underappreciated by authorities dealing with teenagers.

Matt and has father had been planning his Big Ten career for a decade. Along the way, as Brownie was transformed into a football hero, he never lost his natural lethargy. In his junior year, he'd run like a halfback. But since then, he'd partied hard. His weight had ballooned, and he'd stopped working out. "People tell these kids that they can make it to the NFL, but they never add that they'll have to bust their tails," Bennett said. Hoping to ready his key player for his senior year, for some great football and for some attention from college scouts, the Boss had found Brownie a summer job at a health club, with a personal trainer thrown in as a fringe benefit. The first day Matt had gotten on a treadmill, he promptly threw up. He'd walked out and started working at Taco John's.

Laker fans screamed and applauded as Brownie ran out onto the field, beaming. Bennett hated sloth. He hoped for the best but doubted Matt would even make it to All-Conference his senior year.

When the announcer called number 3, the girls in the stands went wild.

"Tony Lorenz, tight end," the announcer proclaimed. Tony Lorenz, Mr. Cool, the king of cocky bravado, was a magnet for female Lakers. Tony was an exercise in a studied indifference that was clearly self-protective, at least to anyone willing to see beyond his strut. Tony made you work to discover that he was smart as a whip, that his mind drifted toward the philosophical, and that he wrote the best poetry in the school. The only person who saw through him was his best friend, Eric Prchal, his cocaptain of the basketball team.

Eric and Tony were the quintessential odd couple. Eric was almost patrician: tall, blond and gangly; Tony—think Marlon Brando before he gained three hundred pounds—was dark, a hint of Mediterranean all the more obvious in Nordic Minnesota, and tight with wiry muscles. Eric was the perpetual good kid, the responsible party—an Honors student, member of student council, leader in the school. Tony was the unbridled one. Eric and his teammates bleached the hair on their heads; Tony was the first to bleach his pubic hair. Eric sucked up to his teachers, bowing and scraping just enough to make them think he felt subservient. Tony dared them to despise him. Eric bristled at his exclusion from the school's In crowd; Tony felt socially invulnerable.

The two were inseparable. "Hey, keep your hands off of him, he's mine," Tony chided any girl he caught flirting with Eric. They were postmodern teenage boys: Although they professed utter revulsion at the mere notion of man-on-man sex, they weren't afraid to walk around holding hands. Eric had set aside that Friday evening to watch Tony on the field, but had been sidetracked by Mary Haugen, who insisted that he work the student council concession stand for at least half of the game. He'd tried to resist, citing his responsibility to his friend. But Haugen was a force of nature, so Eric was heating up pizza when the crowd yelled Tony onto the turf.

Just before they began their senior year, both boys had broken up with their long-term girlfriends, who were off at college. "Senior year, you know, you gotta be free," they explained. They'd organized that freedom around a competition with their friend Jordan Culver to see who could have sex with the most girls. "It's a team game, played by individuals," they said of the contest. There was no doubt that Tony would win.

Tony wasn't a natural football player; he hadn't started playing until his junior year, when his mother relented and signed the permission slip. At his first practice, he hadn't even known how to get into a football stance. But John Bennett eyed him with professional lust. "Fast, great hands, can jump and athletically extremely smart," he pronounced him. "If he'd started earlier, he could have been one of the best players Prior Lake has ever seen."

Everyone was revved up for a winning season, except Bennett, who refused to predict how his team would perform. He wasn't being coy. Vegas can calculate a point spread on college or professional games, but no one in his right mind lays odds on the results of a high school football contest. "Conventional wisdom is that 90 percent of the game is mental, and the ability of most high school boys to concentrate is notoriously volatile," explained Bennett. "Someone's girlfriend breaks up with him, or his dad refuses to buy him a new truck, and the whole game is shot to shit."

Bennett also knew that somewhere along the line he'd lose a couple of players to alcohol, drugs or tobacco. He didn't worry much about losing players to academic probation since they could flunk two courses a trimester and remain eligible. But "chemical violations" were taken seriously. A player caught puffing on a cigarette, tossing back a beer or sharing a joint was suspended from play for two weeks. A second offense, and he was out for ten weeks or the rest of the season. A third meant no sports for a full calendar year.

Around the country, those kinds of rules were under attack from parents and students who insisted that what a kid did outside of school should have nothing to do with his status inside. "Should we pretend we don't know if a student commits a robbery, and treat him as if nothing had happened?" asked Bennett. He knew the fight had only begun. Rickey Higgins, a senior at Warren Township High School in Gurnee, Illinois, had recently filed suit after being barred from playing basketball after he received a second citation for drunk driving. His claim? He suffered from alcoholism, a disability, which meant that his suspension violated the Americans with Disabilities Act.

In eleven years as head coach at Prior Lake, Bennett had never started a year without at least a handful of players on drug suspension. The year before, Buff Busselman's son Dave, the Lakers' star running back, was nailed for drinking on the day of the semifinal sectional game. Bennett was holding his breath, half-convinced that the boy would cross the line once more and be benched for his senior year.

Bennett was no teetotaler, but he had no use for high school football players, especially members of his own team, who drank alcohol. As a high school athlete himself, decked out in flared pants and velour shirts, he'd been Mr. Clean. When the local pizza joint started selling wine and 3.2 beer, he'd stopped going there. When his classmates held bonfires in the country, where the beer flowed freely, he stayed home. "Only dirtballs drank," he said. "And I wasn't a dirtball." He expected his players to follow that example.

"So, you want to know if we're gonna have a great season?" he asked just before the game began. "Beats me!"

Holy Angels won the toss and elected to kick off to Prior Lake. The Lakers' return man watched Holy Angels' perfect kick soar downfield. But he fumbled on the catch, and Holy Angels flew into an early lead, 6–0.

In their disappointment, parents tried to sink down onto the bleachers, but the students had sprawled well beyond their normal center section, talking and laughing, oblivious to how little room they'd left for the adults. The seating was rigorously segregated. No self-respecting teenager would sit with the adults. No adults would dare invade student turf.

The junior and senior girls, Jennifer Aniston look-alikes, posed in the stands, talking on their cell phones while their boyfriends stood on line at the concession stand for yet another Dr. Pepper. Sophomores, seven full days of high school under their belts, actually paid attention to what was happening on the field, or the verse the cheerleaders were trying to lead.

WE AIN'T BAD AND WE AIN'T COCKY, GONNA RIDE ON YOU LIKE A KAWASAKI, they chanted in unison.

Mary Haugen cupped her hands and yelled at the students to move into the band section to open up more space for the grown-ups. The bleachers there were empty, the band strikingly absent. The members of the marching band had been strutting up and down the parking lot all week, their director teetering on a step ladder, bullhorn in hand, trying to get his tuba players to maintain straight lines behind the oboes and flutes. After the long summer, he had barely gotten them up to speed on their instruments since, unlike the football team, the band had no practice until the first day of school. Every year, teaching them to play in unison while marching in straight lines proved to be a Herculean task. The pep band, The Banditos, then were responsible for whatever musical excitement was generated that evening.

Which was just fine with most of the musicians. The marriage of high school bands to football was a match made in hell. Talk about a clash of cultures: band kids who spent their free time listening to Beethoven, or jamming in punk bands, dedicating their Friday nights to the greater glory of football players, who looked down on them, and to football, which most found inexplicable.

Imagine Frank Zappa playing "Ode to the Varsity Squad," which is what he did at Antelope Valley Joint Union High School in Lancaster, California until he was kicked out of the band for smoking. Or Trent Reznor of Nine Inch Nails, who wound up singled out by William Bennett for his assaults on "decency," tooting out the notes to the "Star-Spangled Banner" on his tenor sax at his high school in Mercer, Pennsylvania. Most big-time rock 'n' roll musicians, after all, started out wearing dorky uniforms following drum majors across football fields at halftime.

That was Jake Anderson's musical schizophrenia. Five days a week, during fifth hour, he strapped on his marching drums and laid down the beat for the "Star-Spangled Banner." After school, he and three friends, the members of False Existence, gathered in his parents' garage and beat out loud, grungy, angst-ridden amplified music —with lyrics like *Everyone is made to look like everyone else, We are all the same, yet no one resists—* that they wrote as a group.

The irony was not lost on Jake, a reserved and intense young man. "Jocks and Preps look at kids in the band and see insignificant nerds, irrelevant to them and insignificant to school spirit," he said one afternoon, half-perched on a stool during a break from practicing with False

Existence. "But we make the music that propels their aggression, whether on the football field or in the mosh pit."

Ultimately, it wasn't just the musical schizophrenia that annoyed the band kids about marching at football games. It was also the singularly inexplicable allure of watching eleven well-padded hulks pound each other into the turf over an inflated pigskin sphere. "The game itself is too confusing, stupid and pointless to warrant that big of a crowd on its own, so there is obviously something more going on here," quipped Andy Ottoson. Andy wasn't just a band member; he was a theater kid, which meant that he had two strikes against him in the social hierarchy of the school. "But I'll be damned if I know what it is."

Reilly Liebhard thought he knew what it was, which increased his chagrin at the fact that he was tethered to football not only by his membership in the marching band, but by his participation in The Banditos. "Football bears a striking similarity to military combat and appears to serve as either a subtle, or maybe even blatant, ground for training in the latter. You know, doing exactly as ordered without thinking about it, the rah-rah-team crap, and the obvious physical resonances and ridiculous injuries that come from an all-out fight when you don't really know what you're fighting for. Okay, I know, football players are fighting for a touchdown. But what is that, anyway? It just changes the lights on a scoreboard. They are the same people the next day, with the possible exception of their joints and the fact that the football players get to pork the self-respect-lacking slut of their choice the night before, regardless of whether or not they scored on the field."

Reilly looked out at the throng, inhaled the excitement, then kept going. "And it's just like many wars, where soldiers are fighting neither for freedom nor for some other worthy cause but because 'we gotta kill those G-damn insert-racist-epithet here.' The Laker football team has to beat up on the other guys because they have the audacity to be from Holy Angels or New Prague, and someday, a bunch of 'em might be beating up on Colombian farmers for having the audacity to desire economic autonomy. Either that or they'll be beating up military recruits to break them down and treat them as raw psychosomatic material for the various branches of the service to do with as they please. And heaven help them if they have the audacity to have a simple difference they can't help, such as being gay. There are plenty of automatons marching around just ready to kill 'em for not producing more potential garment factory workers like a good little obedient heterosexual."

His band director, Keith Koehlmoos, a bespectacled Iowan with a bit of mischief to his grin, wasn't unsympathetic to those sentiments. He would have loved to use the time he spent putting students like Jake or Reilly through marching drills to work on their tone and precision, to make sure that the melody chimed through properly. But he was a realist who understood precisely how much Prior Lake loved the full spectacle, the ritual, the tradition they associated with high school, albeit high school circa 1960, which included a full-dress marching band.

Holy Angels' point-after kick split the upright, and they pulled ahead 7–0. Then the Lakers' quarterback threw a long pass down the field, a good forty yards, and Tony Lorenz sprinted to catch it. The fans stood as one, as if connected to the same invisible hand. No one breathed for the split second it took for the ball to traverse the night air. Tony was on the ground, buried under a mountain of Angels, but the catch was good.

The parents tried, once more, to collapse into their seats. Mary Haugen tried, once more, to direct the solid mass of teenagers six feet to their left. But no matter how loud she yelled, her voice couldn't penetrate the crush. "Move over, move over," she simultaneously shrieked and gesticulated. Slim and trim, Haugen looked off-kilter, weighed down by a massive key chain on her belt loop that lent her body a noticeable tilt. A walkie-talkie seemed permanently affixed to her hand. "Hey, you," she cried, grabbing the attention of a boy wearing an orange FUBU sweatshirt. "Move over." He took note of Haugen, listened to her politely, then turned back to his friends without budging an inch.

Haugen called in reinforcements, waving a teacher to the far aisle to help her shift the mass of teenagers. The students listened attentively, respectfully. They didn't talk back, or argue with her instructions. But they did not move. Passive aggression was the teen weapon of the new millennium.

On the path behind the bleachers, Lori Boynton maintained a virtual one-woman receiving line for graduates of the Class of 1999 who still hadn't quite made the transition out of high school. Big Men on Campus, even Big Women on Campus, chafe at the dizzying descent from high school stardom to college anonymity. Stopping by to cheer for the Blue and Gold, to be swarmed over with respect by kids they'd scorned a year earlier, took the edge off the discomfort.

Craig Olson, the principal—Dr. O in student lingo—watched the game from behind the bleachers, occasionally distracted by a gang of Pee-wee League football players who'd shown up in their uniforms. Intent on the action on the field, their parents ignored both their kids' roughhousing and repeated requests from both Olson and the announcer that they rein in their children.

Olson was hardly living out nostalgia for his own high school years in rural Wisconsin. He'd been the only member of his class to graduate without a varsity letter. Growing up, he hadn't been a "high school high" kind of guy in any way. A self-described "mousy nonathletic person who spent time in pursuits nobody else knew about," like climbing mountains or backpacking with his parents, he got good grades without having to work very hard, attended football games only because he played clarinet in the band, and avoided all those dances and pep rallies at the heart of high school life. "I'm still being punished for never going to any of the social events," he said, "because now I have to go to all of them."

The Lakers were on the fifty-yard line, facing a third down with nineteen yards to go. Dave Busselman took the handoff, found a hole in the Angels' defensive line and sprinted toward the left side of the field, a single defensive back his only obstacle. With a good sixty pounds on his opponent, Dave dropped his left shoulder, bowled him over and made it to the three-yard-line before being brought down.

"Way to go, Lakers," the crowd roared. "All the way, all the way, all the way."

The cheerleaders led them in a rousing chant: *GO, FIGHT, WIN TONIGHT, BOOGIE ON DOWN, ALL RIGHT, ALL RIGHT.*

Steve Schumacher waded through the melee, looking for the perfect angle from which to record his daughter Lyndsay's nearly perfect jump.

Steve showed up at every football game where Lyndsay cheered, his video camera in hand, his still camera nearby. In a world of meticulously documented children, Lyndsay was the most meticulously documented of them all.

On the surface, Lyndsay seemed like the cheerleader every high school noncheerleader in American history hated. She had the three *P*s covered—pretty, perky and popular—with a Barbie-doll figure and affluent parents thrown in for good measure. But forget *Heathers* or any bitter memory of the scheming and snooty popular girl in your high school. Lyndsay had spent too much of her life as a quiet nerd to fit the mold. A transfer student from a nearby district, she'd used her family's move to remake herself, to become Olivia Newton-John in her favorite movie, *Grease*. She had pulled it off. "But, inside, I still think of myself as that dorky seventh grader," she said, pulling a strand of hair across her face.

Around the country, cheerleading had been declared a dying avocation. At Stillwater High School just east of St. Paul, the football season had opened with helium-filled balloons rising into the sky, but not a pom-pom in sight. The cheerleading squad had been disbanded at the end of the last school year for lack of interest. Nationally, the number of cheerleaders had dropped from 143,900 in the 1993–94 school year to 130,984 in 1998–99.

Feminism and Title IX, the federal regulation requiring equal spending on male and female school athletics, had dealt a lethal blow to girls leading sideline cheers, cutting out locker decorations and baking cookies for the team at many high schools. Girls strutted their stuff as athletes, not athletic knickknacks. Even where cheerleading thrived, it was a sport, transmogrified into "competitive spirit squads" that tumbled, danced and performed back flips with twists and cartwheel roundoffs. Some teams showed up at local and national competitions as virtual gymnasts. Others moved in synchronized steps to a salsa beat.

But not at Prior Lake. A year before, the local weekly, the *Prior Lake American*, had chosen a cheerleader as athlete of the week. Not everyone was happy. "I don't want to think of myself as an athlete," said Ashlee Altenbach, a member of the squad. Ashlee wasn't crazy about the part of the job that demanded cookie baking and locker decoration. But she didn't want to think of herself as a Jock, but as a saucy dancer who would follow in the footsteps of the Lakers cheerleaders of an earlier era, who'd once shown up at a game against the New Prague Trojans and handed out, well, Trojans. "It loses something by trying to be a sport," she complained.

The Lakers formed up along the line of scrimmage and, first and goal to go, they finally hit the scoreboard. Reilly and The Banditos blasted out a rendition of "The Final Countdown," but the melody could barely be heard above the cheering. And The Banditos? In the scheme of things high school, who cared about The Banditos? All eyes were fixed on Lyndsay as she proudly led the squad,

SHAKE YOUR BOOTY. JUMP, JUMP, SHAKE YOUR BOOTY. JUMP, SHAKE BOOTY. JUMP, JUMP. SHAKE YOUR BOOTY.

The Lakers stayed in the game thanks to Tony, who caught a forty-yard pass in the first quarter, another twenty-eight-yarder in the second, and two touchdown throws to boot. But the team fumbled five more times, threw four interceptions, and forfeited eighty-nine yards in penalties. The final score: Holy Angels 37, Prior Lake 20. The following week's headline in the *Prior Lake American* summed it up in six words: LAKERS SELF-DESTRUCT IN HOME OPENER.

Chapter Four

8:45 A.M., Thursday,
September 30, 1999

One thousand lethargic students bolted from their seats like a herd of wildebeest spooked by the roar of a lion as an alarm pierced the second-hour German classes, Chemistry labs, and study halls. Unlike their counterparts on the savanna, the teenagers weren't terrified by the ear-splitting blare. High school kids love fire or tornado drills, breaks in the monotonous daily routine that guarantee at least ten minutes of fresh air and open sky after hours of the closeness of a school building, so they raced toward the doors with sheer glee.

This drill, however, promised no liberation, which the students would have understood if they'd paid the slightest attention to Craig Olson's appearance on their homeroom television screens the morning before. "You're all aware of the tragedies that happened in schools in Kentucky, Arkansas, Oregon, and Colorado," said Olson, seated in front of the yellow-

and-blue school shield, dressed in an orange striped shirt. He'd spoken quietly, seriously. Tone was everything in forestalling panic, and Olson had considered his demeanor carefully to fend off the anticipated hysteria. "And schools, including us, have examined their security plans." Prior Lake has had very few injuries caused by the violent behavior of students or unwelcome intruders, he reminded them. "We want to make sure it stays that way."

Accordingly, the school had beefed up security, hiring a second "campus supervisor" to patrol the grounds and moving to a closed campus, with all doors but those leading to the administrative offices locked after the first morning bell, he'd announced. Elsewhere, school officials had gone much further, installing surveillance cameras, hiring extra security, distributing student photo ID badges and outlawing backpacks and cargo pants. But Olson had heeded the admonitions of psychologists who'd warned that overkill might terrify students, which was a classic instance of adult projection. The beefed-up security provoked no such consternation; for teenagers, it was just another entry in the long litany of petty, inexplicable annoyances imposed on their lives by mindless grown-ups.

Olson continued: We want to add one more measure, a lockdown drill to help prepare for a "crisis." When the alarm sounds tomorrow morning, go to the nearest classroom, the media center or the gym. We will secure all exterior doors and switch on the magnetic lock that isolates the classroom area on the second floor from the first floor. "So you'll be behind several levels of locked doors," he said, the attempt at comfort ringing through his voice. "Stay quiet and invisible." The goal, he explained, "will be to teach you to secure the building and each person quickly so that we can avoid the mass panic we saw in Colorado."

Olson's carefully wrought explanation had been absorbed into the white noise of daily announcements. Every morning began with the reading of the daily bulletin ("lunch today is hard- or soft-shelled tacos," or "if you're interested in playing girls' hockey, there will be a very short meeting after school in room 102") and the twelve-minute Channel One morning newscast, heavy with commercials, the price schools like Prior Lake paid for the dozens of television monitors they received from that network. Every day, students tuned out that ubiquitous buzz.

Mike Carr stood at the door of his classroom, trying to hold back the tide of students dashing for the nearest exit. "Remember, everybody, this is the drill Dr. O talked about yesterday, so lock the door and move a filing cabinet in front of it." Carr tried to take charge, but the drill had fallen during his Focus time, and Focus kids didn't like to be directed.

"Bang, bang, bang," a boy mimed a gun at Ashlee Altenbach, who giggled and pretended to swoon on a table.

The internal television system was still running, the display reading, HOMECOMING IS JUST AROUND THE CORNER. ARE YOU EXCITED YET?

Roger Murphy helped shove the filing cabinet where Carr indicated, but halfway to his destination stopped and asked, "What if you're taking a dump?"

The drill was a linchpin of Code Blue, a crisis plan ordered by the state of Minnesota and drawn up by Goldy, the campus cop, to teach students what to do if a gun-toting invader entered the school. Goldy had already provided the Prior Lake Police Department with floor plans of the building, copies of keys to all external and internal doors and a photo album containing pictures of every enrolled student. Having combed the roof for points of access to the interior, he'd specified "potentially safe areas" like the gymnasiums, auditoriums and media center, where students could be isolated from any pending threat. The final step in the process was to figure out how to move them to those havens safely and swiftly, which was the point of the drill.

Once they were there, Goldy had explained to the teachers, they should lock or barricade the doors, shut off the lights and guide students into corners from which they could not be seen from the hall. Although Carr followed those instructions, barricading was problematic because the doors swung out, not in. And locking them was a meaningless gesture in a world where teachers regularly handed their keys to student aides they sent on errands, keys anyone could have copied.

Carr tried to keep down the racket, but the laughter rolling like waves up and down the corridors only incited his students. Finally, he managed to gather the kids in a corner, right below his posters from National Women's History Month.

"Did somebody lock the door?" he asked.

"Yeah," answered Critter, laconically. Critter, whose legal name was Chris Clement, tended toward the laconic, except on those days when he was garrulous. "But it's a waste of time, anyone who wants to shoot us can just shoot through the window," he said, pointing to the full-length windows that ran vertically alongside the door.

All semblance of order dissolved as students began dancing and posing in front of the glass.

"How would they know we were here?" asked Carr, hoping to foster a more reasonable dialogue. But he was verbally outgunned.

"Why are you pretending that someone from the outside is going to break into the school and try to kill us?" Critter asked. "Everywhere else the shooters have been from the school and if the shooters are from here, like the kids in Columbine, they'll know right where we are. They'll know the whole routine. Remember last year, that big fat kid? They caught him making threats and shit and the cops came, handcuffed him and dragged him out. If it was somebody like him, we'd all be fried. He'd know exactly where everyone was."

The room buzzed with gossip about that "big fat kid," Dick Tiffany, Prior Lake's own "Columbinelike" threat of the previous spring. A plodding, heavyset transfer student with a lazy eye, Dick was the kind of kid who was a magnet for abuse. After months of being picked on, one afternoon in Math class he'd responded to the day's teasing by muttering, "You're on my hit list." The next thing he knew, he was in Goldy's office being interrogated.

Then, just after Columbine, Dick had mouthed off about his hit list again, to a boy he'd met at McDonald's. "I'm gonna take down any kid on it," the boy reported Dick saying. "Am I on it?" the boy had inquired sheepishly. Dick had said no, but the boy had still told school administrators about the comment. The next day, police officers walked into Dick's classroom, slapped a pair of handcuffs on him and arrested him for making terroristic threats, a felony offense under Minnesota law. No hit list was ever found; no one believed such a list actually existed. "He was too dumb to be dangerous," said Goldy. That didn't stop Olson from suggesting to Dick's parents that he belonged in a "more appropriate environment."

Dick's arrest, in the middle of the day, in the middle of class, had pitted student against student, inviting kids to look over their shoulders, to wonder which of their classmates might take out a gun and shoot them. For the rest of the year, Lyndsay Schumacher had consciously avoided the corridors where Roger Murphy, Jayne Garrison and their friends clustered. "You know what I mean, they look scary," she said, reflecting what she'd learned about the shooters at Columbine. Roger and his friends tried to laugh, knowing that almost everything Lyndsay had heard about Eric Harris and Dylan Klebold was wrong. They hadn't been members of the Trench Coat Mafia, a group that had already graduated. They hadn't targeted cheerleaders or their boyfriends, the jocks. They were equal-opportunity haters on a suicide mission against everyone.

"I have every bit as much reason to be afraid as Lyndsay Schumacher," said Jayne Garrison. "Maybe more, because everyone looks at me like I'm about to take out a gun and shoot them."

The same psychologists and school-safety experts who'd attempted to foster calm, then, had wound up fostering suspicion as they fell into the worst type of stereotyping in trying to help grown-ups distinguish between "the children" deemed needy of protection and "the other children," who needed scrutiny. Beware of kids with volatile tempers or extreme mood swings, who prefer books or movies with violent themes, who are interested in weapons, cut class, curse, drink, use drugs, bully or are bullied, they cautioned. Gripped by images of Columbine, teenagers had listened as intently as adults.

Did that mean that Prior Lake students should beware of Ashlee Altenbach because she was moody and was said to have smoked an occasional joint? Should they report Nick Busse because his favorite novel was *The Fight Club*, or Nathan Bong, a religious kid widely admired by teachers, because they'd seen him studying the explosives section of a chemistry book? Were they supposed to go running to Goldy if they overheard a girl in the bathroom squabbling with a friend, yelling, "I'm gonna fucking kill you if you do that," before stalking out.

Carr didn't have a chance to plumb the students for the full story of

Dick Tiffany, or the names of students who scared them. Roger was refusing to stay in the corner. "This is stupid," he said. "If someone comes into the school, we should go out and fight. I don't see why we're worried. We have Mr. Lachelt."

"Yeah, it's better to die trying than to just sit here waiting to be shot at," his classmates agreed.

At that point, Ashlee was the only one left in the corner. She wasn't anxious to "die trying."

"Having us huddled together in a corner just makes us an easier target," added Critter. "This makes no fucking sense."

Roger devised a different plan. "Wouldn't it be better to leave the door open and stand on either side and neutralize a shooter who tried to come through?" he asked.

Before Carr could find any words to burst Roger's military bubble, Olson sounded the all-clear and invited critiques of the drill. The kids didn't hesitate to offer them. They were much more comfortable batting around realistic scenarios than the grown-ups. And much more sanguine about the results.

"If someone really wants to kill us, they will," said Roger Murphy. "And pretending that's not true is just stupid."

Chapter Five

8:31 A.M., Monday,
October 25, 1999

"Hey, Slick, what's on the agenda for today?" Roger Murphy asked when Mike Carr strolled into his classroom for Focus American Government. The second class of the day, it was scheduled to begin promptly at 8:31, and Roger Murphy was already sprawled sideways out of one of those undersized blue plastic desk-chairs that are the hallmark of American schools. They're the kind of furniture perfect for a business that wants to encourage its customers not to linger. High school students, of course, have little choice but to remain.

Carr gritted his teeth for at least the twenty-fifth time in the ninety-three minutes he'd been at school. Teeth-gritting was decidedly NOT in his nature, but the week before, he'd had a blessed four-day weekend, thanks to the anachronistic custom of granting teachers two days off for a state union convention which none of them attended, and he was having trouble getting back into his rhythm. Looking over at Roger, Carr tried to summon up what little patience he had left. "He's so disrespectful," he said, shaking his head.

Dressed in his usual baggy camouflage pants and overstretched hooded sweatshirt, a full collection of spiked rings, dog collars, studded bracelets and safety pins decorating his body, Roger ignored Carr's frown and buried himself in Nietzsche's *Will to Power*. Carr, dressed in tan corduroy pants and a plaid shirt, read books, but his taste tended toward John Grisham. He'd never read Nietzsche, or Roger's other favorite volume, Sun Tzu's *Art of War*.

Carr didn't know what to make of Roger, who bore no resemblance to anyone he had ever met. He just knew that he hated being called Slick, and that Roger knew it too. In the calculus of teenagers, that equation guaranteed that Carr would be stuck with the nickname for at least one school year.

A seamless fit with comfortable white suburbia himself, Carr had never considered how it felt to grow up a poor, half-black, half-Mexican child in such an environment. Shunned by his peers at Westwood Elementary School, Roger had acted out, and his teachers had responded by declaring him impossible to deal with. Roger, in turn, gave up on them. "They were all too eager to sweep me under the carpet because of my insubordinate behavior," he said. "I'm entirely self-taught. I could never count on anybody else to guide me."

When Roger moved back to Prior Lake after spending most of elementary and middle school in the inner city, nothing much had changed. During his freshman year, naive about Roger's persona as an outsider and his place in the community, John Bennett had taken a stab at weaving him into school life, urging Roger to play football, Bennett's solution to the problems of every outcast or ill-behaved male. "I thought about it, for a minute," said Roger. "Then I thought, 'Wait, I'm not stupid, why would I do that?'" Bennett had given up in dismay.

Open in his disdain for his classmates, Roger provoked them relentlessly, quoting Dante's *Inferno* at them, mocking Christianity, pointing out every factual error or logical inconsistency in their arguments. It wasn't hard, he insisted. "Imagine listening to football players sharing their insights into human behavior. It was so easy to make them look foolish that, in the end, it got boring."

In dealing with teachers, Roger wielded petty insubordination as a badge of honor, and most of the faculty rose unfailingly to his bait. He rarely missed school, but he regularly wandered down to the art room to paint or the writing lab to fool around on the computer rather than attend class. As a junior, he'd run for student council under a Communist banner, hammers and sickles adorning his posters. He and Nick Olson regularly plastered the walls with chess club advertisements like CHESS 3:16: EVEN GOD LIKES CHESS, that somebody inevitably concluded were insulting. And he defied school rules against wearing sunglasses in the building or keeping the hood of his sweatshirt up over his head.

Rather than challenge him head-on, most Prior Lake teachers cringed from confronting Roger's defiance. One female teacher bluntly admitted to her colleagues that she was too terrified of the boy—of the spikes on his boots, his long dreadlocks, his sheer insolence—to even try to correct him. And while extreme, that fear was near universal, which alternately satisfied and puzzled Roger. "I've never hit anyone in my life," he said. "I've never been in a fight. When I break the rules, I'm entirely prepared to accept the consequences. But they're moronic people who don't think that I understand that you don't need a gun or violence if you have a greater intellect. They're too mindless to realize that I'm not dangerous at all."

In fact, Roger understood full well that the teachers' hesitancy in confronting his rejection of authority had less to do with their intellectual capabilities than with a more complicated amalgam of racism and fear of being perceived as racist.

Roger's final year at Prior Lake should have been a total disaster since his best friend and political and musical soul mate, Pete Williams, had run into yet another round of trouble. The June before, on a lark, Pete and his girlfriend Hillary had had sex in the handicapped bathroom off the school auditorium. Just after classes began in the fall, they realized she was pregnant. Hillary refused to consider abortion, so they were planning a Thanksgiving wedding and transfers to an "alternative" educational environment.

While Roger was losing his intellectual confidant to marriage and fatherhood, he'd found a girlfriend, Marissa, the sophomore who'd so intrigued Jeff Hoeg. A "fashion whore," as she put it, Marissa ambled into school wearing purple nail polish, black leather pants with red flames, and a dog collar one day; the next, she appeared in a black bustier with a see-through blouse, a long black skirt, oversized boots and fake purple braids woven into her topknot. The principal was dazzled at her flair.

Roger knew he and Marissa weren't exactly intellectually compatible. She liked soft, romantic music; he hated anything without a furious beat. He read incessantly; she wasn't much interested in books. But they were bound together by their "otherness" in a world of teen conformity. Marissa was a self-proclaimed pagan, a nouveau pose popular among counterculture students more interested in thumbing their noses at the "establishment," which included churches, than in the specifics of any religious belief. Rather than cede her individuality, Marissa had silently suffered through years of peltings with duct-tape balls, flour and empty plastic water-bottles. Finally, she'd gone on the attack, threatening to cast spells on her assailants. When she bought a T-shirt proclaiming, "If I were God, you'd all be dead," even the most macho succumbed to real fear of the young woman who admitted that her style was more fashion statement than political leaning.

Holding hands with Marissa between classes, nuzzling her neck in the media center, Roger seemed almost embarrassed, as if worried that romance would turn him soft. But the seventeen-year-old found a home at Marissa's house, and her mother, a bit of a Harley babe, adopted Roger warmly. When Megadeth came to town, she not only drove Roger and Marissa to the show; she stayed to enjoy it with them. With a stepfather who tried his best to ignore him, and a mother busy with younger children and a regular job on the graveyard shift at a local casino, Roger had long been on his own, following his own schedule, preparing his own meals. At Marissa's, he found a real family.

The first day of school, Roger had taken one look at Mike Carr and dismissed him as another squeakily clean Minnesota kid, a "Mr. Minnesota," as he called them, another pointless teacher. "I wouldn't give him a chance," Roger admitted halfway through the term. "I figured he was just another cog in this wretched and pathetic school system who would adhere to the Prior Lake motto: Let 'em slide by and hope someone else gets 'em."

But something about Carr bugged him. Every once in a while, the young teacher made a comment or posed a question that didn't fit the stereotype. Roger didn't want to be intrigued. But when Carr, who was still experimenting with his teaching techniques, gave a college-style lecture on the Constitution, Roger could no longer resist. Ashlee Altenbach, ever antsy and hyperactive, fidgeted in her seat. The rest of the class sniveled that Carr was putting them to sleep. Roger stood up and screamed, "Shut up so I can hear what the man has to say."

At that point in the year, Roger's growing academic curiosity felt like a Pyrrhic victory to Carr. If he taught to Roger, he lost the rest of the class, which had an attention span of four minutes. When he laid down the law about passes for trips to the school store, where doughnuts and PowerBars were sold first thing in the morning, the kids blithely ignored the edict. Jayne Garrison was unfailingly friendly and funny, but she floated in and out of the room at will. Ryan Langhorst, one of the mellowest kids in the school, leaned back in his chair, smiling, but rarely paid attention, although a long absence from school had already put him more than a term behind his peers.

At first Carr chided the kids if they let out the occasional "fuck," or declared an assignment to be "bullshit," hoping to inch them into cleaning up their language. To no avail. Then he tried putting them on contract, threatening to expel them from Focus. With no luck. Finally, one morning, when another "motherfucker" erupted from the seats, Carr slammed the door. "I'm not paid enough to put up with all this BS." The students nodded their agreement.

"It's a joke," he said. That week's contracts—expulsion notices—had just been posted: more than a dozen students were on the list for overdue work, unexcused absences, tardies, refusal to be quiet and repeatedly belching in class. "They say that the Focus kids learn the same material as other kids, just in a different environment. No way. I can't get through half of what I'm teaching my other classes. I spend three-quarters of my time being a policeman, not a teacher. How does that help these kids?"

Carr wasn't making much more headway with his mainstream students.

In his Honors Comparative Government class, the students had seized control. Eric Prchal sucked him into daily conversations about basketball, which delayed any discussion of the structure of Congress for at least fifteen minutes each period. Or someone would ask him how his training for the Whistlestop marathon was coming, or about his weekend date, which wasted another five. "I have no interest in the personal lives of the teachers," said Katie Keough, a friend of Jake Anderson, "but it's the game, and Mr. Carr's losing."

He prepared lessons he was sure they'd find exciting; they dismissed them as boring. He brought in movies and videos to vary the pace; they fell asleep. He tried to provoke discussions about issues that might intrigue them; they refused to respond. If he lectured, they complained that they hated lectures. If he handed out worksheets, they derided him for not teaching them himself. When he gave them study sheets to guide their exam preparation, they moaned that the print was too small or, if it was large, that the guides ran too many pages. "How is this relevant to my life?" they asked, interrupting a discussion of Thomas Jefferson and slavery. "Why do we have to learn this?" they demanded when he tried to teach them about the electoral college.

That morning, he'd handed back a test and faced a one-woman revolt by the hottest girl in school. "Mr. Carr, why did you take a point off my quiz just because I forgot to write the class hour on the paper?" asked Tina Farrell. Once or twice a trimester, Tina would deck herself out in an outfit guaranteed to push the principal over the edge—a hip-hugging microskirt with halter top that left a good eight inches of skin exposed in the center, or a handkerchief top that covered a small fraction of her chest. She was sassy and flirtatious, a lethal combination for a young male teacher like Carr. "That point wouldn't have changed your grade, Tina," Carr responded, trying to control his exasperation. "So what," she pressed, "it still isn't fair." She had barely stopped whining when a boy in the corner threw his quiz in the wastebasket and mumbled, "This quiz sucked."

Almost a quarter of the students had missed the exam entirely, and Carr was still trying to get them to come in for a make-up. One boy promised to take it the next day. He never showed up. Carr nagged him, exacting an agreement that he would take it that afternoon. He never showed up. "It's now or never, today during seventh hour or I give you an F," he laid down the law the following morning. Again, the young man failed to appear.

No matter how easy the tests, or light the reading assignments, Carr's students complained, seemingly earnestly, about the difficulty of the course. The young teacher was puzzled; he thought he wasn't being tough on them at all. But, reading sincerity in their faces, he lowered the bar—again and again. One morning, the class sent two quintessential "good kids" to confide that everyone was really stressed about an upcoming exam. So Carr spent the hour trying to ease their tension with a game in which he revealed every question and every answer. "It's the easiest class I've ever had," said Katie. "I probably should feel guilty, but I don't. I thought teachers were supposed to know that kids will always take advantage of them if they can."

Somewhere, hidden among the whiners and disrupters, Carr trusted, lurked a handful of students disgusted at the behavior of their peers, perhaps even interested in learning, although they were hard to spot when teen culture celebrated public displays of contempt for education and authority. Tom Maust, the president of the student council, seemed to pay close attention to Mike's lectures, and the German foreign exchange student never failed to respond to his questions and comments. Every once in a while, when the class deteriorated into total anarchy, leaving Mike helpless in the face of so much indifference, some girl would take pity on him and let loose a timid, "Come on, you guys," or scrunch up her face in antipathy to the daily barrage of puerile power struggles.

But, for the most part, even the kids intrigued by the material he presented were shy about brandishing any overt evidence of interest, sensitive to the prevailing disdain for seriousness of purpose, all too easily sucked into the vortex of manifest indifference.

Carr had hoped to use his first parent-teacher conferences, held each trimester just after midterm grades were sent home, to enlist some parental support for an end to the grousing and chaos. Envisioning the kind of meetings his parents had gone to in the not-so-distant past, where mothers and fathers got the ammunition they needed to crack down on their kids, a week earlier, he'd sat optimistically behind one of the dozens of desks that lined the walls of the gym, as parents milled about the center of the room, or waited in line to meet with their children's teachers.

"Why isn't my child getting a higher grade?" the first father at his desk asked abruptly. He wasn't seeking information; he was leveling an accusation and demanding a solution to Johnny's well-deserved C. "My son never got a B before," the next parent in line, a mother, complained. Carr knew she was lying, but in his teaching-methods courses in college they hadn't taught him how to deal with mendacious parents. "What does he need to do to raise it?" the woman continued. A dozen answers sprung to Carr's mind, from "Get a higher grade on his tests" to "Work harder." But the mother was unwilling to listen to anything but an offer to allow her son to submit extra-credit work.

"These parents are really invested in their kids and their grades," Carr said, still startled at the lack of respect he had felt. "But they don't seem invested in teaching them to behave or to work. Didn't teachers use to be able to count on mothers and fathers to be their allies?" His colleagues chuckled at that notion. The alliance of grown-ups, between parents and teachers, had crumbled in the face of a mounting parent-child coalition.

Carr was tired. He hadn't so much as seen a copy of his Government textbook until the week before school opened, and was struggling, day by day, to plan his lessons. He'd just graded a set of essay exams, a six-hour job over the weekend. And he still had quizzes to prepare and worksheets to design.

His students were, for the most part, seniors in high school. But when he brought up the coming presidential election, they had no idea who was running for either party's nomination. Roe v. Wade? A boxing match, right? Margaret Thatcher? Oh, yeah, she designed the American flag, didn't she? After twelve years of education, they didn't know much of anything.

Carr found consolation at lunch in the Elvis-adorned classroom of Lynn Lally, with a small band of teachers who eschewed the more staid ambiance of the faculty lounge. "The Bloods," Strege called them. Carr was looking for distraction, for the loose, playful ambiance of college, and he found it, in spades. The group was energized by the "bad girls" of the faculty, Strege and Schmidty, who reveled in talking about male students who were "hotties," flirting with male teachers, bragging about their own prowess. Their every remark was laced with double entendre and sexual innuendo. During one lunch period, a male student teacher mentioned an oral evaluation he was facing. "I'd like to evaluate you orally," quipped Strege. Another afternoon, Strege accused Carr of trying to steal her student aide, a provocative young woman. "I know you want her," she said, raising her eyebrows.

One of the most popular teachers in the school, Strege was a dynamo of energy with a single mood: exuberance. A former beauty pageant contender—a runner-up for Miss Minnesota—she clearly still thought of herself as the dazzling blonde with the light-up-your-face smile and the flashing blue eyes, despite the poundage she had added over the years. The daughter of teachers in a small town in southern Minnesota, in high school, Strege had been "Miss Goodie Two-Shoes," one of only two kids in her class who didn't drink, smoke dope or party, she said. "I wouldn't have done that to my parents, but I was pretty unhappy."

The minute she enrolled at Mankato State University, however, the lid blew off. Always a fireball of energy, Strege discovered that she could study, work part-time and still explore her wild side. Planning a career as a lawyer or motivational speaker, after college she'd been sidetracked into managing a jewelry store. Realizing that she didn't really care about profit margins, she went back to school and, at the age of twenty-three, landed at Prior Lake as a student teacher. She knew she had arrived. "It's hard because I don't like being taken advantage of, and teachers are being taken advantage of by the community, by the state, by parents," she said. "They think they can just keep piling on more and more. It's getting ridiculous. And then they criticize us. Teachers are always first in front of the firing squad.

"But I love kids this age. I'd sooner set my hair on fire than work in an elementary or middle school. I care that these kids are happy and feel like they belong. It's probably just that I need ego stroking, but I want to be that one person for somebody."

Just a year out of college himself, Mike Carr was besotted with Strege's vitality and popularity. "God, why can't I find myself a woman like that?" he asked in awe, wolfing down a hamburger and milk before telling his cohorts about his weekend, spent throwing up out of the window of the dorm room of a friend at a nearby college.

•   •   •

Mara Corey was too earnest to be part of Carr's clique. But by October, she, too, was desperate for relief. Unlike Carr, she'd begun the trimester with her courses prepared, and she managed to keep her students under control most days. Faced with what felt like a solid wall of contempt for education, she tried to reach out to the quiet ones, to empower the kids who regularly completed the reading, the students she imagined were excited by ideas or interested in developing crisp prose. She knew who they were. In class, they took refuge in utter passivity, too few in number—and too timid—to flout the cultural norm. But they hung back after the bell rang with just one more question or stopped by after school almost surreptitiously to pursue another idea.

Still, the job was grinding her down. She'd just handed back a set of papers to her juniors, and twenty-one out of the hundred students had spelled the word "possessed" "possed." More than a third had written "dosnt" instead of "doesn't." And half had misspelled "needle" as "needel." One boy moaned when he saw the river of red ink across his work, "You mean grammar and spelling count?"

Most of her students were behind in their work and she could find no way to motivate them to make up their assignments. Every day, they fell further behind, excused from school for a never-ending round of field trips. That morning, twenty peer mediators were out of school to help out at a state convention. On Wednesday nineteen seniors planned to spend the day at the University of Minnesota Library, and fourteen more peer mediators would be off at a training exercise. The following week, the student council members were scheduled for an all-day retreat, and the week after, all the sophomores would lose most of a day to testing.

"Field Trip High," Ron Lachelt, Corey's neighbor, called it. The two commiserated regularly as they stood outside their doorways between classes to keep students moving along and to break up scuffles.

On her course-objectives sheet, Corey had made her rule about missed work abundantly clear: It was the student's responsibility to arrange to make it up. "YOUR responsibility, not mine," she emphasized. Like so many of her other rules, that one was ignored. So she was constantly worried: Should I keep bugging them, or should I just give them a time limit and then mark down a zero? Are the students just testing me because I'm new? Am I doing something wrong? How does a good teacher handle this?

Every day at lunchtime, Corey carried those questions in to the teachers' lounge. Her companions were a self-selected bunch. It wasn't just Carr who stayed away. The Physics teacher preferred to spend the time in his classroom playing chess with his students; the band director often ate with his musicians in the cafeteria; and Katie Hallberg, the director of the gifted program, reigned over the Calculus Corner in the back of her classroom. But, unless they were out of the building, Boynton and Olson usually lingered with the faculty who stopped by. Rick Sohler, the senior guidance counselor, leaned back making wisecracks, and Chuck Lundstrom, the cochair of Corey's department, always snagged a couch for a quick power nap.

Just thirty minutes, lunch didn't provide much respite, especially for teachers who didn't brown-bag it and had to sprint down to the student cafeteria to pick up their chicken nuggets or pizza. But teachers work in dramatic isolation, and lunch was one of the few chances Special Education instructors had to get to know the literary crowd, the librarians to carp about student unruliness with members of the Spanish department, new teachers to mine veterans for advice and comfort, and the veterans to acculturate the novices.

The tiny room tucked behind the faculty mailboxes was anything but cozy—just two tables, two couches, two refrigerators and three ancient microwave ovens teachers had brought in when they'd updated their home kitchens. Littered with mugs, chipped plates, plastic containers and random cafeteria trays, the countertop looked like a display at a second-hand store. Leaflets covered the tables, advertisements for Mary Kay cosmetics, Pampered Chef, or some other instructor's scheme for making ends meet on a teacher's salary. And the building's union activists made sure the bulletin board always boasted some reminder—a chart, a clip from the newspaper, a graph—of how far Prior Lake teachers' salaries lagged behind those of their colleagues in neighboring districts.

Even that small space was divided, the far table the turf of the New Age teachers, and the table nearer the door the domain of the hard-asses. The latter, mostly men, were the first to speak up when Corey unloaded her woes that morning. "Your job is to teach these kids to read and write," said Joe Goracke, at the age of forty-five one the leaders of the "Old School" crowd. "They are sixteen, seventeen, eighteen years old. It's time to start treating them that way. How else will they learn to be responsible?"

The women, who dominated the other table, rolled their eyes in collective disgust: Don't listen to Goracke, they protested, call the kids in individually, use "limits," not threats. Goracke laughed dismissively at that advice, accusing his pedagogical adversaries of being wimps by coddling near-adults—although in somewhat milder language.

Like graduates of most education schools, Corey had been well schooled in the kind of "touchy-feely" approaches the women advocated. They sounded just like her teaching-methods instructor at the University of Minnesota, who had cautioned against ever telling a pupil that his answer was *wrong*. "He discouraged us from being that blunt because it might hurt a student's self-esteem," Corey explained. "The notion was that everyone's answer is the right answer for them. One time I asked, directly, 'But what if a student gives an answer that is wrong?' He told me to figure out how he came up with that answer and lead him to the right one. 'If you tell him he's wrong,' the prof said, 'he won't remember the right answer, but he will remember how he felt when you told him that.'"

Although in her first days at Prior Lake Corey had gravitated to the soft-and-gentle group, she had serious doubts about the latest educational fad and feared that her skepticism put her seriously out of step not just with half the lunch crowd, but with many of her own colleagues in the English department, especially with teachers like Strege and Lally, on everything from late work to homework and grading standards.

That Monday, after four blissful days without having to send a single teenager to the office, most of the teachers in the lounge showed at least some sign of rejuvenation. As they helped Corey through her angst, or talked about their minivacation, the bags under their eyes were a shade lighter. Their lunches were more elaborate, as if they had actually had time to cook. Not Corey's. "I spent all weekend, four days, grading papers for College Prep Comp," she moaned, filling the silence after the tension sowed by the competing advice. "I was two weeks behind and I'm still not entirely done."

Her female lunch companions were horrified. "How many papers are you assigning them?" they asked with real concern. "A paper a week," Corey replied casually. Their raised eyebrows and shaking heads spoke volumes: Back off on the assignments. "But how can I teach them to write if I don't make them write?" she pressed. The grimaces on her colleague's faces broadcast their disapproval of that reply. Corey knew it was considered bad form for a first-year teacher to so much as imply that she might be critical of the prevailing standards. She'd sworn herself to discretion. But Corey was not programmed for discretion.

Sensing the disapproval, she quickly moved onto safer ground: the first parent conferences of the school year. "Are the parents always like that?" she asked. The tension abated in a flash. No matter their divisions, teachers like nothing better than to trade horror stories about parents, and Corey knew how to tell a horror story. While Carr was being berated for his grading practices, a couple had confronted Corey over her class policy barring the use of the words "gay" and "ghetto" as epithets for "boring" or "stupid." "I know I'm bucking the tide of teenage slang," she explained to the rapt lunch group, but "offensive is offensive, and I'm not going to allow offensive speech in my class." She'd punished one boy for repeatedly violating her edict and his parents had shown up at the conferences to protest her arbitrary rule. After all, they said, "gays are sinning faggots."

Two female teachers, both devout Christians, kept chewing. Utterly oblivious to their reaction, Corey moved on to her next parental nightmare. A well-dressed couple had sat down at her table and promptly asked, "Are you an atheist?" Corey had refused to play that game, assuming that her religious beliefs were none of their business. "Ah, what seems to be the problem?" she replied instead. The parents had looked over the corrections she'd made on their son's paper and assumed she'd torn it to shreds because he had defended Christianity.

"Does that mean that I'm not allowed to correct spelling if the paper is about religion?" she asked her colleagues.

Before anyone could respond to that question, Joe Goracke leaned forward and smiled an "I can top that" kind of smile. Goracke, who taught both U.S. History and Psychology, never got many parents lining up to meet with him at conferences. Notorious for being tough, and as firm with parents as with their kids, he received phone calls instead, from mothers and fathers clearly intimidated by his imperviousness to whining and pleading.

A week earlier, a student had rambled into Goracke's class late. Reminding him of the class tardy policy, Goracke had meted out a light punishment. "That's not fair, Mr. Goracke," the boy had responded. Goracke remained unmoved. "Well, suck my dick, you motherfucking son of a bitch," the boy exploded. When Lori Boynton called in the boy's parents, his mother had insisted that her son deserved no punishment because he suffered from mild diabetes, which must have momentarily scrambled his brain. "Right," said Goracke, who raged regularly against the "medicalization of bad behavior." "Have you ever heard of diabetes causing a kid to curse at his teacher?"

No one in the room was willing to defend the parents, but they, too, were caught in a web of colliding expectations about the role of schools, about what staff should do and be for them and their children. The relatively few traditionalists among them complained that the other parents were as bratty as their kids, facilitating unacceptable behavior, refusing to hold their children accountable, insisting that teachers and administrators remake every program for the convenience of their progeny. "The school is not there to raise your children, but, unfortunately, too many parents think that it is," said Michelle Lien, the mother of two Prior Lake students. "Too many of today's parents are overly involved in the nitty-gritty of education."

But in an era of extreme protectiveness of middle-class children, of parental hypersensitivity to real and perceived threats to their kids' psychological well-being—engendered, in many cases, by schools themselves—parents no longer felt comfortable bowing docilely to the authority of teachers. In a dog-eat-dog world, shouldn't they at least try to give their children a leg up? If they don't, how will their kids compete against the children of parents who do? If Special Education students have the right to individualized learning plans, why not their kids? Were they really less "special"? How could it hurt to arrange for an easier teacher, or at least one who wasn't so fixated on achievement over effort?

The faculty conversation about parents swirled around Craig Olson, the principal. "It used to be that kids and their parents were grateful for life," he quipped dryly. "Then they wanted liberty, which was great. Now, they've moved on to the pursuit of happiness, and they think that we're standing in their way."

Olson was a mellow guy in a lousy job that put him in the crosshairs between the school board, the superintendent, parents, teachers, students and at least 475,000 state, local and federal regulations. Privately, he hungered to raise the bar on students, to impose more rigor on their education. "We don't need bonehead math, or those types of courses," he said. "We need to stop sending kids the message that they don't have to try."

But he was careful about pushing parents or the faculty too hard. Some of his reticence reflected a naturally gentle, collegial style. The rest was part political savvy and part the legacy of his predecessor, who had pushed too hard for high standards—publicly declaring that the school was not a "participatory democracy"—and been driven out by the staff. It was still not clear whether his sin had been autocracy or snobbery.

Olson understood faculty feistiness. He'd been a pretty feisty faculty member himself at one point, and gotten burned for his candor. As a Peace Corps volunteer in rural Kenya assigned to a small Harambe school, a new school with just three teachers and sixty students, he'd quickly become the de facto headmaster. During his third and final year, however, at his own urging, the board of trustees had hired a permanent principal. That new boss stole money from the school and shifted the blame onto a teacher. He beat children with telephone cable. And rather than teach his own three classes, he regularly excused himself, pleading "school business." Unschooled in the virtues of workplace silence, Olson had complained directly to the board. His reward: a one-way ticket back home to Wisconsin.

Seated next to Olson, Lori Boynton pointedly ignored Goracke's complaint about the diabetic student and latched on to the topic of standards. Boynton, who fit most comfortably philosophically at the table on the far side of the lounge, prickled defensively at any perceived attack on the quality of contemporary education, even one meted out by her boss. Suffused with pride at the quality of Prior Lake's students, she dismissed any suggestion that today's high school students were undereducated in comparison with their predecessors.

Boynton wasn't in total denial. She willingly conceded that during the 1970s, the bottom had fallen out of public education. At Prior Lake, as at many schools, the traditional curriculum had been transformed into a pastiche of electives, as teachers declared themselves their students' friends. But the "do your own thing" culture of that period had faded, she argued, and the continued drumbeat of criticism that kids were ill-prepared was a "Manufactured Crisis," the title of her favorite book.

In that volume, David Berliner and Bruce Biddle posited a near-conspiracy of "organized malevolence" of government officials and their allies who scapegoated educators by "ignoring, suppressing and distorting" evidence about the quality of our schools. Their insidious goal? To undermine support for public education and allow education funding to be redistributed to the already privileged.

"[D]espite greatly expanded student enrollment," they argued, "the average American high school . . . student is now doing as well as, or perhaps slightly better than, that student did in previous years . . . And when comparative-study evidence is examined carefully, that evidence also confirms impressive strengths of American education."

Veteran faculty members had heard it all before: Berliner's statistics, Boynton's gushing about the superior knowledge of today's students—their understanding of DNA and genetics, their math skills, their well-rounded worldview. The dissenters at the other table sniggered. "Obviously, there's some truth to the assertion that kids today know more science than we did at their age, but it's not about the quality of education," said Ron Lachelt, sitting at the hard-ass table with Goracke and his Science colleague, Andy Franklin. "The kids know more science than we did because scientists know more than their predecessors did. And math, well, that's about the invention of the calculator, not about teaching."

The discussions about the quality of education wafted around Corey, who bit her tongue in an uncharacteristic feat of discretion. But away from the lounge, she was openly dubious. "When I talk to my parents, and to older people in general, I know that they learned more in high school than I did," said Corey, who was wearing a long skirt and a knit top set off with a silver apple, a cherished gift from a pupil she'd worked with as a student teacher. She was seated behind her desk in the classroom she shared with a Spanish teacher. Every piece of furniture in the room was adorned with a sign providing its name in Spanish.

"Students of their generation used to be expected to perform at a higher level, to read more books, to learn more history than I did. So I don't know. But I *do* know that these kids aren't learning half of what I did, and I'm not that much older than they are."

Two months into her first year of teaching, Corey was still more confused than chastened. She was dying to ask someone why the English department taught *The Scarlet Letter* as a movie, not a book, or how her colleagues could assign "first-person" research papers. "What's a first-person research paper?" she asked. "How does this prepare them for college?" And she couldn't understand why so few teachers were up in arms about the fact that students regularly copied each other's homework or cheated on in-class worksheets.

She felt befuddled because her colleagues clearly weren't slouches. Lachelt and Franklin, among others, were perpetual students themselves, amassing hundreds of college credits simply because they loved learning. Others read voraciously, in and out of their fields, and called on a real depth of knowledge in the classroom. They pulled money out of their own pockets to buy extra materials for their classes, opened their homes to student study groups and used evenings, weekends and vacations to design new curricula. There were surprisingly few slackers in the bunch, Corey had already noticed, few of the legendary instructors who lectured from ancient and yellowed notes.

They had all the tools to do the job right—the training, the education, the dedication. So why couldn't her students read? The day before, she'd asked the members of her College Prep Composition course to read aloud from an article. One girl stumbled over *Darwinian*, a word she couldn't define, and another didn't know what *autonomy* meant. She'd just read in *Time* magazine that the average American fourteen-year-old had a vocabulary of ten thousand words, down from twenty-five thousand in 1950, and had begun to wonder if the former statistic wasn't too optimistic.

Was she just suffering from first-year teacher blues? Had the poverty of the education Prior Lake students received been obscured by their class backgrounds? Were her dreams for her students absurdly unrealistic? "I can't believe that we can't do better than this," she said, both her confidence and her stubbornness apparent. "I can't believe that this is what passes for an above-average education."

Chapter Six

1:15 P.M., Wednesday, November 3, 1999

Winter was refusing to descend on Minnesota for the second year in a row. The heavy trees lining Fish Point Road were barren of leaves, the fields on the edge of town had lost any suggestion of green and the boats along the shores of Prior Lake had been scraped and drained in preparation for the usual five-month freeze. It was time to think about towing the ice house onto the lake, filling up the propane tank, stocking the cooler with beer and drilling holes in the ice for fishing, or at least for the pretense of fishing. Instead, three days after Halloween, the golf carts were still racing across the fairways at The Wilds.

When Minnesotans weren't talking about how warm the weather would be for the opening of deer hunting season on Saturday, they were fretting about their governor, the state's obsession. Jesse Ventura had just completed his first year in office, 365 days since his improbable victory over politics as usual. His fans—all those teenagers, blue-collar workers and die-hard populists who'd seen his election as a grand experiment in American democracy—should have been celebrating the triumph of the libertarian outsider who'd dared declare, "Government isn't brain surgery."

But Minnesotans are proud people with a deep-seated need to be admired and an almost pathological adherence to the concept of "Minnesota Nice." Jesse had not been nice, at least not if you were speaking the dialect locals call Minnesotan. "Nice" means watching your words carefully so that you won't provoke. It means burnishing the edges off your opinions so they won't scratch the person next to you or, God forbid, offend. Candor might be celebrated in New York. But Minneapolis bears little resemblance to the Big Blunt Apple.

So although the state was riding an economic high and the wonks at the University of Minnesota conceded that the former professional wrestler had appointed an able staff, which was running the state well, Jesse—who'd won the sobriquet "The Body" as a wrestler but been cut down to size as "The Mouth" during his tenure in the governor's mansion—was in trouble. In an interview with *Playboy,* he'd spoken his mind. Perhaps no one would have cringed so tightly at the candor once so admired if Larry King, CNN, and the entire national press corps hadn't aired the state's dirtiest secret—that their new governor had a maw the size of Montana and wasn't reticent about opening it. But the Jesse-isms had become part of the national folklore. Jesse Ventura on organized religion: a "sham and a crutch for weak-minded people." Jesse on the obese: "Every fat person says it's not their fault, that they have gland trouble. You know which gland? The saliva gland." Jesse on single mothers on welfare: "I don't want to sound hard-core, but why did you become a single parent? Is it government's job to make up for someone's mistakes?"

Never mind that the vast majority of those hardy Minnesota populists agreed with most of what Jesse said: that a soldier's sexual orientation is less important than his ability; that college football players are just unpaid professionals; that locking up people for smoking pot is nonsensical; or that the poor need a safety net, not a permanent welfare check. The governor had embarrassed the earnest citizens of the state. Minnesota's honor had been besmirched. His popularity ratings plummeted by half.

Politics, of course, are rarely the passion of high school students. But the Prior Lake students who hung out in room 405 weren't your run-of-the-mill teenagers. In Katie Hallberg's inner sanctum, no one thought it strange for a seventeen-year-old boy to be running differential equations just for fun, for a sixteen-year-old girl to be reading up on funding for the homeless simply because she cared, or for a gaggle of kids to be arguing about Jesse Ventura.

"He's a stupid jerk," proclaimed Mike Rodning, a junior, who was lolling on a black beanbag chair. The half dozen other students crammed into the Calculus Corner, a tight space carved out of Hallberg's classroom by partial room dividers, hung on Mike's every word. None disagreed, although it was unclear whether they seconded his pronouncement or were loath to endure the attack that contradicting Mike, for whom the concept of "legitimate" disagreement was anathema, inevitably provoked.

A quiet girl seated at the table looked up from her homework and broke the silence. "I don't think he's stupid, but I do think he's a jerk," she said, glancing sideways at Mike to see if he would uncoil for the attack. "Why would you want to piss off so many people? He isn't dumb, but, politically, he's an idiot."

Mike's rejoinder was desultory. She hadn't provided him enough fodder for anything more. "What's the difference between being a political idiot and being dumb?" he asked, still leaning back. "Shooting yourself in the foot with the voters is pretty dumb if you're a politician."

Reilly Liebhard, who would have looked like Baby Huey if Baby Huey bench-pressed three hundred pounds, caught the tail end of Mike's comments as he leaned into Calc Corner to check out the company. "I love the fact that Jesse always says what he means," he joined the conversation. "Like the time he was on national TV with the football commentators. They asked him if Minneapolis needed a new stadium for the Vikings, and he replied, 'We just built one sixteen years ago, and we don't build new schools every sixteen years.' That was pretty awesome."

Mike tensed, as if ready to spring. But he knew better than to take on Reilly, who was the school's most serious intellectual threat. "It seems to me that Jesse is more intelligent than he's able to articulate," Reilly continued, not noticing Mike's quandary. "I have the sense that he has a lot of great ideas kicking around in the back of his head, but could express them better."

Katie Hallberg sat behind a desk teetering with papers and projects and videotapes, listening to the swirl of dissension on the other side of the divider, the easy banter, the consultation and chaos. She was grinning like the Cheshire Cat. There was nothing she loved better than intellectual ferment steeping in her room.

The Calc Corner was her own invention, a space set aside for the special study hall her Advanced Placement Calculus students were required to take so they could keep up with the work she heaped on them daily. But as much as a place where her Math students could struggle together through the volumes of solids of revolution, Calc Corner was a safe space for the school's brains, a tiny piece of turf where they could cluster together over lunch, make popcorn in the microwave oven and debate religion and politics without feeling abnormal.

On that late fall day, as the second lunch period was winding up, leaving students and teachers alike just two more class periods before the final bell, Hallberg couldn't sit back and savor the repartee. She had pencils and paper to organize, chairs to set up, her homemade display stand to post outside her door to remind students and faculty of Day Two of her Fall Festival of Knowledge Week, the annual student academic competition sponsored by Synergy, the gifted-and-talented program she directed.

Okay, it wasn't exactly the Olympics, but Hallberg's four Bees—geography and spelling, science and bumble—were the closest thing Prior Lake had to an academic play-off game, and Hallberg did her best to make it at least feel grand. Academic contests, of course, lacked the allure of ice hockey or basketball, so the spectators were likely be few in numbers. It was a spelling bee, for god's sake. Just a few kids lined up in front of the blackboard spitting out letters to words no one ever used or, if they did, they could have spellchecked on their computers. No body slams, cross checks or forty-yard football bombs. No booster club parents sporting buttons with photographs of their children, or cheerleaders waving pom-poms.

Tapped to play Alex Trebek for the day's spelling bee, Dan Jergens, a quiet, low-key chemistry instructor, sauntered into the room, a sheaf of papers, lists of words, in his hand. As the contestants identified themselves to him, all eyes fell on Reilly, the man to beat since Reilly had been reading for a good three years longer than anyone else in the room. When he was just 18 months old, Reilly had started reading spontaneously, with no urging or instruction. By the time he was two, he was quizzing his parents about information he'd gleaned from the daily newspaper. Just after his third birthday, he'd started leafing through his father's back issues of the *Journal of the American Medical Association* and probing his mother about potential life-threatening ailments.

Vegas bookmakers, then, would have put the odds at a hundred to one that Reilly would leave his opponents in the dust. As he took his place among them, Jergens nodded in the boy's direction. "We'll see about that," his smile seemed to suggest.

Round one of the double-elimination competition was uneventful, as Jergens worked down the lists of words in front of him, leading the eight students through *acclamation, analytical, appendices, arraignment, audacious, bizarre,* and *chauvinistic.* Only Lisa Gilbert stumbled, confusing *acquiesce* with *aqueous.* Round two got dicier: *Collateral, conscientious, depreciation* and *disparaging* tripped up four participants.

Jergens kept the mood light, defining words casually, encouraging the students. The participants, however, were tense, scribbling down the words on the small notebooks Hallberg had provided, hoping that seeing them would prevent disaster. Only Reilly ignored pen and paper.

"*Predecessor,*" Jergens asked a boy named Matt. The young man froze momentarily. "You know, predecessor, as in what monkeys were to human beings," Jergens prodded. Reilly couldn't resist. "Not if you go to school in Kansas," he said. The students grimaced: What the hell was Reilly talking about? Catching the reference to the Kansas school board, which had just mandated the inclusion of creationism in the science curriculum, Jergens couldn't hold back a chuckle. But he still threw Reilly a cautionary "come on, don't show off" glare and flipped through the pages of words before him looking for a pointed rejoinder. Finally, he looked up with a smirk.

"Reilly, spell *schadenfreude,*" he said, pronouncing the first syllable like the word "shade."

"*Schadenfreude*," said Reilly, correcting that pronunciation by soften-ing the "a," seemingly deaf to the undertone in Jergens's selection of his word. "The guilty pleasure you get while others suffer," Reilly said, offer-ing an almost textbook definition. He then rattled off the letters of the cor-rect spelling like bullets from a machine gun.

The clock was ticking toward the bell, and four students, three girls and a boy, remained in the contest. It was time to up the ante, so Jergens reached for another, more difficult list. Within moments, the field had been reduced by one, leaving just three seniors standing. As Reilly's turn came, Jergens again scoured his pages for a word that might trip up the acknowl-edged "word nerd."

Again, Reilly appeared oblivious to Jergens's subtext. People in Prior Lake had been playing "Stump Reilly" since he was a preschooler, when strangers stopped him at Hauser's Supermarket while his mother, Joy, was shopping, and presented him with mathematical puzzles. "They were try-ing to catch him in a mistake and there was something almost cruel about it," Joy recalled. Unaware of the ambivalence he provoked in most adults, Reilly had thought it was a game. He still did.

"*Demitasse*," Jergens said, almost triumphantly. "*Demitasse*," Reilly repeated. "A kind of coffee cup, or, perhaps, half a Soviet news agency." This time, even Jergens missed the joke. "D-E-M-I-T-A-S-S-E," Reilly con-tinued.

In what became the final round, one girl bombed by spelling *gendarme* with a "j," and Reilly's only other opponent blew it by mixing up the last three letters of *milieu*. Reilly, the victor, accepted his prize, a coupon for a free pizza, and began packing up his books.

"You're lucky you won on that round," Jergens said, offering no con-gratulations. Reilly looked up, puzzled. "The next word I was going to give you was *fait accompli*," the teacher continued. Reilly didn't hesitate. "F-A-I-T A-C-C-O-M-P-L-I," he noted confidently. Jergens did not smile as Reilly thanked him and raced off to class.

Hallberg watched that final encounter from a chair in the corner where she'd been sitting quietly, seething that not a single faculty member or administrator had bothered to show up to cheer on the students. "It's not that teachers hate the gifted," she said, both steel and resignation heavy in her voice. "It's that they hate the concept of the gifted, at least the academically gifted. They have no trouble with the concept of the athletically gifted. They don't demand that we level that playing field. But hating that concept doesn't change the reality that we have students operating on vastly different intellectual levels, and they all need to be stimulated and applauded. Instead, too many people engage in some kind of perverse logic, like, 'they're already talented, so why do they need something special,' as if you have to give the rest of the kids something to compensate for the fact that they aren't as smart."

Hallberg glanced toward the door, as if she needed to be careful about who might overhear her remarks. Her educational philosophy hadn't won her any Ms. Popularity awards among her peers, especially among the other members of the Math department. "Half of them think that I'm dysfunctional, and most of the rest think I'm either anal retentive or just a snob," explained Hallberg, the recipient of the 1995 Presidential Award for Excellence in Science and Mathematics, the highest honor given to any American teacher.

In the parlance of educators, snobbery meant demanding higher standards and, by that definition, Katie Hallberg was guilty as charged. While Prior Lake students estimated that they spent an average of two to three hours a week doing homework, the average Advanced Placement Calculus student—the average Hallberg student—sweated three or four hours a week on that single subject. The kids mumbled and griped, albeit mildly, but the other math teachers alternately ridiculed and flailed her for that toughness. "They're always complaining that I'm going to burn the kids out," she said, proudly sporting a T-shirt displaying The Theorem of the Mean Calc Teacher, a gift from students in the Class of 1992. "What a ridiculous concept. You don't burn out teenagers by making them use their brains."

The relationship between Hallberg and her departmental colleagues might have remained civil if she'd confined her academic ardor to AP Calculus. It was hard to argue with success, and Hallberg's students won perfect scores on the most difficult AP Calculus tests at twice the national rate. But she was no snob, not in the real sense of the word. Hallberg believed that it was disrespectful not to push all students, not just the brightest, and she waged war with the rest of the Math faculty over the amount of homework they assigned, the number of As they awarded, the amount of Math they actually taught.

It wasn't just the Math department. To Hallberg, the whole school bore too much of a resemblance to Havana, or East Berlin before the wall fell, where nobody did much work because rewards bore little relationship to merit. The students involved in Synergy had never been challenged enough to avoid a morass of self-doubt and, acculturated to low expectations and mediocrity, few of her mainstream students seemed willing to try to find out just how far they could go. "There are too many underachievers in schools, and too many teachers who want to be students' friends," Hallberg said. "If we don't push students, how will they ever discover that if they really work, they can go much farther than they think? Isn't that our job?"

For years, Hallberg thought she was making headway in her crusade for higher standards, with the active support of Prior Lake's former principal. A graduate of Carleton College, one of the Midwest's most elite academic institutions, Fred Blaisdell had praised every blow she struck for more rigor and had upped the ante on instructors of Advanced Placement courses by ordering them to follow her practice of requiring all AP students to take the national AP test. Ultimately, however, his support had been the kiss of death among a faculty who eventually found a way to oust him. Hallberg still suffered for that alliance, although it had been five years since Craig Olson had been installed as his replacement.

No matter the rancor she provoked, after twenty-seven years as a teacher, Hallberg couldn't give up; it wasn't in her vocabulary. And if she couldn't control what her peers did in their classrooms, she could at least do battle on behalf of the kids that most worried her, the gifted and talented—students with IQ test scores in the top 5 percent in the nation. Someone had to prepare Prior Lake's brightest to vie in a fiercely competitive world, and Hallberg had appointed herself that someone.

Synergy, the program she'd created for them, wasn't much, at least not by the measure of the nation's most academically rigorous high schools, where intellectually gifted kids were offered their own curriculum. But in those same communities, parents also bought teachers' answer books to give their children a leg up on Calculus tests, counselors and paid professionals wrote college applications and students were guided to the best universities, prepped for their entrance exams. There, students could choose from ten, sometimes twenty Advanced Placement courses; Prior Lake offered only three.

Working in a district where parental expectations didn't reach that level, Hallberg had to make do with a program that had no real budget, that carried no academic credit, that had, in fact, no regular meeting time. But week after week, Hallberg pulled her kids out of their regular classes for a single period and put them through their paces with speed-reading practices and simulation games. She was a virtual encyclopedia of exercises that pushed young minds to work outside the box, to cultivate abstract thinking in those who tended toward the consequential, or the consequential in those with a penchant for the abstract. Like any good coach—and, make no mistake, she was as focused and exacting as John Bennett on the football field—Hallberg prodded her students to try their hands at chess, to take the risk of making fools out of themselves before audiences and always—always—to compete, not just against each other, but against the most intellectually muscular and aggressive players in the country.

"How else can they see, can they get even a glimpse of how good they can be, or how good they will have to be, if they don't go up against the best and the brightest," she said. She enrolled them in the national WordMasters competition and the Knowledge Bowl. In the Great Auk's Academic Competition, they went head-to-head against the faculty, which often had to struggle to keep up.

In the eyes of her peers, every move Hallberg made on behalf of her Synergy kids was a sign of academic elitism, an affront to the most central tenet of modern education. And, in fact, it was. An entrenched egalitarian bias had swept public schools in the 1970s and, caught up in that idealistic fervor, educators had used bulldozers on the proverbial playing field, wiping away intelligence testing, ability grouping and tracking. Such distinctions created two categories, educators had argued, "the elect" and "the damned," with the former offered novel and rigorous curricula, the latter, usually the children of poverty, shouldered with the burden of failure.

That dismal old landscape might have been revived by removing the racial and class bias built into the practice of tracking and by designing innovative and demanding curricula for students of all abilities. Instead, educators had opted for heterogeneity, the development of a brave new schoolyard in which all students were thrown together in a glorious melting pot. The most gifted would find their reward in helping to teach their less academically talented peers, those peers would be pulled up to the level of the most talented, and nobody's feelings would get hurt.

The reality forged by that utopian fantasy was bleak for Prior Lake's brightest, and it offered mainstream students little countervailing benefit. With group work regularly replacing individual endeavor, students did turn to the smart kids for assistance, but not as teachers or mentors; they simply demanded that they do all the work. And mainstream kids didn't rise to the level of the most talented, as Hallberg's students were the first to explain. "How could anybody rise to my level when I have no idea what my level is because nobody ever forced me to find it?" asked Katie Keough, who looked like a transplant from 1968. "Instead, we're bored because we're pulled down to the level of the least intelligent and the least interested."

And the feelings soothed weren't those of students locked out of the highest-level courses, but those of parents who no longer had to confront the reality that their children were not among the intellectual elite. Their children neither craved nor needed that consolation. They knew that all students were not created equal. They knew who the smart kids were, and it didn't bother them in the least since, in the social geography of American schools, the ideal wasn't to be smart, but to be popular. Who ever heard of a cheerleader or football hero who fell into depression because she or he wasn't accepted into an Honors class? And who *never* heard of an Honors kid who felt excluded because she was snubbed by the cheerleaders? Ignoring differences in intellectual abilities made adults feel better—nobler, more democratic—but it did nothing to challenge mainstream students, and left the brightest kids right where they'd always been, in social purgatory, only without the solace of stimulating classes.

At the age of fifty-seven, Katie Hallberg still remembered that purgatory keenly, although during her own public education she'd at least had significant academic consolation. The daughter of a sign painter from St. Louis Park, a heavily Jewish suburb of Minneapolis, she'd entered school assuming that she was a failure because she was the only member of her family of artists who couldn't draw. In the classroom, though, she discovered math, and a different side of herself. By high school, she was on the fast track, with accelerated courses in Mathematics, History and Humanities, although her destination was unclear since being a female math whiz in prefeminist America was an uphill battle.

Hallberg's academic success did nothing to win her inclusion in the school's aristocracy and was meager compensation for her position at the bottom of a fiercely hierarchical teen society. She thrived only by finding community among the other kids tracked into classes for the gifted—members of the band, foreign-language devotees, kids who didn't feel ashamed of being smart, or those who at least found in academic excellence some comfort, no matter how cold.

If the drive for egalitarianism in an inherently unequal world wasn't problem enough for modern-day Hallbergs, the relentless emphasis on bolstering student self-esteem created an even more untenable situation. Self-esteem training was one of those New Age school concepts that began sweeping the country about two decades ago. The philosophy sounded enticing in an era of EST, rolfing and egalitarian classrooms: People with low self-esteem cause trouble and don't achieve much, so if we want children to soar and behave like civilized humans, we need to teach them to feel good about themselves. Baby-boomer parents convinced that they, unlike their own parents, could raise children without inflicting a single psychic scar, were titillated at that cheery prospect of such universal success.

In one of dozens of waves of idealistic fervor that promised to loft American education to new heights, consultants swept into school districts to instruct teachers in how to eradicate guilt, shame and disappointment from their teaching methods and to replace such allegedly negative reinforcement with positive strokes. If a child fails a test, reassure him that he's not a failure, they preached. After all, you aren't what you do. Don't humiliate a student who doesn't do his homework. Ask him what he was doing instead, encourage him. Elementary school children were drilled in songs like, "Hey, look me over, I'm proud to be me, my perception of myself is strong as it can be!"

Prior Lake had woven those same self-esteem techniques into its curriculum just before the Class of 2000 Synergy students began grade school. The motto of Westwood Elementary School, where most had begun their formal educations, was "Everybody's Thumbody," displayed in all classrooms with smiling cartoon representations of the opposable digit. At Hidden Oaks Middle School, they learned self-esteem in a class called PFLS, Personal and Family Life Sciences, following a workbook designed to help kids "strengthen your self-confidence, manage your emotions, and communicate better with friends and family."

That workbook led them through exercises to turn them into "Dionaraps," the opposite of paranoids, people who think the world is out to do them good. They took peer-pressure surveys, drew up lists of their strengths and their weaknesses and were instructed in building the "three-legged stool of self-confidence," balanced on self-perception and the perceptions of others. The text was laden with quotations like, "There are no strangers here—only friends we haven't met," and "With confidence, you have won even before you have started."

While the coddling made many students feel good about themselves, it provided them with none of the academic benefit promised by proponents of self-esteem training. In fact, feeling good about themselves led kids to achieve less, not more, researchers report. Why work hard and strive to improve if you are praised no matter what you do? The full course in self-esteem, they conclude, had created a generation of risk-averse teenagers who'd been insulated both from the emotional highs of learning how far they might soar, and the lows of failure, humiliation and shame that might have spurred them to work harder.

Furthermore, the new emphasis on kids' psychological well-being hadn't even reduced the amount of trouble roiling through schools. As it turns out, the gurus of self-esteem got it backward: The most dangerous troublemakers aren't people who feel bad about themselves; people who lash out, cause trouble and turn aggressive when they are challenged or confronted are those with an inflated sense of themselves, not the emotionally bereft. In the months after Columbine, the FBI went so far as to suggest that the self-esteem movement might well have contributed to the wave of school shootings in the late 1990s.

The week before the spelling bee, the Synergy seniors plumbed the legacy of that double whammy of egalitarianism and self-esteem training with chilling candor in a discussion of their plans for the future.

"Well, I guess I'm going to get a Ph.D. in Physics," Jake Anderson admitted quietly. Jake always spoke quietly, but the slight young man was almost muttering that day, as if afraid to let his words pierce the atmosphere and become reality. Jake was a young Dexter Holland, a name which means nothing to punk music illiterates. The lead singer and guitarist in a skatepunk band called The Offspring, Holland was more than a punk idol. When he wasn't on tour, he was cloning viruses, part of his doctoral work in microbiology. Like Holland, Jake, who was a musical jack-of-all-instruments, proficient on alto and tenor sax, guitar and drums, was caught between the driving beat of his latest garage band and his fascination with astrophysics. He knew that following in Holland's musical footsteps wasn't a pragmatic career choice, but he wasn't convinced that he had much more of a shot at making it as an astrophysicist.

"But you know, well, I'm not sure that I can do it," he continued, explaining his reticence.

Their desks in an ill-formed circle, the eight other seniors around him nodded stiffly. For almost a decade they'd been bound together by their membership in Synergy, but had never coalesced into the sort of close friendship group that had sustained Hallberg during high school. As they shared their hopes for the future, the conversation was veering a little close to the bone. As Jake talked about his struggle, his uncertainty that his abilities could possibly be adequate to his dreams, he was hardly alone.

For the most part, they were a timorous group, although they would have chafed at that definition. "Well, at least I'm one step ahead of you, I know that I *can't* do what I want to do," responded Lisa Gilbert, a tiny fireball of playful energy who lived and breathed to perform. Lisa had just written a letter to the editor of the *Laker Times*, the school newspaper, in which she'd derided the year's theme, The Sky Is the Limit, as too confining.

"I object . . . I think that to say that the 'sky is the limit' is a step down
. . . . To go above and beyond is a requisite to do well in the big world out
there. How are they giving us the right message if they constantly tell us
that we are limited by the sky?"

But when Lisa got down to her own life, her own plans for the future,
she sounded less like the Man from La Mancha weaving his impossible
dreams. "I know what my limitations are and if I can't act, I prefer not to
be in theater," she said flatly, explaining why she expected to pursue a
career backstage, in television, instead of on the stage.

Only Nick Busse flared in puzzled anger at Lisa's self-styled pragma-
tism and Jake's bashfulness. "Man, if you can't do it, who can?" he
challenged Jake indignantly. Indignation was one of Nick's four major
emotions—diffidence, fury and terror being the remainder. "How can I
possibly know whether my goals are realistic, whether or not people will
laugh at me for being naive about my abilities?" Jake snapped back.

The other students were quiet, clearly siding with Jake. Oh, sure, in his
junior year, Jake had earned a perfect score on the Advanced Placement
Calculus Test—the hard one that almost nobody in his right mind attempted. His ACT scores put him among the top 10 percent of high school
students in the nation. And he was twelfth in his class. But what did any
of that mean?

Half the school had GPAs above 3.0, so the Synergy students couldn't
rely on grades to predict their futures. Reilly Liebhard, a National Merit
Finalist with a long string of national and regional honors, was not even
first in his class. Andy Ottoson, like Nick a National Merit Commendee,
wasn't among the top twenty-five in the rankings because his passion for
theater had no academic outlet and he was unwilling to sacrifice it to
required Phy Ed. They all knew you didn't have to be very smart to get
near-perfect grades if you picked your courses and instructors with care, if
you brown-nosed the teachers and wheedled them for extra credit work.
They could cite plenty of names and phone numbers of Prior Lake students
who'd done just that.

"You can get all *As* without learning anything if you play the game,"
said Lisa matter-of-factly.

Hallberg's classroom was filled with kids who had opted out of Game

Playing 101 as an exercise in boredom. In a Health class, Reilly Liebhard had refused to prove his understanding of muscle functions by filling in the blanks on a worksheet. He'd written an essay instead, and been docked points for noncompliance. Andy Ottoson had submitted more than the required five pages in Creative Writing, and his teacher had refused to read the rest of his tale. Nick had complained to his computer teacher when she turned an Internet class he'd expected to be rich in Web design and programming tips into a cascade of assignments in how to search for Web addresses—and been rewarded with a lecture on intellectual humility and a *D*. In their world, the correlation between ability and honors was tenuous, at best, so their skepticism about their ability to achieve was rooted in realism.

"The problem is that none of these classes is designed for smart kids, and we wind up being punished because we're so bored," said Nick. "If they can have special programs like Focus, for kids who won't work, why can't they have special classes for us?"

Katie Hallberg leaned back in her chair and steeled herself for the onslaught. Nick had mentioned the unmentionable in a room filled with kids well schooled in political correctness.

"That sounds so arrogant, to say that we're more intelligent," said David Glaeser, one of Prior Lake's computer nerds. "You don't want to make the less intelligent kids feel bad. Everybody's gifted in his own way."

Lisa, blazing with animation, interrupted. "But it's okay to make the more intelligent people feel bad?"

Jake's voice actually rose. "If they're so worried about making less intelligent people feel bad, why don't they apply that same principle and eliminate the A Squad of the basketball team?"

David finally found a pause through which he could drive through the rest of his point. "But you can't hurt their self-esteem."

Lisa Gilbert snorted. The only *D* on her academic transcript was from PFLS, and it still rankled. Whenever the subject arose, she became absolutely—unaccustomedly—inarticulate. "Grading people on their self-esteem, teaching them to have self-esteem, like you can dispense it from a bottle, what a ridiculous concept," she said.

Reilly Liebhard tried to lighten her mood. "You're a really bad person because you don't have high self-esteem," he berated her. Lisa couldn't laugh. Even five years after she'd received that *D*, her wounds were still too fresh.

"I had a self-esteem problem although I got straight *A*s and played sports," said Nick. "I thought something was wrong with me. You know, 'I'm doing all the right stuff, so how come I feel so shitty?' You're supposed to feel good if you do what society says. If you don't, something must be wrong with you, and you need Prozac or Ritalin."

Katie Cook sat rigid in her chair. Her body was always tense with focus, but she spoke only with concerted prodding. Adopted by the senior soccer players while she was still an underclassman, Katie, the varsity goalie, had been selected as the cocaptain of the girls' team in her junior year, which brought out the mean streaks of envious parents and peers. Facing her own senior year without the title of captain, she felt isolated, unsure where she fit on her own squad. Although she had received regular awards for her academic accomplishments, Katie was dreaming of four more years as a soccer goalie and had set her sights on playing at a Division I school. John Bennett, her track coach and mentor, was discouraging her. "Isn't it better to be a big fish in a little pond than a little fish in a big pond?" Katie didn't think so. "Why do they always act like we're not good enough?" she asked. "Why do they try to stop us from trying?"

Reilly was quick to respond. "The problem is that the school is so focused on protecting the egos of students that it breeds mediocrity," he said. "If you never let anyone fail, how can they not be afraid of failure?"

Reilly sounded like a clone of his mother and father, Joy and Wayne, the least politically correct parents in Prior Lake—and proud of it. "These self-esteem people seem to think that their kids should never be challenged, that challenges will scar them," said Wayne. "Are they preparing young people for the big ugly world out there? Are they teaching them to handle competition, rejection, harsh realities about themselves?" Joy put it more succinctly in a lesson she'd persistently drummed into Reilly's head: "Self-esteem is a poor substitute for confidence earned from achievement."

Reilly was the only bold member of the group. That was hardly surprising since his parents, fed up with newfangled trends in education that subordinated academic achievement to psychological pandering, had pulled him out of public school when he was in the third grade.

The Liebhards were traditionalists who'd met in 1975 at a dance where the rock band Wayne still played in twenty-five years later was performing. Joy had graduated from Prior Lake High School in the days when her classmates downed Boone's Farm wine every weekend, shared slugs of peppermint schnapps in the bathroom and started fires in the trash can to force breaks from school. Today's Prior Lake looked like a prison in comparison. Back then, two couples met daily in the library during fourth hour for blow jobs, and the librarian assiduously ignored their behavior.

Joy didn't smoke, drink, do drugs, cheat or rebel. In fact, she pretty much wanted the life her mother had—to be an old-fashioned parent raising kids in the country, in a warm house with homemade cookies and hot cider. Wayne was her perfect partner. Although they came of age during an era of "going with the flow," the two planned their lives with intentionality. Wayne, they agreed, would go to medical school so they would have enough income for Joy to stay home with a house full of kids.

After Reilly began dazzling them with his intellectual prowess, their imagined house full of kids was pared down to two children. Their son, they realized, would be a full-time job, and they were intent on not raising a thirteen-year-old university student. "You only get one childhood," said Joy, "and Reilly deserved that one."

Wayne and Joy enrolled Reilly at Prior Lake's Westwood Elementary, but they ricocheted from conflict to conflict. In kindergarten, his teacher called to report that a diagnostic playground test had shown that their son could neither skip nor tie his shoes. Both were true, but Joy wondered why the teacher seemed so much more concerned about skipping than about Reilly's ability to read novels or perform three-by-three-digit multiplication in his head. When Reilly was in second grade, his teacher sent him home with a yellow disciplinary slip, his reward for reading ahead in the *Weekly Reader*. "What was the kid supposed to do? Just sit there and reread the same page over and over again?" his mother asked.

The teachers complained, again and again, that Reilly paid little attention in class, that he made paper "fortune tellers" during vocabulary lessons or read books during their lessons, ignoring the fact that he invariably earned perfect scores on their tests. What about having him skip a grade? Joy and Wayne suggested. "No one skips grades, it's bad for a child's emotional development, and for the other children as well," the administration responded. What about some independent study, or at least placing him in higher grades for certain subjects? Again, the school balked at such a psychologically damaging proposal.

Toward the end of his third grade, the Liebhards brought in a letter from a psychologist specializing in gifted children who insisted that Reilly could simply not be placed in a regular fourth-grade class. Waving the letter aside, Reilly's teachers argued that he didn't need special classes; he needed to spend some time in the "Friendship Club," a special program for kids without enough friends. Wayne and Joy gave up. They pulled their son out of Westwood, enrolled him in an enrichment program for gifted kids at the University of Minnesota, and transferred him to a private elementary school.

Reilly had continued his education at the Academy of Holy Angels, where the nun in charge wasn't worried that placing a seventh grader in ninth grade English, or an eighth grader into pre-Calculus would maim her other pupils for life. Then a new principal arrived, hell-bent on making Holy Angels into a preppie paradise, "the kind of place where you could say 'I'm a Holy Angels man' to some random guy at a party and expect him to go goggle-eyed and start drooling," in Reilly's words. It was hardly his cup of tea.

Reilly's parents decided to give Prior Lake another try, figuring that their son, already intellectually self-motivated, didn't really need much academic stimulation. Socially, however, the transfer hadn't been easy. If his classmates had acquired no other skill at middle school, they'd learned to defend their self-esteem, and Reilly was a walking attack on it. He raced through problems that they sweated over for hours. He pushed his teachers into greater detail, more cogent explanations of their course material. When his fellow students took entirely indefensible positions, he regularly undercut their ill-informed arguments with facts. "Everybody has a right to his own opinion," the other student shot back. Reilly knew better than to offer the favorite retort of Ron Lachelt, "Opinions are like assholes, everybody's got one." But his classmates knew precisely what he was thinking.

Unlike most of them, Katie Keough—the third Katie in the room, although none of the students would have called Katie Hallberg by her first name—didn't misunderstand Reilly's exuberance, the way he thrilled to new ideas, new information, new parallels or possibilities like a strobe light blinking out bursts of pure thought. Not invested in having a towering intellect, she felt no need to keep up with a mind that could process information at the speed of the Concorde and move seamlessly from physics to philosophy to rock music and history without a moment of refueling.

But as she listened to Reilly run down his long list of potential careers—should he become the next John Stossel, a muckraking journalist, or a world-class physicist like Stephen Hawking, an engineer, a political scientist, maybe even a politician—she envied him his family, his absolute certainty that, no matter what path he chose, his parents would support him.

"Well, I just don't get it," she said so quietly that the room stilled. Her voice was always soft, a little girl's squeak. "Adults, I mean. I've worked really hard in school and now my parents say they won't pay for college unless I study math or science." Everyone knew that Katie wasn't a math or science kid. She was set on a career working with homeless children.

"My parents do the same thing to me," Nick said, trying to comfort Katie, not quite knowing how. "I told them that I like writing and they said, 'That's nice but what are you going to do for a living?' I guess they have a lot of faith in me. So much for all that training in self-esteem."

Hallberg winced as Katie Keough and Nick traded family stories. For three years, she'd watched the members of their small group come of age and, as they moved toward graduation, she felt an ache in the pit of her stomach. "People say, 'Oh, we don't have to worry about the gifted kids, they're not at risk,'" she explained. "But they are at risk. These kids tend to be loners, to fail miserably at school or in life, to have a higher rate of suicide, especially if they don't have good family structures."

Reilly and Andy Ottoson, whose mother was the cochair of the English department, seemed on firm footing. As for the rest, that was less clear. Katie Keough was tougher than she yet knew, but easily swayed by guilt, turning her anger into self-doubt and self-loathing. Katie Cook was locked inside a shell, closed off from herself as much as from others. Nick was fiercely private, yet deeply needy of connection; profoundly pessimistic, yet unflinchingly motivated. A closed cauldron of anger and grit at war with, and not yet honed by, sheer intelligence, he'd begun to channel his intensity into achingly sophisticated writing, but he still teetered on the precipice of serious depression and could easily fall over the edge.

Jake Anderson? Hallberg just wasn't sure. He'd grown up with careful, intentional parenting. His father, Jeff, a small businessman whose avocation was performing as a Neil Diamond imitator, had taught him to dream and philosophize, and his mother, Diane, an elementary school music teacher, to learn, to feel pride in his accomplishments. Jake seemed to be thriving. He'd aced high school and was finishing up his application to Boston University. But there was something about Jake, something disquieting in his public reticence, as in the reticence of all of Hallberg's "kids," as she called them.

Only Nick and Reilly showed much willingness to dare, to weave what might or might not wind up to be flights of fancy about setting the world on fire. "What do you expect to find here, bold, independent thinkers?" Nick asked just before the end of the hour. "A bold thinker would be kicked out of most high schools in ten seconds flat. If that's their definition of self-esteem, fuck self-esteem."

Sitting on top of a chair in fashionably baggy jeans and boots with thick rubber soles, Justin Jorgenson pouted. Uncharacteristically, the young man who worried Hallberg the most had said nothing for a full thirty minutes. Finally, unable to let Nick's attack on self-esteem go unchallenged, he emerged. "Hey, what's wrong with protecting kids' self-esteem?" he asked, as if holding on to the concept for dear life. While he'd scored a 28 on his ACTs, one of the top ten scores in the school, Justin, with less than a 2.0 GPA, ranked almost at the bottom of his class. His disciplinary transcript was a four-page testament to noncompliance. In 1997, he'd served eighteen hours of detention, one day of in-school suspension (ISS) and one day of out-of-school suspension (OSS) for truancy, fighting and disrespect to staff members. In 1998, he'd served sixteen hours of detention and three days of ISS for truancy, tardiness, insubordination, leaving campus without permission and misbehaving in class and in the lunchroom. With six weeks of school remaining in 1999, he'd already served seven hours of detention, eight days of ISS and one day of OSS for the same offenses.

In elementary school, Justin had driven his teachers to distraction with an endless barrage of questions that flew off in a dozen directions. In the third grade, his teacher had finally confined him to three questions per day. Then, gradually, his interest seemed to flag. By his junior year in high school, with dozens of Ds and Fs littering his transcript, Justin was in trouble. During dozens of meetings with his teachers, guidance counselors and the assistant principal, he'd been reassured that he was a good kid, that he was really smart, that he just needed to grow up a little and to refine his "study skills." He'd latched onto that rhetoric with a vengeance.

"Yeah, I blew high school, but I know I'll be a success in college and in life, that I'll do something important," he said matter-of-factly. "My friends call me a slacker and lazy. They say that I'm not ambitious." Jake nodded his head solemnly. Nick Busse—who called Justin "the dumbest smart kid I know"—actually guffawed. No one disagreed. "But I know I'll be successful because I have the highest self-esteem of anyone in this high school."

Justin, who'd been raised in a strict Christian home, had penned his self-esteem into a full-blown fantasy for a short story assignment. It was the tale of eighteen-year-old Jon, who drove fast cars, chased women and was destined to rule the world. "I haven't fully realized my potential or what my abilities to see reality will do for me," he'd written, in Jon's voice. "It is rather disturbing to be able to feel people's histories, to see the life threads weaving themselves, to understand the universe in all it's [sic] beauty and horror. This is my curse, my joy and my pain." Jon, however, publishes a master intellectual work, *The Theory of Everything*, a bold vision of the Big Bang theory of human development that brings him instant fame as the only man alive who can truly comprehend reality.

That fantasy wasn't all that far distant from the future Justin envisioned for himself. For months he'd been talking about his Big Bang theory, about reconceptualizing ideas as explosions, and about human social and intellectual development as paralleling the shifts in the physical universe. He hadn't read about the Big Bang theory, of course. It wasn't that he was averse to reading; a copy of *The Iliad* was squashed among the papers in his backpack, although he'd declared the book "a little slow." But his tastes ran more toward Frank Herbert's classic work, *Dune*, or Peter Hamilton's *Reality Dysfunction*, an action-packed "space opera" rife with existential themes woven around a plethora of military hardware.

"I'm not comfortable talking about this kind of stuff with most kids," he explained, flicking a long lock of moussed hair back off his face. Everyone had been nagging him to get a haircut, which was the wrong way to motivate a budding contrarian. "They don't see me as a school person, so they don't take me seriously. Anyway, they don't understand what I'm talking about."

Nick Busse, one of the few students Justin couldn't dismiss as too stupid to be worth the trouble, shot his friend a frustrated glance. "No, the problem is that *you* don't know what you're talking about," he said. "Where's the line between self-esteem and self-delusion?"

Chapter Seven

8:45 A.M., Thursday,
November 18, 1999

Ryan Langhorst's name had appeared in the *Prior Lake American* on November 6 in an announcement of his arrest so insignificant that it got lost between the "Looking Back" column, items from the weekly paper's reportorial past and the regular feature on highway construction projects that froze area traffic into gridlock. Nonetheless, word that the Prior Lake senior was facing a fifteen-year prison sentence still spread through the corridors of the high school, down the aisles of Rainbow Foods and on line at the post office. News, after all, blankets towns and cities long before the presses roll.

"Ryan Langhorst?" students at the high school responded. "No way." To them, Ryan was that stoner boy with the goofy smile. Hardly a danger to society.

"Ryan Langhorst?" teachers asked. "That makes no sense." To them, Ryan was that quiet Focus boy who wasn't much of a student, but was always respectful.

"Ryan Langhorst," called the clerk of the Scott County Court that morning, handing a slim file to Judge Thomas Howe. The silver-haired magistrate peered down from his dais as Ryan stepped forward from his seat in the first row of benches. Then the judge looked back at the file as if trying to make sense of the disconnection between the slight, visibly nervous young man in the gray slacks and open vest and the charges on the sheet: armed robbery, second degree assault, making terroristic threats.

If Jesse Jackson wanted to understand "zero tolerance," he should have been in suburban Minneapolis that morning.

Instead, Rev. Jackson had just been released from jail in Decatur, Illinois, where he'd been trying to coerce the local school board into easing up on its approach to "zero tolerance" by readmitting seven young men who'd been expelled from Eisenhower High School for two years after a brawl during a football game. "[Z]ero tolerance has been exposed as an ugly, expensive and uneducational policy," Jackson had declared, launching a crusade he likened to the struggle to integrate the nation's schools.

"Zero tolerance" had captured the American political imagination in the late 1980s as a handy catchphrase adopted by anyone anxious to prove his seriousness about a cause, whether it be violence, sexual harassment or racial intolerance. The phrase had crept into schools as the battle cry of the crackdown on drugs, gangs, fighting, smoking, and alcohol. And it had been codified into federal law in regard to guns in 1994 with the passage of the Gun-Free Schools Act that required states receiving federal dollars to implement "zero tolerance" policies by expelling any student who brought a weapon to school for a minimum of one year.

In the aftermath of the Columbine massacre, school boards and police across the nation had ratcheted up their "zero tolerance" policies to prove to parents terrified by the images of bloodied students sprawled across the floor of a school cafeteria that they were serious about school safety. Suspensions became expulsions, and violence, or threats of violence, were added to carrying guns or other weapons as intolerable behavior. No more discussions about "student rights" or "compassion." In small farming towns and teeming cities, America's school boards declared war on any kid who as much as looked like he might pose a threat to his classmates.

In Virginia, a twelve-year-old boy was expelled from school for waving a stapler around on a school bus, and a high school boy for having blue hair. A Florida girl was suspended for bringing a nail clipper to class, and an Ohio boy for completing an assignment to compose a fortune-cookie message by writing, "You will die with honor."

Although the chances of a child being killed in an American school were one in two million, 71 percent of adults believed a shooting was likely in their school—and school boards, anxious to be relieved of the responsibility for distinguishing between kids who were real dangers and the stereotypical blowhards, happily caved in to the panic. The dilemma was that while Americans were terrified to drop their children off at the schoolyard, the people they feared were also children. Something has to be done to protect our kids, parents cried in alarm. Somebody has to crack down on those kids, they demanded. "Zero tolerance" policies were fraught with that contradiction.

Before "zero tolerance" landed him in jail, Ryan Langhorst was nobody's definition of one of "those kids," except perhaps for the Prior Lake police. Quiet, with a streak of shyness, Ryan wasn't much for the rah-rah of high school life, or, for that matter, the academics. His tawny hair was gelled just enough to suggest a short spike or two, but Ryan never projected attitude. His music of choice was his dad's favorites, classics like Crosby, Stills, Nash and Young; Pink Floyd; and Bob Marley. Headed to the military after graduation, he hoped that his service benefits would pay for him to train as a pilot.

The local police, however, may have had an ax to grind with the young man that had little to do with his minor arrest record—he'd been nabbed in neighboring Shakopee for possession of pot, a container of "beaners," seeds, to be exact, and he'd been nailed once in Prior Lake for underage drinking. Ryan had been the architect of the department's most public humiliation. Several years earlier, while staying with his aunt and uncle, Ryan had thrown a small party, just seven or eight friends hanging out, the definition of teen life in the suburbs. Someone accidentally, or jokingly, dialed 911. Knowing that putting out an emergency call was no joke, the kids had phoned back immediately, apologized for the accident and explained that no help was needed. Nonetheless, the police appeared at the door. Ryan, who'd been drinking, had taken off at the first sign of a cop car, leaving his friend Ben to navigate the law. "Everything's okay, it was just a mistake," Ben explained. "We need to come in to make sure that everything's all right," the officers countered. "Do I have to let you in?" Ben inquired, his legal knowledge confined to what he had seen on TV.

"What if someone is lying there beaten up," the officer explained, following one of the girls from the party through the door. No one was lying there beaten up. And when the police tested everyone in the house, no one's breath made the Breathalyzer light flash red. But the officers kept looking around until they found something to latch onto: a bomb on a cabinet.

It wasn't a real bomb. A licensed pyrotechnician, Ryan's uncle had been given a bundle of flares with a fake trigger as a gag gift. The Prior Lake police, however, panicked and alerted the bomb squad, which raced over from Bloomington, only to discover a bundle of flares with a fake trigger. The police were helpless to move against Ryan. But he and his family knew that his escape had rankled, and that payback might well be in the air.

That possibility arose on Halloween night, when Ryan and four friends had decided they weren't really too old to go trick-or-treating, that it would be fun to dress up in character and roam around town. Ryan had turned eighteen a month earlier, but the two girls in their group were younger, and they were all looking for a lark to break the tedium of suburban boredom.

Ryan's nine-year-old brother had decked himself out as a ninja, slicing his sword through the air at every door. Ryan opted to play cat burglar, cloaking himself in black pants, a black sweatshirt and a stocking cap. His dad lent him a pair of his old Marine Corps boots and cut off the fingers on a pair of old leather gloves. His stepmother, Jodie, gave up some old stockings he could pull over his face. A toy pistol completed the outfit.

Ryan and his friends had hit the town with aplomb, stopping by the houses of friends and relatives, playing their roles to the hilt. Just before nine P.M., with the evening winding down, they were driving along the northern tip of the lake, down Shady Beach Trail, when they spotted three younger boys lugging bags full of goodies. Back up, one girl in the car demanded, let's make those kids give us some candy. The driver obeyed, and the girl jumped out to confront the middle schoolers. Ryan, sandwiched in the middle of the back seat, leaned across another boy, stuck his "gun" out the window and cried, "This is a stick-up."

It is unclear how scared the boys, ages thirteen and fourteen, actually were. Ryan's cap gun had a fluorescent orange tip that would have made it hard to mistake for a real weapon. The boys didn't run, and they certainly didn't hand over the loot. They did let their female "attacker" take a few handfuls of candy, but as they raced away into the night, they yelled, "We're gonna get you for this" to the older teenagers.

Fifteen minutes later, Ryan and crew were hanging out in the lot at the PDQ, one of those gas-station-and-convenience stores that have replaced drive-ins as teen hot spots, when they found out precisely what the boys meant. Two police cars pulled up, their blue lights flashing. "Do you have a weapon in your vehicle?" the officers demanded. "Just my cap gun," responded Ryan, pointing to the faux pistol on the floor of the back seat. He was promptly escorted to a squad car and locked inside. "This is a bunch of bullshit," he protested. No one argued. An hour later, he was at the Scott County jail being Mirandized. The next thing he knew, Ryan was facing Judge Howe and three felonies.

Ryan was the latest Prior Lake teenager to be caught up in the adult zeal for "zero tolerance." The school and the community had jumped on the national bandwagon, vowing to expel students found guilty not only of possession of a weapon, whether a firearm or a nunchaku, but of possession of a weapon look-alike. And doubters skeptical about the school board's collective backbone were quickly appeased. During the 1995–1996 school year, the board had ousted five students for weapons possession. The following February, it kicked out two more, one a high school student found with a pocket knife, the other a thirteen-year boy discovered with a loaded BB gun and an unopened pack of cigarettes in his backpack.

When a middle school student brought a toy gun to school, a Blue Nintendo gun, and pointed it at another student, they fell into murkier waters. How could they throw a kid out of school for brandishing a blue plastic light gun with a wire hanging off it, many community members asked. The board hung tough. Look-alike weapons can be just as dangerous as real weapons, the school liaison officer, Duane "Goldy" Goldhammer, had insisted. The youngster joined the other seven students expelled.

One member of the board, however, had begun having second thoughts about "zero tolerance," wondering if indiscriminate expulsions might actually create more danger than they prevented. Dick Booth was an unlikely dissenter. At the age of fifty-four, the mild-mannered business consultant and member of the Minnesota Valley Community Church was no Jesse Jackson. Until "zero tolerance" became an issue, Booth's most rebellious stance was his advocacy for more equity in extracurricular spending, which meant less money for athletics and more for the arts.

But Booth had been chewing on one of his first votes as a board member, a vote to suspend a seventh grade boy who'd walked out of a classroom carrying a pair of scissors. "The year before we expelled that boy, he was a student at Grainwood Elementary School, where every kid had a pair of scissors in his desk," he said. "Suddenly, the same pair of scissors he'd thought of as a tool was being treated as a weapon. What lesson did that boy learn? What did that suspension mean for the rest of his education? How much anger and confusion did that suspension create, and how will he respond?"

Booth was sitting in Fong's Chinese restaurant in downtown Prior Lake. Fong's was the only restaurant in downtown Prior Lake, one of those towns-turned-suburbs that have lost their centers to malls. The boy with the scissors had been expelled four years earlier, but he still haunted the baldish man whose seriousness was burnished by real warmth. Booth was convinced that he'd finally put his finger on what had been troubling him. "Some day we're going to kick a kid out of school for a pair of scissors or a cap gun and he'll come back with a rifle," he said, leaning forward over his lunch. "We're on the road to where we no longer use common sense."

Outside, the traffic was light on Route 13. Cars were pulling out of the lot at Hollywood, where the regular Optimist Club meeting had just ended. The possibility of a school shooting in the tranquil suburban town felt surreal. In a community of 14,723, the Prior Lake police dedicated most of their time to handing out speeding tickets or citations for drunk driving. Despite the rapid growth, the crime rate was actually falling. Only one student had ever pulled a gun at Prior Lake High School, and routine teenage scuffles and fights were rare. Goldy, the campus cop, acknowledged that he didn't do a lot of traditional policing beyond dealing with locker break-ins, spats over boyfriends and a flurry of minor problems with middle school kids, kids at the age when *Lord of the Flies* becomes a believable scenario. "Most of my job is preventive," he said. "And my mere presence does a lot for prevention."

Booth had first voiced his concern about the district's take on "zero tolerance" in the spring of 1998, when the expulsion of Cole Welchlin was brought to the table. Cole was a striking senior, a good student with spiked hair of regularly changing hue, torn tank tops and T-shirts with ripped blue jeans, or leather miniskirts and combat boots. Her crime wasn't her garb, at least not officially. Rather, on the second day of her last trimester before graduation, a parking-lot attendant had spied what he thought was a gun on the front seat of her 1984 Caprice Classic, a huge black boat that she'd painted with pink leopard dots. The other attendant, a retired police officer, wasn't so easily fooled by the black plastic weapon in its black vinyl holster. The orange caps sticking out of the back of the "gun" were a dead giveaway.

But the first attendant remained unconvinced, and the next thing Cole knew, Goldy was pulling her out of U.S. History for a meeting in the principal's office. "Do you know why you're here?" Lori Boynton demanded angrily. "No," said Cole, truly puzzled. "What's in your car?" Boynton pressed. My car? Cole thought. "My Walkman and some tapes," she said, forgetting the souvenir a friend had brought her from Texas. "Do you have a gun?" Goldy asked, going straight to the point. Cole was flabbergasted. "A gun? Why would I have a gun?" she said, still confused. Finally, she realized that the police officer was talking about the tiny toy pistol and began laughing—but not for long.

Goldy escorted her to her vehicle and ordered her to stand back while he confiscated the toy. Stunned, Cole was told that she was suspended from school, barred from reentering the building even to grab her backpack. If that wasn't bad enough, she was arrested and charged with a gross misdemeanor for carrying a replica firearm onto school property.

Ridiculous, said Dick Booth when the board was asked to expel the girl permanently. If we're going to expel kids for toy guns, shouldn't they at least be guilty of pointing them at somebody, of using them to terrify or intimidate? His fellow board members entrenched themselves in tough talk. He managed to sway just one vote.

Bent on crafting a more reasoned approach to "zero tolerance," Booth couldn't have timed his campaign more imperfectly. Eight days after his confrontation with the board over Cole Welchlin, Columbine was etched into the national lexicon of horror. With television sets blanketing the nation with images of hysterical teenagers and frantic parents, it was not a propitious moment for Dick to convince the district to relax its stance, at least on fake weapons. Nonetheless, he pressed forward. "Look-alikes are not the same as deadly weapons," he insisted at a special meeting devoted to "zero tolerance." "And the policy doesn't address whether the look-alike is even meant to scare anyone."

Sue Bruns, a first-term board member, lashed back. "How would we know if someone was threatened?" asked the mother of twin boys, who held a master's degree in sociology from the University of Wisconsin. Booth, a soft-spoken but intense guy, almost snorted. "Obviously, the kids will tell you." Other members of the board supported Sue, convinced of the importance of holding firm. Craig Olson sided with the majority. "We're seeing very little violence because students know they'll get clobbered if they bring anything to our school," he said, assuming that the policy was responsible for the calm.

In fact, evidence from other districts suggests that "zero tolerance" has not proven to be much of a deterrent. Research suggests that schools with rigid "zero tolerance" rules in place for four or more years were still less safe than those without them. And school violence had fallen off dramatically long before the current wave of inflexible responses was instituted.

When Prior Lake's school board met for a final vote on its "zero tolerance" policy, however, the only concession made was to give principals more discretion over what to do with kids in kindergarten through the fourth grade who brought weapons to school, perhaps inadvertently, or without understanding what they were doing. Even that was too much for Martha Hoover, another board member, who protested that they were creating a gray area that "street-smart" elementary school children might exploit.

Months later, that decision still rankled Dick. "Our definition of weapons makes it too easy for us and too hard for the kids," he said. "Are we going to ruin someone's life over an inadvertent weapon, something most people don't even think of as a weapon? We're making things easier for ourselves, but we're not making kids safer. Probably quite the contrary. I can't imagine what kids think of us."

Tony Lorenz, for one, would have been happy to answer that question. "It feels really remote," he said about the possibility of a Columbine-style assault on Prior Lake. "But, mostly, all those policies are so contradictory that you wonder whether everyone has gone crazy."

Like most of his peers, Tony knew that he was more likely to be hit by lightning than to be shot in school, and that his home was a more perilous environment than his classrooms. Nonetheless, their parents pleaded with them to be meticulously careful, at least when they were not reassuring them not to be afraid. For the students, then, the mixed messages became yet another sign of adult insanity. Were they being protected or cracked-down on? It was often impossible to tell. Under the law, they were children; they couldn't vote and could be locked up for drinking. But if they behaved like kids and brought toy pistols to school, they were treated like grown-ups. Grown-ups, however, could carry briefcases, the adult equivalent of backpacks, into their offices. And they could blow off steam and yell "God, I want to kill that guy," without being sent to a police officer for a chat.

The rules were in flux, and they were caught in the crossfire. The most vivid symbol of change was the fate of a Prior Lake student named Mark Person. When the Class of 2000 were freshmen, a junior boy, Mark Stier, the son of a local pastor, had been shot, execution-style, by Person, then a sixteen-year-old sophomore. The murder had occurred one wintry afternoon when the two Marks were riding around with some friends, and Person, angry over a $75 drug debt, pulled out a .25-caliber semiautomatic pistol and brandished it at Stier, who was sitting in the rear luggage compartment.

"Just shoot him," one of the other boys urged Person. "We'll make up a story, and I bet you can get away with it." When Person didn't respond, his friend goaded him harder, accusing him of not having "the balls to shoot" a "worthless nobody" like Stier.

"You don't know how bad I am," Person responded. He then fired the gun, shooting Stier in the left temple. The young man died five hours later.

Person and his friends quickly concocted a tale of a game turned sour and called 911. When the police found physical evidence contradicting the hastily constructed tale, the boys recanted—although they later claimed that the police had interrogated them for fourteen hours without food or drink, and that their confession, obtained through coercion, should be suppressed. Those were the days before America became afraid of its own youth, when teenagers, in suburbia, at least, were supposed to be treated with compassion. So the confession was irrelevant. The judge ordered Mark Person tried as a juvenile and sentenced him to be released from prison on his nineteenth birthday. For the most part, the community was satisfied by the tender mercies of the court.

Shortly after he regained his freedom, not two weeks after Cole Welchlin had been expelled from school, Person had sauntered into Prior Lake High School without a peep from the administration. The occasion was the pre-prom Grand March, the annual presentation of prom-goers and their dates. It was a favorite parental moment, a chance to watch their kids all cleaned up, elegant and demure. The Gold Gym in the high school had been transformed for the evening. The lights were soft, a pin spot dramatically focused on the stage. Like five hundred other parents, Elaine Stier sat excitedly in the stands, waiting to see her daughter Amy, a sophomore, emerge in her floor-length gown. Instead, she saw her son's killer, Mark Person, climb the steps onto center stage, escorting Becca Crooks, a graduating senior. Elaine and Amy fled from the auditorium, hysterical. "The administration's attitude seemed to be 'forgive and forget,' you know, 'he served his time, so let's move past it,'" Amy said. "Like there was nothing wrong with letting a murderer run around the school."

Students heard a different message, although they could make no sense out of its logic: You'll be kicked out of school if you have a plastic water pistol in your car, but you are welcome on school grounds even if you're the convicted murderer of a Prior Lake student who served no serious time for your crime.

The dissonance of those messages, whether cognitive or intuitive, reached a new pitch when the news about Ryan Langhorst hit the school. "How can they try him for second-degree assault when he didn't even hit anybody, didn't hurt anybody?" students asked when they learned about the initial charges against Ryan. But the grousing didn't go much beyond "that's lame," since everyone assumed Ryan wouldn't get more than a slap on the wrist.

Then two more charges were added: armed robbery and making terroristic threats. If convicted, Ryan faced a maximum of fifteen years in prison, a minimum of four. No legal action was taken against his companions, a puzzling omission given the seriousness of the charges against him. "Has everyone gone crazy?" the students asked. "He didn't even have a real gun!"

Three weeks later, Ryan's father, Randy, stood outside the Scott County Courthouse, smoking a cigarette, seconding that perplexity. Ryan had received a citation to appear in court at 9 A.M., and Randy was pacing up and down waiting for the judge to arrive; his wife, an attorney, struggled to reduce his rage.

It was a steely gray morning as Randy poised himself for Ryan's hearing, but he was breathing fire. "They better start marking toy gun packages, 'Dangerous for kids over the age of ten,'" he said. "What the hell's going on here? We can't treat kids like this."

Unlike Ryan, Randy had been a high school hellion, at least by contemporary standards. In those days, in the late 1960s and early 1970s, kids were expected to skip school, drink, drive, and live, at least occasionally, on the wild side. So when Randy and some buddies tipped over an outhouse with the occupant inside, they weren't taken to jail. They were given a stern lecture. And when a cop caught him and some friends with a twelve-pack of beer in the back of his old 1968 Cougar, he took the beer and ordered them sternly, "Wash my cop car or I'm taking you in."

Randy stubbed his cigarette out and watched the jury pool file through the modern building. They looked remarkably like him: working men and women who would still remember what it was like to be young. "No way anyone's going to convict Ryan for armed robbery. For Chrissake, charge him with disturbing the peace and get it over with."

Inside, the district attorney was making no such plans. A tough-on-crime kind of guy, he was going after Ryan full bore, and the police were cheering him on. "[T]he gun looked real and it accomplished the same thing as a real gun—it scared the hell out of those kids," Prior Lake Police Chief Bill O'Rourke said.

At Prior Lake High School that afternoon, anti-Ryan sentiment was running just as high in the teachers' lounge. "He scared those kids, he deserves to be tried," said a Special Education teacher, although she did not focus on precisely what he should be tried for. "He should be locked up," Lori Boynton, the assistant principal, declared flatly. Dan Edwards, a young Social Studies teacher interning in school administration, remained quiet. Growing up in Prior Lake in the '70s, he'd been mugged for candy by older kids, and nobody ever went to jail for it.

Randy stood at the courthouse door, dreading the coming encounter. "If this is 'zero tolerance,' 'zero tolerance' is bullshit," he said. "This is Gestapolike tactics against youth."

Chapter Eight

10:14 A.M., Wednesday,
December 8, 1999

Mary Wenner's tongue was hanging out, her finger pointed down her throat, her eyes rolling. Everyone in the narrow administrative office complex understood that look: the attendance secretary was on the phone with yet another parent handing out yet another bogus excuse for why Jessica or Daniel wasn't in school. Leaning back in her chair by the attendance window, Mary knew. She always knew—from the initial stammer when she called to ask about the absence of a son or daughter and the hasty "Oh, yeah, I forgot, he had a doctor's appointment," or the less fluent "Ah, eh, I left the house before he got up, let me call my husband and see what happened." Covering for the kids again. Just great. Terrific parenti.g.

Keeping track of a thousand students, hour by hour, day by day was a task that would try the patience of Nelson Mandela. Teachers were supposed to fill out Scantron sheets for each class period, reporting the presence or absence of every student, but they were notoriously lax. Student aides were assigned to pick up the materials, but they were routinely distracted on their rounds. And parents were supposed to make sure their kids went to school, not whisk them off on vacation in the middle of the school year, or curtly tell Mary, "I don't know where my son is, that's my wife's job."

Beyond the occasional grimace, Mary remained cordial even with the most obstreperous parents. But her omniscience was laced with a hefty dose of irony and humor when kids showed up at her window with written excuses scrawled in stilted language on notebook paper. She didn't nail them. Fierce authoritarianism wasn't her style. She just leaned forward and handed back the note with a flip, "Gee, Jason, doesn't your mother spell her name with two *n*s?"

In September, with a mob of new students at her window, the game was almost fun. By December, Mary was weary of its familiarity. Everyone in the office was weary by December. A flu bug had taken hold of the school. Teachers were being felled at a record clip and the substitute list was woefully inadequate. Substitutes had to be licensed by the state, which required them to submit college transcripts, the results of teacher licensing exams, clearances from the state police and hefty processing fees. If they made the cut and were called in to work, they were paid $85 a day, about $20 less than they could earn delivering pizza. Karen Barclay, the senior secretary, was shifting teachers from hall monitoring to classrooms as she struggled to find more workable solutions.

It was just that season. School years have rhythms and, for most, the beginning of the long winter is a dreary ebb. The promises of the new year are long forgotten, the burst of energy of the last weeks of school impossibly distant. Among the staff, the mood vacillated between ennui and downright hostility. Joe Goracke was slugging it out with the school board over the new teachers' contract, brimming with fury over the prospect of losing benefits. Ron Lachelt was firing off letters to Minnesota's commissioner of education, attacking the Profiles of Learning. Lori Boynton, whose penchant for the positive was balanced by a thinly disguised temper, was losing her patience with students whose primary interest at school seemed to be testing her limits. Even Nancy Jans, a secretary shared by the Focus and activities offices, was snarling, and Nancy never snarled.

For the sophomores and juniors, life had fallen into a dull routine of worksheets and quizzes, teachers carping about overdue assignments, and administrators nagging them about passes. But for the seniors, that tedium was riddled with anxiety. After all, it's not easy to indulge in idle boredom when an eighteen-year free ride, eighteen years of preordained certainty, is giving way to weighty decisions that will define the trajectory of your life.

Even three months earlier, when 180 Prior Lake seniors boarded yellow school buses and headed into downtown Minneapolis for the National College Fair, that reality felt impossibly distant. The early fall was still summer memory rather than winter misery. Their final year of high school seemed interminable. The trip, then, was more lark than business, and dozens of students who'd already completed their college applications hopped onboard, onto buses filled with an equal mix of kids serious about college and those who had no intention of spending a minute of the following year in the classroom.

The vast Minneapolis Convention Center was crammed with rows of booths staffed by college representatives handing out brochures and contact cards, clamoring for attention, offering catalogues and financial aid advice. Matt Brown, the football player, saw none of it. He and his friends had strolled from the bus through the double doors, made a hard left off the lobby, circled back out through a side door and taken off into the warren of downtown streets. A few students wandered the aisles, stopping by dream schools like Hawaii Pacific University, whose catalogue enticed lifelong Midwesterners with photographs of palm trees, lush rain forests and pristine beaches. The more ambitious headed for the booths of private colleges in Iowa, Wisconsin and the Dakotas, but the big draw was the section set aside for the University of Minnesota and the Minnesota State Colleges, their banner proclaiming, "There's no place like home."

Most students roamed the aisles aimlessly for a few minutes, as if picking a college were like shopping for new tennis shoes, then followed in Matt's footsteps. By lunchtime, the throng of teenagers from across the Twin Cities had dissolved into lines at dozens of downtown restaurants and shops. The only sign that thousands of teenagers had been there was a salesman from Sunbreak Student Vacations, perched outside the auditorium, soliciting stray seniors interested in spending Spring Break in Cancún.

By December, however, with college application deadlines looming and their parents pushing for some serious decision-making, denial was evaporating. At lunch in the cafeteria, after school at Burger King, in the morning after nightly lectures from their fathers, students were succumbing to a senior anxiety that even the Christmas decorations scattered around the school couldn't blunt.

Suddenly, the restless anxiety, the grouchy shortness of temper, and the incessant ringing of telephones and bells were cut by the sweet lilting sounds of forty young women singing, *Welcome here, welcome here, All be alive and be of good cheer.*

Stationed directly in front of the main office, Tom Hassig, baton in hand, was leading his concert choir through their paces in preparation for the following week's holiday performance. Several times a year, he transformed his students into roving troubadours, singing on stairwells, in front of the office, even in locker rooms rather than in the choir room or the auditorium. Different acoustics, a chance to hear themselves in a new way.

Come, all good people, enter in, The wind blows high, come in, come in.

Hassig knew his choirs were good, really good. He also knew they could be better: that their enunciation could be crisper, that their pronunciation on the Cuban carol "A La Nanita Nana" or the Nigerian "Betelehemu" could be less American. Standing on his toes as he directed the group, dressed, as always, in perfectly pressed pants, a starched shirt and a colorful tie, he stopped them again and again, begging them to listen, directing them to punctuate, to relax into the tune.

Hassig could be mercurial, rattling the walls with anger one day at behavior that he would ignore the next. But the students couldn't resist him. When the bass section held an eighth note for a full quarter-note value, he accused them of acting like "whole-note Nazis." Rather than seek comments, he solicited "criticisms, witticisms and aneurysms." He was an utter perfectionist, which simultaneously impressed and frustrated his singers. If they arrived at school for an evening basketball game, they always saw the lights on in the choir room. For every concert, he decorated the auditorium elegantly. And in his programs he included a stern warning to parents about the difference between an appropriate "bravo" and an inappropriate catcall.

Ding-a-dong-ding, a song to sing, Let the merry music ring.

Students began filtering out of their study halls and classes well before the bell signaling the end of class and the beginning of the first lunch period, changing Hassig's captive performers back into distracted teenagers. Jayne Garrison stopped her friend Anna Bican midnote with a friendly jab in the ribs. And Shannon McGinnis drew a stern Hassig stare when Tony Lorenz sauntered by and picked her up just as she was trying to finish the alto part on *I've got a pie all baked complete.*

Shannon had been on a roll all year, juggling a schedule that looked like the weekly Franklin planner of a corporate executive. As vice president of the student council, she was saddled with grunt work without an iota of glory—running the student concession stands at football, soccer and basketball games, keeping the cafeteria vending machines stocked and maintaining the books. She also played varsity tennis, worked part-time at Subway, served on the National Honor Society executive board and had still earned straight *As* the first trimester.

It wasn't unusual to find her sitting on the floor in front of the student council office half-asleep at 6:45 A.M., or finishing up paperwork for concessions at ten P.M. She didn't read books or watch the news. She had no idea who was running in either the Republican or Democratic presidential primaries. But Shannon glowed with energy as she raced around the building, her hair pulled back in a small pony tail, bobby pins adorned with metal flowers keeping the short ends out of her face, reveling in the respect of teachers.

Tall and almost stately, Shannon exuded a well-earned self-confidence without a trace of the "aren't I the coolest girl in the school" pretense. She would have been easy to hate, if she hadn't been born without a catty bone in her body. Raised in the wealthiest section of town, in a house on the lakefront, Shannon was the daughter of a bank officer and a businesswoman. Her boyfriend, Jon, a freshman at the University of Wisconsin, was both enviably handsome and entirely devoted. And she was even the reigning Miss Teen Minneapolis, although the latter status was a bone of contention in the McGinnis household.

Shannon's parents had been less than enthusiastic about their daughter's entry into Pageantland, fearing that she'd take to a diet of carrots and celery lest an extra ounce lose her a title. Their permission for her to compete had been provisional, then: If we see you getting caught up in your looks, you're out, they'd decreed. And Shannon had stuck by that deal and still emerged with the crown in June. She was scheduled to fly to Orlando for the national competition in ten days.

In those weeks before Christmas, when her friends were still wracked with doubt about where they should go to college and whether they would be admitted to their top choices, Shannon wasn't breaking a sweat. Going far from home wasn't an option. "I'd be nervous and homesick," she said, as a matter of fact. Considering a career in chemical engineering, she wanted to study at her parents' alma mater, at the prestigious Institute of Technology at the University of Minnesota. Her ACT scores were a mediocre 24, but when balanced by her 4.0 grade point average, she knew she qualified for an automatic admission.

Tony was also riding high, despite a bitter end to the football season. The team had picked up steam and, in their section semifinals, had met the New Prague Trojans in a dramatic confrontation, a chance for the Trojans to avenge their loss to the Lakers earlier in the season. The Trojans had been out for blood, and the New Prague police out in full force to make sure none of it was spilled off the field.

From kickoff through halftime, the Lakers had dominated the Trojans, racking up twenty-eight points to New Prague's seven. Then, with 1:18 left in the third quarter, the Trojans turned the tide, scoring twenty-one points to tie the game. There was only a minute left, and Prior Lake was in the driver's seat, the ball in its possession, the clock on its side. As the seconds ticked down, the offense moved quickly down the field, well into Trojans' territory. One long completion—one charmed pass—might put the team in the end zone. The quarterback took the snap, dropped back and lofted the ball high into the air. Hundreds of spectators held their breath. Then the ball came down—smack in the arms of one of the Trojans' defenders. The interception threw the contest into overtime.

That meant that each team's offense would be given four downs, from its opponent's ten-yard line, to try to score. The Trojans got the first shot, and they almost made it work. But just six inches from the goal line, the Lakers stopped them. The Trojans had no such luck. On second down, one of the Lakers' backs broke free and scampered into the end zone.

The victory pitted the Lakers against Hutchinson, their most reviled rival, in the match for the conference title, and the players loped onto the field swollen with confidence. But just forty-nine seconds into the game, their quarterback went down, his leg hurt badly enough that he had to be helped to the sideline. Then the Lakers blew a promising scoring opportunity, fumbling on Hutchinson's fifteen-yard line. One misfortune or mistake seemed to breed another, and the play that would have given them a game-tying touchdown, a sixty-seven-yard run from scrimmage by David Busselman, was called back because of a penalty. That was that; Hutchinson's 13–6 lead held. On the last day that the boys would ever play together as a team, the last day that many of them would ever put on football helmets and shoulder pads and lean into a huddle, they left the field in tears.

Tony was not among the weepers. Basketball, not football, was his passion, and the season had just begun. Tony had planned his senior year with care. Utterly indifferent to his grades, he was doing just enough work to stay eligible to play Division I basketball. Unlike his friend Eric, he wasn't seeking out scholarship offers, although he was willing to entertain any that came his way. Otherwise, he figured, he'd join the Marines, proof positive—more to himself than to others—that he was among the toughest.

Eric and Tony were still joking with Shannon when the bell finally rang and five hundred students, Lyndsay Schumacher among them, raced toward the cafeteria. Tony caught his girlfriend's eye for an instant and moved just an inch away from his old friend Shannon. Off the field and court, Tony had fantasized spending his senior year winning the "who can have sex with the most girls" competition against his friends Eric Prchal and Jordan Culver. But getting involved with Lyndsay in the early fall had put a serious crimp in his competitive style. Her jealous streak was a mile wide, and just as deep, and Tony struggled to keep it from flaring. It wasn't easy. Its major focus was Eric, Tony's almost constant companion. Lyndsay couldn't stand playing second fiddle to anyone, especially not to a boy.

•　　•　　•

That foursome weren't the only Prior Lake students on a roll. Roger Murphy had turned an academic corner, Mike Carr the ironic agent of his reformation. Day after day, Roger had nagged and whined about Carr's low expectations of his Focus students, about how easy the work was. "Okay," Carr had responded one morning, out of sheer frustration rather than a lightning bolt of insight into how to manipulate Roger. "If you're so smart, give me a five-page paper instead of a three-page one, and from now on, I'm going to make up special tests for you."

"Fine," said Roger, rising to the unplanned challenge.

First, he submitted a paper on gun control and the Second Amendment to the U.S. Constitution; it was rife with sentence fragments and misspelled words, but clever and incisive. "It's not really that we need this amendment," he wrote. "It is more the fact that we have it. Owning guns is our right, and Americans push their rights to the fullest extent." When he followed that up with an essay on John Locke, the philosopher, Carr knew that something special was happening, although he still didn't quite understand what had turned Roger around.

Roger, on the other hand, understood full well. He enjoyed popular teachers like Sara Strege, whose Speech students had just completed their lip-synching unit. Watching his friends Jayne Garrison and Kelli Clausen pretend to belt out "The KKK Took My Baby Away" had given him a good belly laugh, and Strege was always a blast. But he didn't confuse such assignments with academic rigor. "There are teachers who are fun, and there are teachers who teach," he said. "I just never had one of the latter before Mr. Carr."

For years, Roger had strutted his intellectual superiority; but he'd never proven it to anyone, including himself. "Carr's the only teacher I've ever had who pushed me. If I'd had someone like him in the ninth grade, everything would have been different."

That afternoon, he'd haltingly admitted to Carr, and himself, that he had begun to think about the future. "So what do you think about my becoming a teacher?" he'd asked the young Social Studies instructor. Too stunned to respond, Carr stared at Roger's dreadlocks and long chains, and laughed. "Have you even taken the ACTs or thought about applying to college?"

But Roger, like Tony and Shannon, was an exception. His friends were imploding en masse, both academically and socially. Their academic

ignominy surprised no one since, these days, young rebels intent on proving their disdain for "the system" act out on the only system that controls
their lives: school. Cutting class, ignoring papers, blowing off tests were
familiar countercultural rituals.

But, personally, they weren't doing much better. Pete Williams and
Hillary Haxton had married just after Thanksgiving, in a formal ceremony for which Roger donned a tuxedo. At the urging of the administration,
Hillary had left Prior Lake and enrolled at a school for pregnant teens, and
Pete at an alternative school with no classes, no requirements. "They give
me credit for setting and meeting my goals," he explained, "for getting a
job, an apartment and paying my bills. That's all I've done for the last three
months in high school, and that is enough."

No one on the staff was sorry to see Pete go. For him, Prior Lake
schools had long been a revolving door. He'd been suspended for the first
time in the eighth grade, for carrying a pocket knife, and later for dealing
drugs and for fighting. He'd tried studying in a neighboring, more rural,
district, but had been expelled for refusing to submit to a body search for
cigarettes. Then, in his junior year, back at Prior Lake, he'd taken his Social
Studies teacher seriously when she'd instructed her students to "break a
norm." Pete had found an American flag, doused it with lighter fluid and
lit it on fire just outside the front door during lunch hour. With the full
encouragement of the administration, he'd dropped out, intending to prepare for his GED, then changed his mind once more.

Pete had been in drug rehab for heroin use and a psych ward for
attempted suicide. On a normal day, he might pop a dozen NoDoz with a
liter of Mountain Dew, go to school, come home to a few lines of coke and
smoke a bowl or two of pot. "I've learned all about gateway drugs," he
said, his long legs stretched out in front of him, his demeanor as Jim
Morrison-like as possible. Morrison and Hendrix, Pete's heroes. "My gateway drug was caffeine. I drank my first Dr. Pepper at the age of four, and
it's been downhill ever since. Dr. Pepper led to cigarettes, when I was nine.
That led to alcohol, and I was tripping on acid by the time I was thirteen."

His final departure, then, had been a relief for all sides. "Prior Lake
High School is filled with conceited, overbearing, arrogant, rich, Christian,
self-righteous, holier-than-thou pricks," he said the day he'd walked out
the door forever.

Jayne Garrison and her mother were wrangling almost daily over her ever-changing hair colors and styles. And she and her boyfriend, Randy Henke, had broken up in a blaze of anger, hysteria and melodrama that spilled into classrooms, offices, even the teachers' lounge. Jayne had sliced her wrists, although not deep enough to provoke real alarm. She was untethered—picking fights with her friends, refusing all help—and, from week to week, on the verge of being kicked out of the Focus program, her only real lifeline. "Have you made plans for the next year?" her teachers asked. Jayne was having too much trouble coping to think about anything that far away.

That morning, the seniors had met to choose their senior song and flower, the first steps in the six-month march toward graduation. Nick Olson had cast his ballot for the pansy and Alice Cooper's rendition of "School's Out." The purple rose and "I've Had the Time of My Life," from *Dirty Dancing*, won the most votes. "I'm clearly 'other,' and I'm proud of that," Nick said, seated in Mike Carr's classroom for study hall, leafing through an application for Gustavus Adolphus College. Carr was too programmed to understand Nick's disaffection. "What's wrong with school spirit?" he asked, curiously or defensively, it wasn't clear which. Nick rolled his eyes. He liked Carr but knew that, like most of the adults who worked in the school, he was clueless when it came to the feelings of teenagers who did not think of high school as the high point of their lives.

Nick Olson was simply fed up: fed up with teachers wearing whatever they wanted and students being sent home for their attire; fed up with acing exams but getting Cs at the end of the trimester because he refused to do the worksheets assigned in order to help students study so that they could ace exams; fed up with watching his classmates plagiarize and cheat their way to passing grades. He was keeping count of what percentage of Mike Carr's students were copying their papers off the Internet—23 percent and rising, he said. He probably wasn't wrong.

It wasn't just the "alternative" kids, the ones who were so far out of the mainstream that they were beached on some distant asteroid, who were struggling in the weeks before Christmas break. Ashlee Altenbach, the most fresh-faced girl in the school, had been careening from disaster to disaster all year. First, she was kicked off the cheerleading squad for repeatedly showing up late to practices, and no amount of reasoning or pleading would change her coach's decision. Then, she'd been caught stealing from the clothing store where she worked as an assistant manager. Expelled from the school work program, which gave her high school credit for her job, Ashlee had also been charged with one count of felony theft. "One foolish mistake," she said, sitting by the attendance window in the office two days after her arrest. In her blue nylon warm-up pants and gray sweatshirt, Ashlee—generally the quintessence of perkiness, talking a thousand words a minute, verbally slaloming from school to her boyfriend to last weekend's big bonfire—looked . . . deflated. "It sounds sad to say, but I'm glad that I got caught, at least that I got caught now instead of when I was twenty-four-years old and it would stay on my record."

Utterly convinced that she was helpless in the face of her diagnosed hyperactivity, a victim of a force beyond her control, Ashlee followed the script of the remorseful teenager flawlessly. Her dark blue eyes filled with tears. She looked so entirely innocent that each time she recited her dialogue, the adults around her relented. "Everybody makes mistakes," Lori Boynton reassured her when she was called into the assistant principal's office. "But that doesn't mean that you're not a good person."

Having raised flakiness to a high art, however, she was cursed with the habit of getting caught, which forced her into perpetual façade-maintenance. "I wouldn't want a kid like me," she said earnestly. "Maybe a kid with my personality, but I lie all the time." Her parents hated her boyfriend, so she snuck out to be with him. When they found marijuana paraphernalia in her car, she convinced them it was someone else's.

Ashlee couldn't decide whether she wanted to be a little girl, a bad-ass rebel or an entirely conventional suburban housewife, which was the future she said she had outlined. "I want to get married, give birth to a boy a year later, have a girl, wait three years and have another son and, then, two years later, another daughter," she said, I POKE SMOTE scrawled across her hand. It took a few minutes to decipher the code, I SMOKE POT. "I want to stay home with my kids and make supper, tuck them in and read stories like my mom did. She made me grilled-cheese sandwiches and Spaghetti-Os while we watched Mr. Rogers."

College deadlines were upon her, but Ashlee hadn't sent away for any applications. She hadn't browsed through the small library of college catalogues or filled out the College Exploration Inventory the guidance office had prepared. She knew she was going to college. But, like most of her friends, lacking any experience in initiative, she just hadn't gotten around to thinking about where or how.

It wasn't that the students were uninterested in college. For decades, suburban kids have been taught that they *have* to go to college. It's become a doctrine of faith. So 87 percent of them—straight-*A* students and middle-of-the-roaders, kids at the bottom of the class and the utterly indifferent—expected to continue their educations the following year, despite a roaring economy that offered them salaries of $12, $15, $18 an hour without any further education.

"The press for college is absurd," said Bill Bond, one of the senior teachers in the district, as he listened to students with no interest in learning or in professional careers chatter about the fraternities they would pledge, the dorms they would live in. "We keep getting parents of kids with straight *D* averages telling us that they're worried about how their kids will get into college. We can't say what we want to say, which is 'your child shouldn't go to college, he should go to a technical school or get a job.'"

Bond was riding the School-to-Work train that had gained steam across America in the 1990s, a movement that not only encouraged schools to guide students to formulate career goals early, but to address the reality that some kids just weren't made to follow the mainstream "academic track" that would move them along the educational conveyor belt from high school to a liberal arts education. The demise of tracking of all sorts had dealt a near-death blow to traditional Vo-Tech programs designed for kids not deemed "college material." School-to-Work advocates, then, were trying to recapture the best of the old system—the recognition that high school should prepare non–college bound students as well as those planning on continuing their educations—even while updating the definition of Vo-Tech with a new technological twist.

Prior Lake still maintained a few vestiges of the old Vo-Tech in shops at the back of the building where three teachers offering classes in woodworking, welding, automobile repair and drafting hung on for dear life in a community where kids weren't supposed to grow up to get their hands dirty. For a small group of boys, those shops were comfortable ports in a storm of required academic courses that felt like utter tedium. "They're the only classes I care about," said Scott Vig, the son of a mason, who filled his schedule with as many woodworking and cabinet-making classes as possible. "I'm not going to college and, for people like me, there should be more courses like this, more of a chance to work with our hands."

But a seemingly innocuous, pragmatic program had become one of the most contentious issues in American education. Ultraconservatives had woven the School-to-Work initiative into an elaborate conspiracy: Big Brother converting schools into tools of Big Industry, with teachers deciding which kids would be among the "elect" who would receive full educations, and which would be channeled inexorably into menial jobs. In Minnesota, a grass-roots activist group called the Maple River Education Coalition had mounted a vigorous lobbying campaign against this alleged Communist plot.

For the most part, Prior Lake's teachers agreed with the Maple River folks, although without the conspiratorial underpinnings. Most already derided the "work study" programs that awarded high school students credit toward graduation for managing retail stores or ringing the cash register at Burger King—although few could explain precisely how kids were gaining less useful knowledge there than they did in Weight Lifting or Aerobics classes. But when the principal invited a School-to-Work representative to talk with teachers about the career opportunities open to students not interested in college, the faculty brimmed with hostility. "We're not in the business of turning out little worker bees for industry," Sara Strege snapped, to the enthusiastic nods of her peers.

Few parents were embracing School-to-Work either. They might not have seen the evil hand of the Corporate State behind the program, but the vast majority had bought into the notion that their kids *had* to go to college if they were going to build successful and financially stable lives. Which colleges was a matter of widespread indifference since, like parents in all but the most affluent suburbs, where economic success was built on high-status university educations, few Prior Lake mothers and fathers worried about the prestige of the college stickers on the back windows of their SUVs. Most were small-business owners, midlevel business employees or high-income, dual-career, blue- and pink-collar workers—Northwest airline mechanics married to senior secretaries, skilled construction workers wed to teachers—whose economic comfort had little to do with the quality or prestige of their education. So while they spent money freely on weddings, on boats, ATVs and snowmobiles, when it came to higher education, they became curiously pragmatic. College was pretty much just college. No matter where their kids studied, they'd emerge with a four-year degree that would be a magic ticket up.

That same message was broadcast by their high school. "All that Stanford, Harvard, Yale nonsense is absurd," said Rick Sohler, the senior guidance counselor, dubbing it alternately a "yuppie obsession with status" and a "waste of money." Sohler, a serious caffeine-aholic whose day was incomplete without at least eight cups of coffee, had wound up in education in order to avoid the draft, although he'd still been conscripted since the Selective Service ultimately changed its rules to permit the drafting of teachers. By the time he finished a stint in the Air Force, Sohler already had too much time invested in public schools to change gears, so he'd pursued a graduate degree in counseling. "I wanted to stay in education without all the grading and preparation," he said, his eyes laughing.

When he arrived at Prior Lake in 1973, Sohler had homed in on the "kids who don't fit the mold," and designed the Focus program. "We needed something to allow a group of unsuccessful kids to survive in the mainstream high school environment, to get their diplomas while still staying with their friends," he said. The "successful" kids, then, were not his primary concern.

In meting out college advice, Sohler wasn't suffering from Coastophobia. He was equally skeptical about the best students' investing so heavily in the University of Minnesota or local private schools like St. John's University or Gustavus Adolphus College. "In some programs, they can do as well at

Mankato State, at least for undergraduate." And schools beyond the Minnesota-North Dakota-Wisconsin-Iowa corridor? "Don't waste your money," he told parents directly. "The kids who go away all come back."

Sohler's colleague, John Bennett, the football coach, was divided on the issue. He bemoaned the lack of adventurous spirit in college selection. "They're a bunch of pansies," he said, reading down the list of colleges to which seniors had applied. Mankato, North Dakota State, Normandale Community College, University of Wisconsin-Eau Claire, Moorhead State. "They're being overprotected," he continued, before doing an abrupt about-face. "Look at my sister," he said in a refrain familiar to many of his advisees. "She went to Yale and the University of Massachusetts and wound up teaching at Winona State. What was the point?"

Parents at the Twin Cities' most prestigious high schools could have answered that not-so-rhetorical question. They had bought into the concept that college wasn't just about education; it was about the doors that "name-brand" institutions open, and Mankato could not. Many could even recite the comparative graduate school admissions rates from the University of Minnesota and, say, the University of Chicago, off the top of their heads.

New Prior Lakers, who were changing the community into one of the Twin Cities' tonier suburbs, were injecting that same collegiate snobbery into the town. "I worried that if they didn't leave, they'd be too narrow, too conservative, since everyone around here believes that this is Panglossia, the best of all possible worlds," said Lucy Lamp, curled up in a chair in her cluttered living room. After her children's first forays to the career center, which had little information on Ivy League schools, Lucy had encouraged them to do research on their own. "You can go to school anywhere," she taught them. "There are plenty of scholarships out there. Go after them, shoot high." Her eldest daughter had graduated from Cornell University, her son was a freshman at Columbia University and her daughter, Johanna, a Prior Lake sophomore, was looking at Harvard and Massachusetts Institute of Technology.

"I'm constantly shocked at the community's acceptance of school mediocrity," said Elaine Pagels, whose family had moved to Prior Lake from a university neighborhood in Indianapolis four years earlier. "It's disrespectful to kids not to expect more of them. It takes away their hope and motivation. You'd think none of these kids had the ability to do anything special."

The students gleaned that very message from the college advice they were receiving. When teachers and counselors told them "Small is better," they heard, "You'll get lost if you try to compete in a big crowd." When they were advised not to go far away from home, they understood, "It's dangerous and unfriendly out there." For years they were encouraged to play sports, diversify their activities and maintain good grades so they could get into good colleges. When the moment of truth arrived, they were funneled into schools that would have admitted them with no activities, or with decidedly inferior class ranks.

Chapter Nine

12:50 P.M., Monday, January 17, 2000

Lori Boynton was in a foul mood, and things weren't about to get any better.

Christmas was supposed to have been a glorious trip accompanying the band to London, where Prior Lake's musicians were slated to march in the millennium parade. She hadn't been back to England since she'd studied there as a college student. Her husband, Jim, was coming along. Her younger daughter, Bria, was in the band. And Rian, her oldest, home from college, would watch the house over the break.

The trip had gone without a hitch for five days, unless you consider four underage piercings and one tattoo to be hitches. Some of the boys had discovered the midnight pornography broadcast on television and the sex shop around the corner from the hotel. But no one went missing during bed check, and the band had done themselves proud as they marched through Trafalgar Square.

Then the phone rang in her room at the Thistle Hotel in King's Cross. With her mother's permission, Rian, a freshman at Luther College in Iowa, had thrown a small New Year's Eve party, just eighteen kids and, well, the cops had shown up at the door with a Breathalyzer. Rian had gotten nailed, and there was probably no way to keep the fiasco out of the newspaper.

Okay, so your kid gets slapped with a $135 fine for underage drinking. It's not a big deal, unless you're the assistant principal of the high school filled with students you discipline regularly and your daughter had been a "perfect kid," a member of the executive council of CLASS, the Chemically-free Leadership and Student Strength group. The previous spring, after the Minnesota School Survey suggested that Prior Lake's students were consuming significantly greater quantities of drugs and alcohol than their peers across the state, Rian had been interviewed by the *Prior Lake American*. "I think a lot of parents are sending inconsistent messages," she said. "The parents might say, 'Oh, don't do this,' but there's really no punishment, so when it happens it's not that big a deal."

Teenagers can have long memories, and when school resumed on January 3, Boynton could feel the derision aimed in her direction. "Did you have a nice New Year's Eve, Ms. Boynton?" they asked with a heavy touch of irony. "How's Rian, Mrs. Boynton?" Boynton even received an anonymous letter she was sure was from a parent whose child she'd punished for drinking, mocking her skills as a mother.

Typically, Boynton was coolly self-assured. A self-described "alpha female," she still thought of herself as one of those '70s political types who jumped onto the tail end of the antiwar movement. An unrepentant liberal who had never missed a Rolling Stones concert in Minneapolis, she dreamed of leaving behind her custom home and oversized kitchen after retirement, to join the Peace Corps.

But, in this case, she flinched, which was all the students needed. The "gotcha" echoed down the hallways each time the grimacing assistant principal emerged from her office. Then she flinched again, trying to protect her daughter. The kids had just shared a bottle of champagne to celebrate the millennium, she told anyone willing to listen. They were very responsible, she insisted. None of the boys who drank drove a car; most of the girls stayed the night. Boynton publicly obsessed about who had called the Prior Lake Police Department about the party, and quizzed anyone who would play that game. Seniors who'd shown up, but been turned away? Students at a raucous, drunken blast across town who'd heard about the gathering and phoned it in out of spite?

"It's so unfair to Rian," Boynton pleaded. At that point, Rian was 150 miles away in Iowa, which only made the bid for sympathy ring more hollow.

The 1999–2000 school year was not the idyllic session Boynton had been hoping for. The class of '99 had been fantasy seniors: "smart, obedient, easily manipulated," she called them. Thirty-three had finished with grade point averages above 4.0, and the school had handed them the highest number of athletic and activity awards in its history. They'd been a proverbial breath of fresh air after the class of '98, the hellions who'd besmirched the good name of Prior Lake.

But the fall of the 1999–2000 school year had been an unrelenting parade of dress-code violations, tardies, unexcused absences, willful disobedience and just plain youthful stupidity. One senior had stayed home sick but driven to school to pick up some books, leaving a six-pack of beer displayed prominently on the seat of his car. A girl nabbed by Craig Olson for meandering around without a pass had given him a raspberry before declaring, "Bite me."

Throughout it all, Boynton and Olson generally maintained remarkable senses of humor. "Well, did you bite her?" Boynton asked Olson when he told her about the wandering girl. Olson had, in fact, been tempted to take the young woman literally and nibble at her hand. He regularly indulged fantasies of taking his students literally. But, a dyed-in-the-wool Midwesterner, he was a master of self-restraint. Boynton, whose church and neighborhood activities gave her an encyclopedic knowledge of students' families, suggested a more benign alternative for dealing with the errant teenager. "She just wants attention, why don't you make her your office aide?" Olson bore little resemblance to mythical stern, by-the-book principals. He had ten thousand ideas for rewriting that book, and was never shy about being clever with students.

But he'd tried using attention as a substitute for punishment during his first months as a young teacher and still regretted that folly. While he was student-teaching in Harford, Wisconsin, in 1976, on the very day his supervisor was visiting from the University of Wisconsin, an eighth grader named Cindy had managed to push her lab table in front of the door to the classroom while

Olson was off at the supply room. Then she doused it with alcohol and set it on fire. His supervisor's advice was candid: Figure out what makes her tick and deal with it or she'll accuse you of rape, or something worse, he counseled. When Olson pleaded for a more concrete suggestion, his supervisor explained that Cindy might feel deprived of attention. Spend more time with her, get to know her, make her your aide, he advised. Although skeptical, Olson bowed to the wisdom of the experienced.

First Cindy mismixed chemicals in order to ruin his experiments. Then she dumped honey all over the seat of his chair. Finally, during a unit on breadmaking designed to show how yeast worked, she mixed up a batch of dough in the drawer of his unlockable desk, ruining all of the student tests he had stored there.

"What I learned from this exercise was the importance of getting kids to believe that you can be even more evil than they are if you have to," Olson said. Which meant that he wasn't about to follow Boynton's suggestion.

Boynton's mood was not helped by the fact that the district was just gearing up for the referendum for a new high school, or that the "senior problem" was fast approaching, the time of the year when the almost-graduates start boinging off the walls. "You're seniors, you're supposed to boing off the walls," Boynton told them. It was not clear whether she was preserving the self-esteem of kids about to be punished or reassuring herself that it would soon be over. "There'd be something wrong if you weren't."

That did not, of course, make the reality any easier to cope with. She and Olson finally developed a plan to keep the school civilized during the remaining five months, starting with a major crackdown, the first hints of which Olson had introduced at a department heads' meeting the previous Wednesday. Teachers are supposed to be in the corridors before, after and between classes, not in the mailroom, the lounge or their classrooms, Olson reminded them. Your job is to supervise, not to chat with your colleagues or catch up on grading. "Kids don't misbehave when they know they are being watched," he announced. "Visibility" was the new watchword, "accountability" a close second. And stop the epidemic of "motherfucker" and "bullshit" polluting the environment. It's the teachers' job to maintain order. It would be Boynton's job to police the policemen.

When trouble struck, however, it didn't come from the ranks of the students, but from the teaching staff, the last place Boynton expected to raise her blood pressure. But Joe Goracke wasn't just any teacher. He was the die-hard enemy of liberal ThinkSpeak, and Boynton was the paragon of political correctness. Oil and water would understate the antipathy. Potassium and water was closer to the mark.

Name any newfangled educational fad—from the self-esteem movement to block scheduling—Joe Goracke derided it. He derided them all because they gave students and their parents excuses, and he hated excuses, unless they were serious and to the point. He expected kids to do their homework, complete the reading, show up on time and behave appropriately. When they did not, he expected adults to punish them. Boynton was in charge of punishment, and Goracke was fed up with what he considered to be her mollycoddling of adolescent miscreants. During the fall, she'd let the student who'd called him a "motherfucking son of a bitch" off with a single day of in-school suspension. Several weeks later, she'd banned Justin Jorgenson from the cafeteria for just two weeks after Goracke had caught him throwing food for the second time. "It's so inconsistent," he said. "The first time she threw him out for seven weeks. So how does it make sense to give him a lesser punishment for a second offense?"

A denouement to the Goracke-Boynton drama seemed inevitable. The other teachers were practically laying odds on what spark would light the fire.

That morning, Boynton had waltzed into school with her guard down. The students had been given a holiday for Martin Luther King's birthday, and the teachers were having one of those quiet workshop days where they actually got to create some semblance of order out of the chaos in their classrooms. The staff gathered at 7:30 A.M. for coffee, bagels, and a little staff development. The next item on the agenda was a districtwide luncheon at Hidden Oaks, followed by a brief meeting about insurance. Then one more short gathering back at the high school and the day would be done. What could possibly go wrong?

Joe Goracke raised his hand.

The teachers and administrators had just finished eating a lunch that would have horrified anyone but public school teachers, and endured a tedious explanation of their insurance options. Moving the session toward conclusion, Jerry Spies, the director of curriculum and personnel, sort of the vice superintendent of schools, had just asked if anyone had anything they wanted to add.

The crumbs of a sandwich still on the table in front of him, an empty milk carton off to the side, Goracke responded, "If you're finished, I want to say a few things about the contract." As always, his voice was low, almost a whisper. Goracke rarely shouted.

The members of the Prior Lake Education Association, the union representing all of the teachers in the district—at the five elementary schools, the middle school and the high school—had just approved their 1999–2001 contract. Goracke, who'd served on the negotiating team, considered it a complete sellout, shoved down teachers' throats by union copresidents more concerned with being "nice" to the school board than with serving the interests of their members. Goracke asked for the floor to make sure that the teachers who'd voted for that contract understood precisely what they had accomplished.

Jerry Spies froze when Goracke began talking, trading glances with the superintendent, Les Sonnabend, who sneered. Both knew what was coming. Boynton, who'd spent two months talking about how generous the school board's offer had been, went rigid. Her nostrils actually, literally, flared. "How dare he," she whispered under her breath. Boynton was covered under a different contract, which had given principals and senior administrators 24 to 28 percent raises over the previous five years. During that same period, the teachers had received a 16-percent pay increase.

Imbued with her share of New Age thinking, Boynton hated the standard negotiating process, the wrangling, divisiveness and backbiting. The notion of consensus bargaining—the collective-bargaining equivalent of marriage counseling, or the self-esteem movement, in which both sides were supposed to emerge feeling good—had piqued her interest. Joe Goracke, however, acted as if he were a steelworker wrangling with Andrew Carnegie.

Prior Lake teachers had taken a beating during their 1995–97 and 1997–99 contract negotiations. During the first round, Goracke's team had met with the school board's negotiators eleven times before they were able to eke out a raise that was half of what most teachers in the metro area had won. The second round had turned ugly, and teachers had moved to "work to rule," a bargaining tactic in which they performed only their basic, required tasks. Eight-hour days and required committee meetings. Not a minute more. They'd still emerged with a salary schedule that placed the district 126th in the state for salaries of teachers with twenty years of service, on par with educators in remote areas, on the Iron Range or in farm country, rather than those of surrounding metropolitan and suburban towns. Starting salaries had been rising; new teachers, straight out of school, with no graduate education whatsoever, began at $27,000. But unless something changed drastically, they couldn't hope to keep up with their peers in other fields; veterans in the district topped out at $58,500.

"They say that they are concerned with keeping quality teachers in the district," Goracke sputtered. "How can they expect to do that during a teacher shortage when our teachers can walk out and get a $2,000 or $3,000 raise across town?"

Goracke had entered negotiations for the 1999–2001 contract loaded for bear. He'd prepared charts comparing salaries of teachers at a dozen levels with the salaries of teachers of like experience in surrounding districts. He'd calculated average and median pay increases across the metro area, and even put out a flier showing how Prior Lake raises compared—negatively—with Social Security cost-of-living increases. In other words, he'd done the home-work necessary to sit down at the negotiating table, slap down the statistics and bring the teachers a package he could be proud of.

In the end, he had been the only teacher negotiator in that frame of mind. The other members, all middle or elementary school teachers, had been looking for cordial agreement, not a knock-down, drag-out fight. The contract they'd taken back to their members just after Christmas was billed as a victory which would increase their salaries by 3 percent each year. The fine print provided a bleaker picture. The district would no longer guarantee full payment of the insurance premiums for teachers' families, or for retirees' spouses. Teachers looking for full dependent cov-erage would be expected to pay a substantial percentage of their "family" premiums. And new retirees would have to pay for their spouses them-selves. By Goracke's calculations, those premiums would cancel out many of the teachers' meager raises.

"I'm not sure that you understand what you have done with the con-tract," Goracke said as he stood before scores of teachers in the HOMS cafeteria. The air sizzled. Everyone knew that Goracke could be, well, "opinionated" was the word used most frequently. Abrasive, in fact, was the unspoken adjective in a culture where public displays of anger were studiously discouraged, among adults as well as children.

Most of the elementary school teachers had no idea what Goracke was upset about. Their building reps hadn't presented the contract as a major triumph, but they'd sold it as a realistic agreement in an era of skyrocket-ing health-care costs. Goracke's take was entirely different: You don't give up something for nothing and pretend that you've won. Districtwide, 159 teachers had voted for the agreement, with 95 dissenting. Most of those 95 came from the high school, where only ten teachers supported ratification.

More than half the room fidgeted as Goracke laid out his case. Some elementary school teachers actually got up to leave. Unsure what to do, Jerry Spies, still hanging on to the microphone, traded looks with Boynton and Sonnabend, then performed a well-amplified throat clearing. "The contract has been ratified," he said, interrupting Goracke, "so I'm not sure what the point of this is."

Boynton smiled in agreement, as if to say, "Good, shut him up." Back in her office, she seethed. "He's lost his mind. I really think he needs psy-chological help."

But as the high school staff left the meeting, Goracke was surrounded by well-wishers. "Good for you, somebody needed to say that," one sci-ence teacher congratulated him. "Thank you for speaking up for us," an English teacher patted him on the back. "Jerry's interrupting you drove the point home more forcefully than you ever could," another colleague added. "Your point was that we're being demeaned and he certainly treat-ed you like a disobedient student."

Sitting in the faculty lounge after the luncheon, Goracke was not consoled by the support of his colleagues. After twenty-two years teaching social studies at Prior Lake, he was almost beyond consolation. It wasn't just the biennial struggle with the board over salaries and benefits. It was the constant insults to his professionalism—by the school board, the administration, parents and students.

The late afternoon sky filtered a gray light into the room as a dozen senior teachers sat chatting with Goracke, exhausted in the face of so much change, so little progress. The sole neophyte in the small gathering was Mara Corey.

For years, they had all recommended their profession highly, but their enthusiasm had seriously waned. Even as he lived with the constant fear that he might let his kids down, Lachelt felt undermined by "loosey-goosey" educational trends that meant kids graduated without knowing enough, or by "experiential" education that left his classes half-empty while kids drove off on somebody else's field trip. Before the Christmas break, he'd actually blown up in a faculty meeting over the new graduation standards, which, he was sure, would wind up hurting his students. It had been a chilling moment. No one at Prior Lake had ever seen, or imagined, the stolid and centered biologist losing control. "What do you want?" Olson had demanded, his frustration with Lachelt's ire apparent. A new job, Lachelt responded, and a continuation of my current medical benefits.

That afternoon, seated next to Goracke in the lounge, Lachelt was weighted down by resignation. "It's just not the same, every year it seems less about learning, every year they make it harder for me to do my job."

As usual, Goracke was more blunt. "I wouldn't trade the experience for anything, but I wouldn't do it again," he said. He had warned his four children away from teaching.

The tradition throughout public education had long been one of teacher autonomy and at Prior Lake, as at almost every school throughout the nation, teachers still insisted that kids would be better off if everyone— parents, administrators, politicians, bureaucrats and school boards— would just leave them alone to do their jobs. We're professionals, treat us like professionals, they argued. In an era of Medicare and HMO oversight of every prescription a physician writes, every test he or she performs, that argument carried more than a whiff of arrogance.

The teachers' room crackled with hypersensitivity to real or perceived attacks on teacher professionalism: contract negotiations that left them behind Social Security cost-of-living increases, Olson's recent threat to make tardy teachers provide weekly attendance sheets, school board attempts to pressure them into block scheduling—the new fad that would give them fewer courses with longer periods during which students inevitably flagged.

Corey sat quietly, soaking in the conversation. In the classroom, she'd finally hit her stride, that comfortable balance between casual and in-command. But her relationship with other members of the English department had grown more strained by the week. No one was openly rude, but her entrance into a chattering crowd cast a noticeable pall over even the most casual discussions. Several colleagues studiously avoided her. Others broadcast their distaste with gestures and glances.

Corey's refusal to play the "new teacher," the humble, unopinionated novice, was a thorn in her department's collective side. She edged in on conversations about curriculum and standards and flaunted a not-so-veiled disdain for prevailing custom. Disgusted at the prospect of teaching *The Scarlet Letter* as a movie, as the English department required, she dared broach the matter with her cochair, who'd dismissed her with a perfunctory "who the hell are you, a newcomer, to tell us how to teach" response, his nose seriously—seemingly permanently—out of joint.

But the antipathy for Corey went deeper and felt decidedly more personal. Although a native Minnesotan, she was too candid and too fond of hyperbole for an environment where understatement was the sine qua non of politesse. Hearing her talk about a stint as an oversized model, about living in France, even playing soccer as a teenager, her peers pegged her as a cocky braggart. Rather than pull back or tone down, her insecurity piqued, Corey overcompensated. Laced with the melodrama and exaggeration of the need for acceptance, her every attempt to win approval backfired.

Privately, Jeff Hoeg consoled her. But, in public, even he kept his distance. She'd begun to question whether the problem might not be Prior Lake, as if there wasn't something in the town's air that was making the kids lazy and bratty, the parents obnoxious and the teachers entirely too lax. At least she was trying to believe that. The discussion with the veterans—the hard-ass traditionalists of the school—wasn't making it easy.

Goracke was obsessed with union issues, but Corey understood that they were, in fact, just one of dozens of indignities that he tried to put behind him as he entered class each morning. For many, none of the threats to their view of professionalism loomed larger than "accountability." Politicians across the state and the nation were ganging up on teachers, trying to force them to prove that they were doing their jobs. Aside from teacher or student testing, the most popular proposal for doing so was merit pay, an anathema to teachers, who'd long been paid according to their experience and education rather than any evaluation of their work. Why should we pay good teachers the same amount as bad teachers? politicians had begun arguing. Students don't all get the same grade; they're rewarded according to the quality of their work. Why shouldn't teachers be subject to the same sort of evaluation?

Few proposals hit more raw nerves. They're implying that we're holding back, that if the school board dangled a check in our faces, we would be better teachers, more dedicated and creative instructors, several teachers argued that afternoon. It would breed competition, others said, appalled at the concept.

"Would they judge me by my grades and tell me, 'if they're low, you must be doing a bad job'?" Corey asked. "Oh, great, more money for more *As*," a Biology instructor added, assuming, with Corey, that merit pay would be based on such simple criteria.

Predictably, Joe Goracke had a different concern. "It would become a popularity contest," he said flatly. "Teachers who the administrations like would get raises, which means that those of us who stand up to them would be in big trouble."

But while the teachers vented their anger at proposals for merit pay, it was difficult for them to expend much energy on a distant insult when they were buffeted by so many closer to home. "I can't even worry about merit pay right now, it's the least of my problems," said Sally Davis, a Spanish teacher who'd sat quietly during the discussion of accountability. "The worst insult to teachers today isn't even the school board, sorry, Joe," she said. "It's the parents. They're this antiauthority generation and they're still mad at authority figures from when they were in high school. So now we're that authority and they have to protect dear little Muffy from the mean teachers who don't appreciate her."

Andy Franklin never interrupted. A soft-spoken, gentle man and, like Olson, a former Peace Corps volunteer in Africa, he was punctiliously correct. But Davis took a breath, and parents were everyone's favorite topic.

"It used to be that when I had a problem with a kid and called home, the parents would say, 'I'll take care of it,' and they did," he said. "Now they say, 'How dare you!'" A father had recently stopped by Franklin's office at 7:15 A.M., as he was preparing his notes for the day. "I need fifteen minutes," the father announced. "I'm sorry, this is not a convenient time," Franklin had responded. The man had left in a huff, leaving Franklin speechless but livid. "Would he have barged into the office of his doctor or lawyer without an appointment?" he said.

Davis had her wind back. "They talk to us like dogs who should obey," she continued, "or waitresses at expensive restaurants who serve up cold steaks."

Goldy, who'd been hovering at the margins of the conversation, shook his head, his gelled flat top backlit by the sun streaming in through the window. "They're the same way with the police," he added. "You should hear the calls we get, parents demanding that a squad car come by because their son won't cut his hair, or because their daughter won't get out of bed to go to school. They're not willing to accept responsibility for their children, so they want to foist it off on someone else.

"It's too much Oprah and Jerry Springer. No responsibility, no consequences."

No fan of today's parents, Goracke still wasn't about to let teachers off the hook. Parents, like their children, could scream and complain all they wanted, but if teachers stood firm, what could they do? "Look what goes on here," he blustered. "Passing is a given, even when you want to say to parents, 'Your daughter couldn't pass gas.' And if students are a point or two from a C, all they have to do is whine about how hard they are trying, and teachers give in. We need to say, 'Don't tell us how hard you work, SHOW us how hard you work.' But too many teachers won't. And it's the same with standards. Politicians and bureaucrats are trying to raise standards because there aren't any. Or, there are, but we don't hold kids to them because we're hung up on protecting their self-esteem or rewarding them because they say they are trying. So we're part of the problem. We're a dysfunctional community."

•   •   •

Mike Carr stood at the doorway in jeans and a flannel shirt, eavesdropping intently. He no longer knew what to think. Over the weekend, some college friends had stopped by, but he'd been too swamped with papers to spend much time with them. "They're all out partying and making money with no homework to grade. And it made me feel like a sucker."

The only fun he'd been having at Prior Lake was a two-on-two basketball competition he and his roommate, Nate LeBoutillier, a long-term substitute in the English department, had begun with Eric Prchal and Tony Lorenz. Those few hours, and the easy camaraderie it created with students, were his vision of teaching—although he'd been less convinced that it was worth the price after the first game, when the boys won 22–20 and informed the entire school that Carr and Boots, as they called the substitute, were "losers." Carr, who still thought of himself as eighteen, had been flabbergasted at the defeat. "We're much better players than they are, we know how to play a thinking man's game," he'd insisted. He was deadly serious, desperate to save face.

The boys had agreed to a rematch, and Carr and Nate had pounded Eric and Tony across the court, emerging triumphant, 21–11. The third game was planned for Wednesday, and Carr had vowed to finish the kids off permanently, to leave them in the dust in utter humiliation.

That competition was tepid consolation for the fact that his students had never heard of Anita Hill or Clarence Thomas, for the daily grind of indifference that had eaten away most of his enthusiasm. He'd tried talking to Paula Gaffney, who'd been assigned as his mentor, but she was in a funk of her own.

Paula's problem wasn't so much in the classroom, where she ruled with a firm hand and a quick wit. It was the soccer mothers who were driving their varsity coach crazy. Soccer was the "in" sport for Laker girls, especially after Mia Hamm and the other members of the 1999 Women's World Cup Soccer Championship team became national sex symbols. And it didn't hurt that the boys in the school, titillated by the physicality and aggression of the game, turned up regularly to watch them play.

But the most ardent fans, and Paula's greatest frustration, were the soccer moms. Nowhere was the nature of parental involvement in the school—and the changing relationship of parents to teachers—thrown into sharper relief than in the sports program. Even parents who remained shy about trying to dictate to teachers how to run their classrooms didn't hesitate to order around their children's coaches.

The mothers of the female soccer players, many living out varsity sports fantasies denied them in the days before the passage of Title IX, couldn't be accused of disloyalty to their daughters; they showed up at every game, home and away. But they picked apart every call that Paula made. They phoned her at home and stopped by her house uninvited to protest because their daughters weren't getting enough play time, because senior girls weren't guaranteed starting slots, because Paula was discriminating against their kids, giving too much recognition to the offense or ignoring the girls who played defense.

When Katie Cook, who'd served as a captain during her junior year, was denied that responsibility as a senior, her mother, Pam, climbed the complaint ladder, from the coach to the athletic director to the principal. "What message does this send?" she asked repeatedly. "I hope your child never has to go through something like this," she said in a message she left on the coach's answering machine. But then she openly sneered at other soccer mothers for trying to tell the coach how to run the team or for demanding that the captaincy rotate to allow all the girls the same opportunity to serve.

"It's hostile and dysfunctional, with a capital *D*," said Elaine Pagels, the mother of a junior on the squad. "Parents scream because their kids are on the B squad, not the A squad. And then the girls get into the same backbiting, the standard set by the adults." That understanding, however, did not restrain Elaine—who, like Pam Cook, was hyperprotective of her daughter's self-esteem—from trying to mount a mini-insurrection against Paula when she concluded that her daughter was not being given enough playing time.

Even as she struggled to keep the soccer mothers at bay, in the classroom, Paula was veering toward boredom. "I'm an overachiever who gets depressed if I'm not challenged," said Paula, who had married the day after she graduated from college, then found a job and signed up for a graduate program all in the same week. She was pregnant with her second child, due to deliver in late March. "I wanna save 'em all. I won't give up. I want to be the one. I haven't lost that yet. If I get indifferent, fire me."

But Paula couldn't keep her mind focused exclusively on her students. She kept looking at the big picture, at the state of education, and was horrified.

"We're afraid to raise the bar because it might make us look bad, so we accept mediocrity. But we're teachers, how can we be worried about looking bad?" Having taught elsewhere, she knew that the problem was not unique to Prior Lake. "It's everywhere. It's like we're giving up on the kids.

"Everyone wants to create homogeneity in education, and that's ridiculous. They want to make uniform rules. You can't do that. Equality is not sameness. So we don't push the higher-level kids because it's not okay to treat them differently, even though they would thrive. And, in the same way, we try to treat all schools the same rather than ask what is the basic dysfunction in a given area and dealing with that. We know that reading and writing levels are poor at Minneapolis and St. Paul schools. But you don't solve that problem by mandating basic-skills testing for all the students in the state when 90 percent of those students are doing fine. Instead, spend that money on the schools where you're having problems."

Carr couldn't wrap his mind around the larger issues. He needed a way to cope, day by day, with Jayne Garrison's constant comings and goings, with Ashlee spacing out during his lectures, with Roger falling asleep because he was excruciatingly bored.

"Why put the time in when they don't care?" he asked Sara Strege one morning, unloading the frustrations accumulated during a single class period. During student presentations on the amendments to the Constitution, his Focus students had dug in their heels and refused to cooperate. "Can't you just sit and listen?" he'd finally yelled. "No," one boy replied. Meanwhile, Critter was slouched at his desk, mumbling "Fuck you," to everyone in the room. Finally, someone else chucked a Gatorade bottle across the room and hit Carr in the leg. "That's it," he declared. "I'm putting you on contract." But Critter had hidden the contracts, leaving Carr with no visible weapon. When he found them, the bottle-thrower refused to sign the form.

"Sometimes, I feel like a baby-sitter," said Carr, clearly torn. "And I didn't go to college to baby-sit."

Strege smiled, knowingly. "Way to go, Carr, way to kill their self-esteem." She was only three years older than Carr, but she tended toward the motherly. "Everyone begins with aspirations and it's hard to let go in face of twinkle-tits and glitter-dicks.

"Why didn't you just laugh at Critter when he hid the contract, or at the kid who threw the bottle? It would have made them feel guilty. Lighten up. These Focus kids have tough lives, with divorces, abusive families, you know."

Carr interrupted. "I'm supposed to be their teacher, not their parent."

It was Strege's turn to interrupt. "You're paid to teach them and you're obviously not doing that either."

"Yeah," Carr responded, "but are we really doing them a service by just helping them get through? Does that prepare them for real life?"

Less than five months into his teaching career, Carr felt caught between the two schools of thought at Prior Lake, and was struggling to reconcile his personal comfort with the playful energy of the Streges and his affinity for the tough standards of the Gorackes.

"I want to be like Goracke," he said regularly. But Strege, well, she was Carr's idea of fun. On Fridays, it wasn't unusual for her to interrupt his class, or the classes of other colleagues, by bursting in, chanting, "It's Friday, it's Friday, it's Friday."

Two weeks earlier, she'd walked into another teacher's study hall, where the students had tuned in to *The Maury Show* on television. The substitute in charge had thought the fare bizarre for a study hall, but he'd been told directly by the regular teacher that students should be free to turn on the tube. Strege watched from the corner as Povich's guests, all executives, talked about what their spy cameras had caught employees doing—a woman urinating on her boss's chair, another Xeroxing her breasts. "Did you ever see the one where the guy stirs drinks with his member?" she asked the students when the show faded to commercial.

But Carr couldn't decide if Strege was his role model for a teacher. In her Speech class, students had recently finished their lip-synching unit, Strege's own design for spicing up the course and calming student performance jitters. Carr had listened enviously to the laughter spilling out of her room across the hall as the kids mimed their way down the Top Forty playlist.

But Ashlee Altenbach had given him pause when he asked her what she had learned from Strege's assignment. "I don't have a clue," Ashlee said, scrunching up her face in puzzlement. "But it was fun."

Chapter Ten

1:45 P.M., Tuesday
January 24, 2000

Mary Haugen was imbued with the supreme self-assurance peculiar to those who spend their lives ruling over teenagers subject to punishment for so much as questioning their authority, which left her little inclination to self-doubt or remorse. But that Thursday afternoon, regret seeped from her every pore.

Three weeks earlier, the idea of holding a student forum had seemed like a stroke of genius, a sure-fire strategy for defusing the nagging hostility pervading the school. Haugen wasn't seriously worried that the discontent would boil over into anything approaching meaningful revolt—like a student strike or a blow for "student power." Those concepts had vanished from youth culture along with communes and Jefferson Airplane. But Scott Vig, she'd heard, was plotting insurrection over Prior Lake's treatment of eighteen-year-olds, Tina Farrell, the queen of the microskirt, was stirring up trouble over the dress code, and the student council members Haugen counted on to control adolescent restlessness had lost all credibility, if they'd ever had any to begin with. It seemed prudent to devise some way to clear the charged air, and a full day of open-mike gripe sessions in the auditorium, each devoted to a different burning issue, would vent the steam from the pressure cooker of petty rebellion. Or so she had thought.

Her planning had seemed flawless. Student council members would chair the meeting, providing them with "leadership" experience—and insulating administrators from student wrath. No one would be permitted into the auditorium for even one of the seven forty-two-minute sessions without being punctiliously obedient; interested parties would be required to obtain advance permission to attend the sessions from every teacher whose class they would miss. And, no matter what, a supervisor would be on hand, not only to field questions, but to make sure things didn't spiral out of control.

On paper, then, it had sounded like the sort of enlightened, progressive activity Prior Lake wanted to endorse. Instead—predictably—the auditorium was packed with scores of teenagers sporting spiked hair and Harley-Davidson T-shirts, chains and pierced tongues and, with the school's most notorious druggies and partiers, and the affair was turning into a mud-slinging brawl.

Things had started off mildly enough during the first hour—either because the session began at 7:45 A.M. or because it was devoted to traffic and parking, hardly the catalyst of youthful passion. But the second hour, set aside for an exchange about the school dress code, had developed into a Felliniesque drama. Chairing the session with Eric Prchal was Lyndsay Schumacher, decked out in black leather pants, a hot-pink sweater set and clunky black shoes. "Miss Boynton suggested that Dr. O should model some of the skirts that students have worn," she said, setting the tone seriously but casually. "But, since he's not here, I guess he decided not to take the risk.

"So the questions are," she said, referring to her printed list, "should there be a limit on how short your skirts or shorts can be? Should the school control and monitor what you wear? Do teachers have the right to tell you if your clothes are inappropriate? And do you even know what the current dress policy is?"

Every eye in the room sought out Tina Farrell, who would have won any contest for the Student Most Likely to Be Sent Home Because Her Skirt Was Too Short. In September, she'd been called to Boynton's office for wearing a hip-hugging miniskirt and a skimpy leopard-print blouse that left no doubt that her navel was pierced. Fully aware of why she'd been summoned, Tina had planted herself in Boynton's doorway and performed a pirouette before sitting down. "If boys make comments about you, we'll punish them, but you gotta work with me," Boynton tried to reason with her. Tina raised her eyebrows, as if to say, "What makes you think I would mind those comments?" Boynton then attempted to engage Tina in a sociological discussion about the meaning of clothes. Tina's eyes glazed over. She was sent home with instructions to change quickly and return to school.

In December, Tina had pulled the same stunt again. She wasn't a female Eddie Haskell. In most ways, she was a conventional girl with conventional dreams about a husband and seven kids. She was just pushing the limits, trying to provoke the adults in authority. And they rose to the bait every time. That wintry day, Tina had dangled the bait once more, and Rosalie Schaefer had bitten without a second thought.

A prim woman who taught courses like Creative Foods and Fashion Impact, Schaefer had been waging a running battle over girls' clothes all year and had even suggested to male teachers shy about the overtones of castigating scantily clad females that they find some pretext to send the offenders to her room. When Tina sauntered into class wearing a Lycra dress that would have showed every bulge in her physique if she'd had any, Schaefer had stopped her at the door with her classic line, "You look like a garden hoe," and sent her down to the office.

That time, Boynton played good cop to Olson's stern administrator. "Dress is an expression of who you are and this is how I choose to express myself," Tina said, grinning. "No," answered Olson. "If it were such an expression, I'd never wear a tie." He offered up a lecture on dressing in a manner "appropriate" to the setting, as if imparting an insight that actually might make Tina say, "Wow, I never thought of that." He elaborated on Boynton's exegesis about the sociology of clothing. Tina yawned. "Just send me home and get it over with," she finally demanded. That had been her goal in the first place.

As she walked toward her car that afternoon, she'd laughed. Ashlee Altenbach, who lacked Tina's curves, had worn that same dress the day before, and nobody had said anything. "It just bothers Mrs. Schaefer that I'm so shapely," Tina said.

Tina had signed up for the forum in order to blast the administration about the dress code policy, and Lyndsay had just handed her that opportunity. "I don't think the school should limit the length of your skirt unless, literally, your butt is hanging out," she said. Hers was not. It was a scruffy day for Tina, blue jeans and an oversized sweater. "And all this stuff about no chains is ridiculous," she continued, pointing to a group of boys with long chains dangling off their belts. "Chains are cool unless they're being used to choke or hurt someone. You can kick the person out of school for choking another student, so you don't need chain or spike regulations."

The students burst into applause.

Seated next to Lyndsay, Eric Prchal writhed. Since she'd broken up with her boyfriend, Tina had been flirting with him, and Eric was wowed, both by her energy and by the entree she gave him into Prior Lake's top social circles. Behind his back, Lori Boynton was appalled at the prospect of a Prchal-Farrell connection. "He's such a terrific kid and she's, well, you know," Boynton said. Eric, of course, cared nothing for Boynton's opinion. That morning he was just worried about getting through the session without alienating Tina.

He needn't have worried. Dressed in a navy-blue business suit, Boynton leaned over to the microphone before he was forced to respond to Tina's comments. It seemingly never occurred to Boynton to respond to Tina's rant with the words the vice principal of her own high school might have used, something along the lines of "I don't feel any need to justify these regulations. We make them, and you will follow them." Instead, she heaved a minor sigh and said, "Several years ago, our attorney advised us to watch the length and size of chains and spikes because of what had happened elsewhere. And we also have to be careful about spikes because they scratch chairs in the library. And, come on, we haven't exactly been tough on enforcement."

Pulling at the chains hanging from his pocket, Nick Olson followed up on Tina's remarks, creating an ironic alliance between two students with nothing in common except, perhaps, their antipathy to the dress code.

"The safety issue is absurd," he said. "You can strangle someone as easily with a cord as you can with a chain, and you can poke someone's eye out more easily with a pen than the spikes on your jacket."

"Mine aren't even sharp," yelled a boy in a leather jacket heavily studded with spikes. "And who sits on spikes and damages chairs? That wouldn't be very comfortable."

Ryan Sauer took the floor. A junior, he had recently become the school's poster child for personal redemption. The year before he'd been a wild man, cutting class and talking back to his teachers. A walking encyclopedia on student drug use—on the price of Kine buds from Oregon, the tendency of Ecstasy users to become "E-tarded," and the number of kids who sucked on "one-hitters" (single drag pipes) during outdoor education class—Ryan had decided that he wanted a real future. That didn't mean that he had sworn off partying. But, hoping for a scholarship to college, he'd modified his behavior, as he put it, and pulled up his grades to a 3.8 that trimester.

"These policies make it sound like we're bad kids," he said, almost pleading. "Come on, it's the year 2000. Expression is a HUGE thing with kids. Times are changing. Get with it."

Boynton smiled, as if to say, "Students are so predictable." No heat or real ire. Just the usual whining, the perennial adolescent naiveté.

"I assume you'd kick out a guy who came to school wearing a prom dress," said a boy dressed in a black T-shirt, his baseball cap worn backwards. "Of course he'd have to be a moron, but . . ."

The comment came out of nowhere and would have led in that same direction if Mary Haugen, standing at the back of the room, hadn't bitten. "The advice we get is, and the legal precedent in terms of athletics, at least, is that we would not allow cross-dressing because it violates the norms of society," she said.

The audience erupted. Adults need to be careful with terms like "norms of society."

"If a girl can wear a shirt and tie, how come I can't wear a miniskirt?" yelled a boy with a pierced eyebrow.

"Bigotry and hypocrisy, that's what it boils down to," Ryan Sauer added.

With that, a member of the National Honor Society tried to move the conversation in a more serious direction. "By banning cross-dressing, you're pointing a finger at gay people," she said. "They're not hurting anybody."

Outfitted like Morticia Addams, but holding a baby doll in her lap—an assignment for her Family and Consumer Science class—Marissa Clausen continued in that same vein. "Years ago, all men wore dresses. So you're punishing people just because fashion has changed and homosexuality is not accepted."

Struck broadside in her liberal principles, Boynton squirmed. Right, like they wouldn't tear a cross-dresser to shreds! Should she reply to the serious questions when she knew most of the kids were just playing? At times like that, old-fashioned authoritarianism sounded pretty good.

"Would you kick a person out of school for cross-dressing?" someone asked her directly.

"It's hard to say what we'd do because we have no policy," Boynton answered. "At some pep fests and Laker Capers we've had boys dress as girls, and we don't allow that. But that was obnoxious, not expression."

Haugen interrupted her. "The point here is respect, not disrespect. It's like black face. You can't mock another person," she said, assuming that Prior Lake could never have a student who was a sincere cross-dresser.

Boynton picked up where she'd left off. "The question is whether someone is being offensive."

"How would you know if he was mocking or genuine?" a voice shouted.

"I'd talk to him," Haugen replied.

"What if he didn't want to talk to you about it? What would you do, interrogate him?"

Bored with what seemed a digression into irrelevancy, Ryan Sauer veered back to daily life. "Last year, not long after Columbine, I wore a 'Psycho' T-shirt from Universal Studios that had, you know, like fake blood stains on it. I was sent to the office and told that it was the most offensive thing anyone had ever seen, that I was associating myself with the Columbine kids. No, I wasn't, and I'm offended at being told that I am like them."

Boynton was back on familiar territory. "The problem is that we have to think about more than the nine hundred students at the high school. We have to be sensitive to the entire community. And some kids complained and said that they were scared for their safety, and some parents were worried. We couldn't ignore those concerns."

Lyndsay deflected the conversation onto the question of "Playboy" T-shirts, which had been banned from the school, an addition to the ban on clothing advertising alcohol or drugs. Students regularly sported T-shirts reading "Remember My Name, You'll Be Screaming It Later," "Steel Erection," or "Pimp." But those had not yet become contested terrain.

"They were banned at the request of female teachers who found them offensive," Boynton responded. The students tittered at her use of the plural. They all knew she was talking about Tina's nemesis, Rosalie Schaefer.

"Just because one teacher finds something offensive, that shouldn't mean it is," said Tina, reentering the fray. "What if one student found something offensive?"

"Oh please, everything is offensive to somebody," a student shouted in exasperation.

The clock was moving toward the end of the hour, and resolution did not seem imminent. Then again, resolution was not high on the agenda. No one protested when the bell rang and the dress code was taken off the table, replaced by the question of early release from school. That discussion, however, was perfunctory, a warm-up for the main event, a debate about special rights for eighteen-year-old students, which was coming up in the fourth hour. The rights of adults was the hottest issue on campus, and all heads swung toward Scott Vig when it began promptly at 10:19 A.M. It was Scott Vig's insistence that, when he turned eighteen and moved out of the house, the school should treat him like an adult that had ignited the grumblings that had worried Haugen in the first place.

Scott was a walking attendance nightmare who'd managed to rack up sixteen unexcused absences since the end of November. The administration had finally forced him to sign an "attendance contract," which specified that if he missed four more days before the end of the trimester, he'd lose all his credits, no matter his grades. He'd already exceeded that limit.

A self-contained guy who spent his free time hunting, fishing or racing his snowmobile across the plains, Scott loved cabinet-making and construction, but he hated school, which he considered to be a useless pastime. Although raised in a devout Christian home, he was a serious partier, fond of beer and good pot. "This school is run for the student council kids and the academic types, and I'm neither," he said candidly. His reserve was palpable, as was his pain.

But Scott's antipathy to school was not the root of his attendance problem. Scott was locked in a power struggle with the administration and had staked his personal honor on victory. The issue was his seventh-hour study hall, a massive gathering of students in the auditorium at the end of the long school day. Scott, who bristled with energy and chafed at confinement, hated it. And he couldn't think of one good reason why he shouldn't be allowed to leave at the end of sixth hour rather than spend forty-seven more minutes locked up in a class where nobody ever studied.

His guidance counselor had provided what she considered to be a perfectly good reason that he should remain until the final bell: Them's the rules. The only students permitted to leave early were ones with notes from their parents or those who'd earned Honors Passes by keeping a 2.8 grade point average and staying out of trouble. Scott did not qualify for a pass on either count. And, over the age of eighteen and no longer living with his parents, he refused to run home to mommy for a note. Which was where the conflict began to heat up.

Scott had caught up with Lori Boynton at the entrance to the office one day and asked why he couldn't write his own notes. "After all, I'm a legal adult and I don't live with my parents," he insisted. Forget it, Boynton replied, and moved on with her business. Scott exploded. "How dare she walk away from me?" He stormed out of school steaming, "If she can walk away from me, I can walk away too." His, then, was a serious case of refusal to accept the basic power dynamics of high school.

That departure won Scott another day of in-school suspension, his definition of torture. ISS students spent all seven periods in a windowless classroom with other errant kids and a rotating cast of teachers. They were not permitted to speak. If they had exams, the materials were brought to them by their teachers.

Scott showed up for school the next day, his ISS day, but defied the mandate to the ISS room. During second hour, Boynton called him into her office. "Didn't you know you had ISS?" she asked. "Go down there right now." Scott refused. "You can give me out-of-school suspension if you want, but I will not go to ISS." Boynton stood firm. "Either you go to ISS tomorrow or you have to attend Saturday school," she insisted. Scott stood and declared, "You do what you have to do, but I won't attend either."

The faculty was divided over the Vig flap. Half agreed with Boynton that rules were rules and shouldn't be changed just for Scott. Others took a more pragmatic view. "Is this really smart?" wondered the teacher who supervised the mega–study hall. "No one does anything there anyway." Joe Mestnick, a Social Studies teacher, moved closer to the heart of the matter. "What's the point of getting into a power struggle with him over a study hall in which nobody can possibly study? They're just making it worse." But no one addressed Scott's underlying question: Why should a legal adult need a note from a parent?

Boynton decided that Scott was trying to get kicked out of school. Why else would he be so openly disobedient? she asked. She was wrong. He wanted to finish high school and didn't want to do so at an alternative high school, an adult education facility, which the administration had been urging him to consider. He didn't want to drop out. He just wanted to be released from his seventh-hour study hall, and be treated like a grown-up. Every day he was thwarted, he became more defiant.

In fact, Scott believed that the administration was trying to force him to leave. "They bend the rules for some people, so why not for me? They're taking away my rights as a citizen, as an adult. Every year the rules around here have gotten stricter. They're treating us more and more like little kids, so we're acting more and more like little kids."

Olson had bent the rules for Kristin Murphy, a senior girl who was also living on her own. But she hadn't moved away from home in any sense that the school considered to be "voluntary," as had Scott. And, in fact, her personal struggle had won her wide-eyed admiration. When Kristin was just ten years old, her mother, a cocaine addict, had died of a brain aneurysm, leaving her father, a long-distance truck driver, to raise her. Once her father remarried, she and her older sister both fell into a not-so-unusual tumultuous relationship with their stepmother, and Kristin had finally been kicked out of the house when she was a sophomore. That was not a unique approach to parental responsibility in Prior Lake, where a dozen or more students were booted out of their homes in any given year.

In Kristin's case, her expulsion from home proved toxic. A friend's mother provided kids with alcohol, and the same friend's older sister turned them on to drugs. Needing to understand what had enticed her mother to risk death,

Kristin experimented with cocaine, although she finally settled on meth as her drug of choice. "It was easier to get and cheaper," she said. For months, she lived in a blur, snorting drugs at school, conducting buys in the bathroom. She had plenty of company. "Sophomores and drugs, they go together, we were like little kids with new toys," she explained. By the summer, Kristin was in trouble and entered a twenty-one-day drug treatment program. When she was released, Prior Lake didn't want her back, so she transferred to a neighboring district. But after she broke up with her boyfriend, she relapsed and spent two weeks in an inpatient psychiatric facility, trying to claw her way out of the desire to jump off a cliff. She got that far, but not much farther, transferring to an alternative high school, the worst possible environment for a kid struggling to stay away from illicit substances.

By then, Kristin was terrified that she was following her mother's path. Wracked with constant headaches, she'd lost her virginity and contracted a host of STDs. She became a poster child for the dangers of teen drug use. Through sheer grit, Kristin had begun to rebuild her life. Intent on showing up her parents, who were convinced she'd never graduate from high school, Kristin had talked her way back into an extremely skeptical Prior Lake High School; enrolled in the work program; taken at job at PDQ, a local convenience store/gas station; and rented her own apartment. She lived with a grueling schedule of school, work and family, which meant her sister and nephew—and had been clean for eight months. "Am I proud of myself?" Kristin responded to the question. The pierced rod on her tongue flashed every time she began a new sentence. "Not yet, talk to me in ten years."

Olson had allowed Kristin to get around the "note from a parent" rule by assigning Kristin's sister parental authority. Scott wanted similar consideration. "What's going on here, why her and not me?" he asked, although he knew, or suspected he knew, the answer to that question. It surfaced in one of the endless meetings he had with Boynton and his guidance counselor, at least until he started refusing to appear when they summoned him.

"Do you think you'd be taking this same position if you didn't have all that money?" Boynton asked.

There it is, Scott said to himself. My money. As a member of the Shakopee Mdewakanton Sioux Community, Scott was part-owner of

Mystic Lake Casino, one of the most successful Native American casinos in the country. Like all tribe members, on his eighteenth birthday he'd received $250,000, a lot on which to build his house and the first of what would be his ongoing monthly share of the take, which was running about $70,000.

When his father was growing up, membership in the tribe had meant life as an outcast, as an object of ridicule and overt racism. And Scott had started elementary school in Prior Lake as "just another Indian kid who was bullied by the white kids," as he put it. But as the small Indian bingo parlor grew into a multimillion-dollar operation, everything had changed. "Suddenly they all started kissing my ass. Watching the change, it became hard to trust anybody."

The worst offenders, in Scott's view, weren't his fellow students. He was a stalwart of the most popular group of kids in the school and had been elected Homecoming King in November. It was the teachers. Few hesitated to make cracks about all his "toys," his Harley and ATV, his snowmobile and massive truck. And he regularly overheard them discussing how terrible it was that kids like him had all that money that "they hadn't earned."

"Do they have a problem with the fact that the Kennedy kids or the Rockefellers have 'all that money' that *they* didn't earn?" Scott asked.

At the Forum session, Scott stood proudly at the microphone and pleaded his case in public for the first time. "I'm eighteen years old, which makes me an adult. I'm living on my own. I pay my own bills. Why should I have to get a note from my parents to leave school early or when I'm sick?"

Knowing that Scott would be loaded for bear, Olson had scheduled himself to attend that session of the Forum, but before he could respond to Scott, Tina Farrell jumped in. "I agree. I'm eighteen years old. I can go to the casino and gamble without my parents' permission. I can buy cigarettes without my parents' permission. I can go to jail as an adult. I should be able to leave school without a doctor's note. I can leave school for good but I can't write my own note? That's lame."

Half the students in the room had passed their eighteenth birthdays, and every voice chanted in agreement.

"Tell us what the law says about this," Scott challenged the principal.

Olson had boned up for the session. "It doesn't say much. Just that we need an attendance policy and that we can decide whether or not to excuse an absence."

Kristin Murphy rose. "Your policy presupposes that a student has no family problems. We can't get emancipated, since we're already eighteen. So you need to change your policy."

"Kids should be able to do what they want when they're eighteen," a voice from the back added. "We're old enough to accept the consequences. If we don't come to school and don't pass, don't give us diplomas. It's as simple as that."

To Olson, it was not simple in the least. "Look," he continued, "we have legal liability if a child does something a parent doesn't want him to do."

"That's the whole point, we're not children," Scott shouted.

That was a debatable assertion. These days in America, eighteen-year-olds live in a netherworld of second-class adulthood. They suffer all the downsides of adulthood: being required to register for the draft and facing the stiffer legal penalties of grown-ups. But, other than the rather theoretical privilege of the vote, they are treated like children. They can't drink. They're carded if they want to buy cigarettes. In Minnesota, even their driver's licenses are provisional.

Easing up for a moment, Olson promised to check what kind of policies other schools had.

"Why don't you just try it out and see what happens?" Scott pressed.

"Change comes over time," Olson chided. "We can't just give in to the pressure of students. We have a duty to respond to others in the community, to parents and the board."

The bell rang. Disgusted, Scott walked out, muttering, "We're going to end up paying his wages. I'm already paying his wages. Why can't he just do this? Nothing is going to change."

Seated on the edge of the stage, Lyndsay Schumacher and Eric Prchal breathed a joint sigh of relief. This wasn't quite what they'd anticipated, but at least the anger was being deflected onto administrators, not onto them. From the beginning, Eric had suspected that he and Lyndsay were being set up, that Haugen had chosen student council members to chair the sessions in order to avoid being the target of student wrath. Thus far, they'd been safe, but they both knew their turn was coming.

The next session was devoted to a wide array of school policies, from suspensions to drug enforcement, and one of the most touchy questions posed was favoritism toward student council members. Neither Lyndsay nor Eric denied that they received special treatment, that they were less likely to get hassled in the halls or questioned about their whereabouts than their peers. They girded themselves for the onslaught.

It didn't come, at least not at first.

"Why are pep fests mandatory? They're entirely stupid. Why are we required to be peppy?"

"Why can't we save stuff to disk in the media center without special permission from Mr. Hurni?"

"Why can't we leave study hall for the media center without a pass? Don't you want us to study?"

A dozen insults, perceived or real, flooded the auditorium.

"The rules here are really stupid," a girl added. "If you sneak out to smoke a cigarette in your car and get caught, you get an automatic three-day suspension. But if you sneak out and drive your car away from school to smoke and they catch you for leaving, you only get one day of ISS."

"Yeah, and think about this, how stupid the drug policy is," a boy added. "If you're caught smoking a cigarette, you get the same punishment as you get if they find you with heroin. That's so ghetto."

Tina Farrell had her own agenda. "I put up posters for my friend's eighteenth birthday and Dr. O took them down. The posters read, 'Now You Can Go to the Nudie Bar Legally.'

"What about our right to free speech?" she asked. Like her friends, Tina was a virtual constitutional scholar, but also a constitutional literalist. She knew, or cared, little about how the Supreme Court had interpreted the document. And she was not above asserting rights that the Constitution failed to mention.

Curtailment of freedom of speech and expression was the students' most constant complaint. Especially after Columbine, what little freedom of speech they had under the law was severely diminished in the name of safety. Every muttered "I'm gonna blow up this school," every shouted "I hate Jocks," suddenly sounded ominous to adults, who reacted swiftly and mercilessly. No one seemed to realize how much tension the crackdown was provoking.

Assigned to design a house for his Architecture class, a baby-faced sophomore—a seriously good kid, a certified Eagle Scout—handed in finished drawings with a chemical-weapons laboratory behind the home and a nuclear-missile silo in front of the garage. "I'm liable if you shoot up the school or kill someone and I don't stop this kind of thing," his teacher told him, instructing the boy to redo his work. The boy was livid. "Did he really think I was planning to build a nuclear silo? That would have been a little expensive. So why didn't he call my bluff and make me engineer it or cost it out?"

Ultimately, he didn't put up a fight, but he'd learned cynicism. In his revised project, he converted the chemical-weapons laboratory into a cherry-paneled library containing copies of the First Amendment in every known language and a thousand treatises on the importance of free speech.

The problem went deeper than Columbine fears, however, with which many students sympathized openly. Administrators felt free to interfere even in students' private conversations. One afternoon, a boy named Alex Hershey was standing in the cafeteria at lunchtime talking to Jayne Garrison, complaining about Sara Strege, whom he called "a motherfucking whore." Strege was one of Jayne's favorite teachers, a shoulder she cried on regularly about Randy, her on-again, off-again boyfriend. Jayne reported Alex to Strege, who'd gone up the chain of command to the principal. Alex had been forced to apologize and spend some time in in-school suspension. Even the most ardent supporters of administrative prerogative weren't sure that a perilous line hadn't been crossed when a boy was punished for what he said in a private conversation.

But it was political correctness that was the most constant thorn in their collective sides, and Nick Olson turned the discussion in that direction. "I don't know why they even teach us about free speech in school since every time we turn around, they limit it," he said. Nick's complaint arose from the school's reaction to the clever posters he'd crafted to advertise the chess club, which he ran. Every one of them had run him afoul of Mary Haugen.

ARE YOU TOO ANGRY AND HOSTILE TO JOIN THE PEP CLUB? JOIN THE CHESS

CLUB BECAUSE WE'RE DYSFUNCTIONAL was inappropriate because it demonstrated contempt for other school activities.

BURY THE WOOD, a locker decoration on the day of a big match against Woodbury High School, had "inappropriate" sexual innuendo.

DID YOU LOSE YOUR ELIGIBILITY TO PLAY SPORTS BECAUSE OF DRUGS? JOIN CHESS. WE'RE OPEN-MINDED—well, that was a no-brainer.

The only poster that hadn't earned him a threat of being banned from school activities was, TIRED OF DEFENDING THE UNIVERSE? PLAY CHESS AND LET 'EM SUFFER.

As he told his story, Nick's point became lost in a sea of grumbling at the mention of Mary Haugen's name. The arbiter of offensiveness, inappropriate conduct and, most importantly, eligibility for activities, she was widely referred to as "Little Gestapo"—and not just by students. There was something about Haugen that forced even mild-mannered students like Nick to exercise serious self-restraint.

For some, it was the aplomb with which she tried to interfere in their personal lives, the utter certainty that she had the right to comment on their social activities, on the crowd they hung out with, on which boys they were dating. "When I first got here, she called me in three times in less than six months because she didn't like the guy I was seeing, because she thought I was hanging out with the 'wrong' people," said Heather Hoersten, who'd been captain of the girls' ice hockey team until Haugen took away her title after she was caught at a New Year's Eve party where alcohol was served. Heather's was not an unusual story. Haugen regularly offered unsolicited social advice.

For others, it was the way Haugen wielded her power over their captaincies and their eligibility to play sports or participate in activities. Haugen regularly called students into her office and grilled them about rumors she had heard about their "extracurricular" activities. They were convinced that she would believe anything about a kid who hung out with what she considered to be the "wrong crowd," and the Wrong Crowd was demanding an explanation.

"I absolutely do not practice guilt by association," Haugen insisted when the students began barraging her with examples of disparate treatment. No one was about to allow her to slip away from the issue that easily. "I don't need a confession," she finally admitted when confronted directly about operating on the basis of rumors. She was hardly alone. At high schools all across the nation, schools were informed by police, other kids and parents about drug and alcohol use by students. And activities directors regularly took the rumors to heart.

"Come on," said Tina, "if a Goth kid reports something about, say, Lyndsay, who are you going to believe?"

"This isn't about rumors," Haugen said, although it clearly was. "I think it's a bad idea for you to be at a party where there is drinking, whether you are drinking or not. But am I punishing you for guilt by association? No."

Every eye in the room rolled in unison.

Perched on the edge of the stage, Lyndsay didn't try to control the discussion. She had her own issues with Haugen, dating from her pre–student council days. During her junior year, a boy seated next to her in a class had stolen a test. Haugen had called Lyndsay in and accused her of receiving a copy of it. "That's not true," Lyndsay had protested. "You have no proof." The issue, of course, was not proof but suspicion. Although Lyndsay suffered no punishment after the meeting, the memory of being unfairly accused still rankled.

The minute the conversation began centering on Haugen, there was no way that the privileges of the student council members, *her* kids, were not going to be questioned. Eric and Lyndsay inched closer together on the edge of the stage. "How come they can go out to lunch and we can't?" one boy asked directly. Several times each trimester, Haugen took "her" officers to Burger King or Perkins. "Those are working lunches," she replied firmly. "Yeah, right," someone shouted. "And if I want to have a working lunch?"

The bell rang. Haugen breathed a sigh of relief. The next session was about the length of the lunch period, which gave students thirty minutes to navigate the lunch line and wolf down a meal, and about the quality of the food. She'd ducked the fire once more—until the final hour, the time set aside for an open discussion.

By then, Olson and Boynton had disappeared. Haugen was the only staff member left in the room. The seniors were in the middle of a bitch fest about their class song when Scott Vig strode through the door and up to the microphone. Anxious to get out to his fish house, which he'd just moved to Fish Point Lake, he'd run out to his truck to drop off his books so he could make a quick getaway after the final bell. That quick trip to the parking lot constituted truancy, since students were not allowed to leave the building without permission. Seeing him come back into the building, Mary Haugen had threatened him with detention, then added, "You have no right to try to rile everyone up."

Scott was in no mood for lectures about his lack of rights. "I have the right to say whatever I want," he responded. "This is supposed to be a student forum, and lots of people agree with me."

"No they don't," Haugen informed him. "You need to go somewhere you'll fit in better. You're out of control. You don't want to live by the rules, and we're not going to change the rules just for you. You need to go to an alternative school."

Scott had checked out alternative schools, the places where troublemakers and misfits were sent. "I'm not going to a place where I have to get a pierced eyebrow to fit in," he declared as he stomped off into the auditorium and directly up to the microphone.

"I just bumped into Mrs. Haugen outside and she said that they're not going to change any of the rules, so what's the point of all this?" he asked.

Just then, Haugen's cell phone rang. "How come she can have a cell phone in school and we can't?" Ashlee Altenbach asked. "I have multiple jobs and people have to be able to get hold of me," Haugen answered.

"Yeah, there are always different rules for the staff," Tina complained.

"What's Mrs. Haugen doing here anyway?" a voice from the back of the room shouted.

The crowd was turning nasty. Not nasty in any cosmic sense of nasty. Just pissy. But what makes a rumble in a suburban high school? Eight dozen pissy teenagers and an administrator who doesn't know when to leave. Haugen made a beeline for the door.

The session degenerated into a tangle of grumbling. Ashlee Altenbach griped, to no one in particular, about being kicked off the cheerleading squad for being absent from one game and late to another. Scott's friend Jon Fox tried to steer the group into a conversation about more generalized disrespect for students, but another senior boy wanted to know why high school seniors were served the same amount of milk at lunch as kindergartners.

Lyndsay tried to reestablish order by pleading with the seniors to allow the underclassmen a chance to speak. "We need to do something about the weird kids," said a sophomore wrestler, seizing on the opportunity. "They don't belong here. They should have to stand during the National Anthem. And if the administration is gonna make Tina go home and change because they say she breaks boys' concentration, they should make those girls with Barbie heads on their backpacks and spells and shit stop it. They're what breaks my concentration."

Everyone knew he was talking about Marissa Clausen, who decorated her backpack with doll heads and who was widely feared as a witch. She'd come to school that day wearing three T-shirts, her hedge against a teacher ordering her to take one off. The top one read, "If I Were God, Everybody Dies." The wrestler, it seemed, had taken that literally. He hadn't seen the bottom two, which declared, "No Salvation, No Forgiveness," and "Do Me a Favor, Ignore Me."

Ashlee, however, hadn't finished her laundry list. "Mrs. Boynton called me into the office because she said she'd heard a rumor that I smoked pot before school. I'm sick of her and Goldy and Mrs. Haugen saying, 'I heard this,' or 'Rumor has it.'" It had not been a rumor. Mike Carr had told Ashlee's parents that he suspected that she was coming to class stoned. But his evidence was that she appeared more hyperactive than usual, which demonstrated how fluent he was in drug behavior. "Anyway, what business is it of hers what I do before school?"

The clock had just moved past two P.M. The final bell would ring in twelve minutes. Edging out Ashlee, Lyndsay tried, in vain, to end the day with some semblance of order, but a dozen different insults still had not been aired.

Ryan Sauer reached the mike thirty seconds before the bell rang. Everyone was too busy packing up books and backpacks to hear his final words: "Keep pushing the limits, never stop."

Upstairs, in an English classroom, someone scrawled on the blackboard:

QUESTION AUTHORITY. BUT FIRST RAISE YOUR HAND

Chapter Eleven

8:30 P.M., Wednesday, February 2, 2000

There are whiners and there are rebels, or at least rebel wannabes, and, at Prior Lake that winter, the rebel wannabes didn't show up at forums or whimper to Boynton and Olson about honors' passes or their own mistreatment. Late at night, they drove around town, smoking cigars, talking about the politics of being teenagers.

In a different age, they might have been riding buses to Selma, marching against the war in Vietnam, or railing against apartheid. But theirs was an era with no burning political issue to spark their passion, no national cause celebre to forge a youth culture. It was a shitty time to be a restless kid, and they knew it.

"We live in a world totally defined by the mass media, it's like mass media fascism," said Nick Busse, sitting on a bench outside the high school in a "Freedom from Religion" T-shirt, courtesy of his favorite band, The

Dead Kennedys. "You can't escape it. The minute an alternative view, an alternative culture starts to arise, MTV commercializes it and it becomes shit. So we think what we're programmed to think. We know only what we're programmed to know. We buy identities off the rack at the mall— you know, like the punk stores, quality rebellion at affordable prices.

"Even in school, we segregate ourselves according to mass marketing. Tommy Hilfiger doesn't sit next to combat boots, who hate Abercrombie and Fitch, who despise the Goths, who can't stand anyone who wears a team shirt. Prepackaged cultures. Prepackaged identities. Does anybody really care who anyone else is, or is it all a response to what we've been marketed to feel?"

Nick knew what he felt. He had a long list of adjectives: oppressed, stifled, wasted, ignored, bored, depressed, angry, lonely, confused, fearful, jealous, underappreciated. "I've always felt superior in some ways because I knew I was smart, but I also felt inferior because I had no friends and never had any fun. I felt totally alone. I'd sit alone in my room at night with the lights off, listening to music and scribbling some prose in a notebook."

A natural idealist, Nick had begun his descent into cynicism at the age of seven, when his mother was killed by a drunk driver. Taught to obey the rules lest he be punished, he assumed that adults were subject to the same equation of responsibility. So he'd expected the man to be sent to prison; instead, the killer had served just two months in jail. Then a family friend embezzled his mother's insurance money, which he'd allegedly invested for Nick's college education. Once again, Nick watched an adult pay nothing for his crime.

By the time he reached middle school, he felt inundated by hypocrisy. "A neighbor of ours was into Wicca, another guy was dealing drugs out of his house and some kids on crack stole a car. There are religious fanatics with arsenals in their basements. Racism and sexism didn't disappear; they just went underground. Then you come to school, and Jocks and Preps speak Ebonics and act like drug dealers, but they call people Jews, niggers and faggots."

When Nick read about the school shooting in Jonesboro, Arkansas, he concluded that the world was spinning utterly out of control. "This is chaos, this is hell," he thought, "this country is hell."

Fed up with being a "perfect kid," with treading the dutiful path toward good grades and playing sports because that's what he was supposed to do, he'd given up on the Prior Lake ideal, at least the one his dad had scripted, which included a future at the Air Force Academy and a crisp, pressed uniform. A decade after his mother's death, Nick was crisp and pressed, but in black chinos, a "Black Flag" T-shirt and hair ever-so-slightly spiked. For a while, he'd thrown himself in with the hard-core punks who reveled in anger for anger's sake. But he was too smart and, at heart, too wedded to traditional values, not to see behind that façade.

So he was steeped in loneliness, desperate to fit in—somewhere, any-where—but oblivious to the reality that refusing to reshape himself into one of the five or six acceptable teenage molds was a choice, no matter how unwitting. He ached for community and hadn't found it beyond the tenuous theoretical connection he'd felt while reading books like *The Fight Club, 1984* and *Clockwork Orange*. But real community, physical and tan-gible? "It feels impossible. Our whole society is like a giant dysfunctional family. We've lost faith in religion, government, schools, cops, especially the family. Everything. So how can we have community?

"All we have is a façade."

Nick had no role model for teen rebellion. "I can't identify with the counterculture movement of the 1960s because it was all about love and peace," he said, a telling reflection of what today's teens are taught about yesterday's radicals. So there he was, at the age of seventeen, rage seeking an outlet, a rebel without the hint of a practical cause, spending his evenings riding around smoking cheap cigars because it seemed like the bad-ass thing. Then it came to him: I need to create a Prior Lake e-zine, a Web site that might sow a few seeds of resistance, provoke some contro-versy and discussion, maybe even forge a little community.

Within a week he had a Web address, an e-mail account and a proto-type Web page, thanks to the skills he'd acquired as the cadet commander of the Minnesota Valley squadron of the Civil Air Patrol. He chose *Social Castration News* as his title, parodying *Student Council News*, the monthly student council newsletter. "Why bother?" Nick asked on the page outlining his purpose. "Our school never gave us a forum for free thought, so we invented our own. We, the intellectually gifted students, are basically getting cheated out of an education because the school system is designed to serve only the needs of the average students. We don't intend to leave high school without sharing our opinion about this.

"We are also concerned with the current trends of materialism, consumer excess and nihilism that dominate popular culture. These concepts threaten to uproot the moral foundations of our democracy.

"We are fighting back in the most constructive way we know how—disseminating information. This is what the Internet was made for!!!"

The kicker to that page was an MTV logo with a red slash across it and the notice, "This page is anti-MTV for a cleaner less corporate bullshit world wide web."

Elsewhere, he advertised for contributors: "WE WANT YOU! Help Us Fight Ignorance. Remember: They might have the numbers, but we have the brains."

Nick's idea was to build the perfect Web site in black and red, the anarchist colors, with articles by Prior Lake students, links to his favorite political and punk sites, and the best visuals he could cull from Adbusters, the Center for Commercial-Free Education and a host of antiestablishment organizations. When he was ready, he and his comrades would blanket the school with fliers, and rock that staid, self-satisfied institution.

Not one for small talk—really for any talk unless he had something substantive to say—Nick was incredibly good at secrecy. The other guys he'd recruited, however, were not. One told another, who blabbed to a third. The next thing Nick knew, before he had three articles loaded, *SC News* had received an e-mail from the principal. Three days later, Mary Haugen followed up with a firm dressing-down about two inaccuracies in an article about problems on campus. "Don't individuals have any responsibility to seek information?" she wrote. "As I see it, I always have a choice. I can base my opinions on hearsay and gossip or I can go to a credible source and get the correct information. Then my opinions are based on fact." The communication was signed, "Mrs. Haugen."

Olson, on the other hand, sounded thrilled that his students, even if just a handful, were actually spending time debating ideas and politics, although he was a bit concerned about the community's reaction to an electronic publication rife with anarchist links. He sympathized openly with Nick's lead article, which dealt with the commercialization of public education. His example was Channel One News, a commercial television network that bought advertisers access to twelve thousand American classrooms by providing their schools with televisions. "Channel One News is the most ingenious mass-marketing tool ever devised," Nick had written, reminding readers that it was owned by "the same corporation that owns RJR Nabisco, the propaganda ministers behind the notorious 'Joe Camel' ad campaign.

"YOU ARE BEING EXPLOITED," he'd continued. "Although our teachers are not even allowed to talk about religion, school administrators preach materialism to us by making us watch this crap."

Olson seconded Nick's concerns. "As your principal, I am constantly being bombarded by requests from other commercial organizations to gain access to you students. They know where you spend your day, and they work hard to come up with ways of getting into your wallets. I strongly oppose that, in general, and am doing as much as I can to prevent the school from becoming commercialized."

The principal's only real quarrel with the publication was the anonymity with which Nick had shrouded the authors of the e-zine. Nick had learned his Thomas Paine well and believed that by concealing the identities of the students involved, he might force greater focus on their ideas. Olson missed the point, assuming that the editor was "hiding behind a pseudonym," and chided Nick gently for his own pen name, Jimmy Sporenko. "You may use your real name as I'm using mine," he wrote before signing himself, "Craig Olson, Principal."

More self-assured than he realized, Nick refused to yield. "I'm sure it won't be difficult for you to figure out who I am," he responded, before offering Olson his own page on the e-zine, "and I sure wouldn't want to spoil the fun."

Olson tried to divine the identity of the editor and wound up thinking about Reilly Liebhard rather than Nick. That was logical, since Reilly was not only passionate about politics, but possessed the technical skills and the literacy to have pulled off the venture. In making their guesses, the teachers, however, were less savvy, ignoring the expertise behind *SC News* and homing in exclusively on the tone. Lynn Lally, then, read through the site and decided that Jayne Garrison must be editing the e-zine, although Jayne clearly could not have designed a Web site or crafted the site's articles. John Bennett, the football coach, seized on a boy who sported multicolored spikes in his hair— seemingly unaware that that student had purchased his anger off the rack at Hot Topic, a faux punk chain store that catered to comfortable teenagers looking for the latest in antiestablishment attire.

Nick didn't care that no one figured out that he was the driving force behind *SC News*. He wasn't looking for attention; he was having too much fun writing articles, editing his own magazine and inciting debate. "We definitely thought there would be enough pissed off kids to support us," he said, "and pissing off the kids who disagreed with us was part of the fun."

Every day, he posted new contributions, most of them raising serious questions, although a few were just run-of-the-mill teen carping. Falling into the latter category, Johnny Berserker sent in a thinly veiled "story" about a student's confrontation with a teacher whom he'd kiddingly called "an ass" in a conversation with a friend. Overheard by the teacher in question, the young man—Danny—was accused of "verbal harassment, use of foul language and insubordination." How dare the school be so petty, so arbitrary! Berserker said in passionate indignation. "The next time Danny is sent for punishment he will not serve it. He is prepared to fight it until the end and has many on his side that are willing to fight with him. It is time to stop letting these people run our lives and dictate to us like we are sheep."

But most of Nick's authors opted for more gravity. In his first submission, Nick's original coconspirator, Kurt Milberger, attacked the Student Forum as "a pathetic attempt by the student council and the administration to silence the student body . . . It was a lot like arguing with your parents, no matter what we said, the student council/administration had some form of justification and reason as to why nothing can change." But in his next article, he took on the anarchy fad sweeping the nation. "Every time you turn around nowadays you see someone claiming to be an anarchist," he wrote. "From the hippest band on MTV (namely Korn) to the fourth-grade kid that lives down the street from you. Everyone is jumping on the bandwagon. Spending their hard-earned money on products supporting anarchy produced by some huge corporation for sale in their chain stores all across the country."

Jake Anderson, who was still see-sawing between going to the University of Minnesota and flying off to Boston, added his voice with a piece about the commercialization of the Internet and the danger that it would become as bland as television. Figuring that if he was being blamed for the e-zine, he might as well join its ranks, Reilly Liebhard, under the pseudonym Sam Radley, churned out three articles in a single evening. The first, about the perniciousness of Nike ("the omnipresent swoosh" of a corporation that had gained a "stranglehold over young American minds"), was a plea: "We must fight for a world in which propaganda, slave labor and conformism can be regarded as sad, bygone hallmarks of the twentieth century . . . Taking a principled stand prevents one from becoming a sheep—whether it's under the swoosh or under the swastika."

After Mike Carr's sociology class erupted into a battleground during a discussion of the Boy Scouts' refusal to allow gay men to serve as troop leaders, Nick weighed back in with "Intolerance, Prior Lake–Style," a treatise provoked by the fact that every girl in the class had supported gay rights, but only two boys. "Hate," he wrote, "has less to do with ideology or values than with trying to feel superior to someone. In our society, it is not macho to tolerate homosexuality, and in our media-driven culture of male violence (think football games and action movies), young men must always act macho.

"What this is really about is a group of machoistic teenagers with low IQs, trying to feel superior to someone. That's all it is." He concluded with a stanza from The Dead Kennedys, *Behind the muscle mask is a scared little boy called Macho Insecurity.*

That, at least, provoked a response.

"[Y]ou seem to have taken the worst the class had to offer and post it for everyone to see," wrote a junior boy who called himself The Thinker. "In a nutshell, you have labeled them intolerant and rude and small-minded bigots. . . . [Y]ou who promote freedom of speech need to be careful that you don't limit it to only yourselves. . . . If these people abhor homosexuality, isn't that their life choice, and one you should accept?" He concluded by reminding Nick of the "many commandments against homosexuality from the beginning to the end of the Bible."

If The Thinker had read the full Web site, he might have known that the latter argument would have been unlikely to move the editor. Beneath a photograph of Jello Biafra, the lead singer of The Dead Kennedys, Nick had included one of his favorite quotes: "Change is possible. Are you trapped in an unhealthy Christian fundamentalist lifestyle? Think that you don't have a choice? The truth is: Christian political extremists can change. It's not about Hate. It's about Hope."

If *SC News* had been scripted by television or Hollywood screenwriters, the e-zine would have taken Prior Lake by storm, galvanizing students to radical action—to marches and protests—or inciting parents or administrators to crusade against the new publication. But today's screenwriters haven't spent much time in today's suburban high schools. Rebellion—real rebellion, not just carping at petty rules and regulations—has no consumer niche among contemporary high school students. They are Stepford Teens, cloned from a generation that has turned suburbia into a cushy cocoon. Parents negotiate house rules with their children. The school administration plans forums where students can air their grievances. And all values are relative.

"I have my own car, plenty of spending money, sex whenever I want it and my parents finance everything," one boy said. "What's there to rebel about?"

In Pleasantville, then, where old-fashioned authority dynamics have been banned as politically incorrect, or potentially injurious to children's mental health, intellectual ferment, even pseudointellectual passion, rarely sprouts in that alkaline soil. The students aren't defiant, except about the most immediate indignities. What rebellion they practice is in the form of passive aggression, which hardly makes for tidy dramatic denouements.

In an e-mail, Christy Gold, whose father was the youth pastor at Friendship Church, thanked Nick for "giving us our right to freedom of speech back." Otherwise, most of the response was along the lines of "Dudes! at least keep the site up." Few students came out of the woodwork to jump on, or throw tomatoes at, Nick's bandwagon, or to comment on his links to the American Civil Liberties Union, Adbusters or the National Organization for the Reform of Marijuana Laws. Even the "Follow the Flock" poster, a photograph of a herd of sheep posed in front of an American flag, a Tommy Hilfiger logo emblazoned in the corner, was roundly ignored.

Ultimately, *SC News* died with a whimper rather than the proverbial bang. By early spring, Nick was fed up and ready to get back to work on his novel. On April 16, he posted his resignation from his e-zine. To Craig Olson, he extended warm thanks for understanding "that education goes beyond the classroom, and involves self-expression and individualized think-ing." To Mary Haugen, although not by name, he posed a pointed question: "Can you not see that anyone who would take the initiative to do something like this should be praised for their creativity and concern for their school? Would you rather we be placid, acquiescent retards who didn't care?"

To the students, he said, "We gave it our best shot. *Quod scripsi scripsi.* What I have written I have written."

Chapter Twelve

1:34, P.M., Friday,
February 4, 2000

The deafening beat of a drum machine reverberated off the towering ceiling as the lights in the gym dimmed. TJ Douglas strutted across the cavernous room in an oversized sweatshirt, his baseball cap worn fashionably backward, with Dwyne Smith, in pants so baggy that they seemed bound for his ankles, following four steps behind. The spotlight found the two boys as they met at the center of the floor.

"What's up, y'all," TJ greeted the crowd. The response was a stunned silence. "Come on, y'all, stand up, get up off your duffs," TJ urged the students. "Come on, nig . . ." TJ caught himself midsyllable. It was the wrong crowd for the word "niggaz"; there were only four black faces in the room. He and Dwyne segued quickly into their rap.

*Two of a kind, we're gonna blow your mind, Dwyne and TJ
sending chills down your spine, down through your vertebrae,
leaving the people in the crowd not knowing what to say, but to
stand on their feet to celebrate and hear what these two intelligent brothers have to say.*

"Oh my god, these kids are actually rapping," exclaimed Chris Feist, a
senior boy. "They're rapping about Prior Lake." It was something the students had never seen their peers do before, and their eyes widened. Their
hearts beat a little faster. Should they be appalled? Excited? The latter reaction prevailed, and they stood and shouted, the gym erupting with the
energy of a thousand teenagers released from their own conventional
expectations. Pep fests were always stultifyingly predictable. TJ and
Dwyne were anything but.

The occasion was the annual SnoCapades, the pep rally-cum-student
follies that marked the beginning of SnoWeek, Prior Lake's antidote to the
midwinter doldrums. The script for the event had been etched in stone during some historical moment beyond the memories of even retired teachers.
Senior boys, always prominent Jocks, served as emcees for the two-hour
pageant. Student clubs performed skits and the cheerleaders tried to remake
themselves into a dance line. Pupils chose a teacher to roast, then a group of
them played the parts of contestants in a parody of the game show du jour.

Mike Carr was the teacher in the hot seat, his lack of prowess on the
basketball court serving as the brunt of the joke. Many students already
knew that Eric Prchal and Tony Lorenz had been humiliating Carr and his
roommate in a series of two-on-two games. The rest had received full
details of the adults' latest ignominious defeat that morning, when Eric
had used the public address system during daily announcements to report
on Carr's most recent embarrassment.

The roast had been followed by Prior Lake's own version of *Who Wants
to Be a Millionaire?*, with Tom Maust, the student council president, playing
Regis Philbin. The questions all revolved around the lives and likes of students who belonged to the In crowd. What was Melissa Conzemius's middle
name? Who could name Kristen Holmes's favorite song? Half the audience
had no idea whatsoever who Melissa might be, or whether Kristen preferred

No Doubt or Britney Spears, and they tittered nervously in their ignorance, reminded of their estrangement from the center of social gravity.

But for all the students, the forty-five-minute event was growing tedious, and by the time the cheerleaders grabbed center stage, Biology class was sounding pretty appealing. Then the spotlight hit TJ and Dwyne.

> *So honeys get up and move that booty round and round, make*
> *it jump up and down to this funky sound.*

In the few short weeks they'd been at the school, TJ, a transfer student from Kansas City, and Dwyne, who'd moved to Prior Lake from inner-city Minneapolis, had become Big Men on Campus. The Asian students, who dressed like LL Cool J, followed them around like sycophants. The Wiggers, white suburban BOYZ who pretended to speak Ebonics and studiously mimicked the hand gestures of the 'hood, were their most devoted groupies. And half the girls in the school were vying for their attention, rubbing up against them, handing them their telephone numbers.

> *You be askin' is the party really hot? Hell, yeah, me and Dwyne*
> *are blowin' the spot. So just you grab your shorty and proceed*
> *to this party.*

Seated on the gym floor, John Bennett, the football coach, was visibly shaken. "Is this our future?" he asked, almost plaintively. A Chemistry teacher nervously paced the bleachers, clearly worried that the "situation" might get out of hand.

"Diversity has finally come to Prior Lake," Lori Boynton announced as the SnoCapades ended, ecstasy juicing her voice.

Roger Murphy had no problem with the boys who'd increased the black male population of Prior Lake by 200 percent, but he couldn't help mocking Boynton's self-satisfied glee. "Yep, ain't it great that we got our own NE-groes now," he deadpanned. "And ain't it fun to watch 'em dance! NE-groes are such talented entertainers! It's the Organ-Grinder-with-the-Little-Monkey Syndrome."

●   ●   ●

"So aren't you impressed with the diversity at Prior Lake?" Tom Maust inquired of a long-term substitute one evening. Blond-haired and they blue-eyed, Tom was too doughy for his preppy clothes, which looked freshly pressed but inevitably wrinkled. He was stunningly serious. Good liberals, Prior Lake's teachers and administrators valued diversity, and they had passed that theoretical value along to the kids. The Social Studies department had recently added a required course in Eastern and Western Studies, a twelve-week trimester devoted to India, Africa, Asia, Russia and Latin America, which its instructor, Paula Gaffney, taught as an exercise in the eradication of ethnocentrism. Martin Luther King's birthday had finally been declared a district holiday, usurping Presidents' Day. The choir sang in Spanish, French and Ibo, and was about to depart on a trip to New York City, where they were scheduled to rehearse with a gospel choir in Harlem. And at the annual student council retreat in November—held downtown in Archangels Hall at St. Michael's Catholic Church—Mary Haugen had even prodded the thirty student leaders assembled into adding the encouragement of diversity to the group's mission statement.

But the kids couldn't miss the disconnection with their own reality. Only .5 percent of Prior Lake residents claimed non-European or non-Christian backgrounds. Whenever Hmong and Hispanic residents of Minneapolis began fishing along Prior Lake, the town fathers had responded by virtually eliminating parking in the area. The voices of locals dripped with contempt whenever conversations turned to the subject of the "rich Indians," or "those fat cats on the reservation," referring to people like Scott Vig. And when Martha Hoover, a member of the school board, talked about the burgeoning student population, she moved smoothly into a discussion of the three new apartment complexes being built in Savage, which had attracted large numbers of Somali residents. "We have no trailer parks here, but they just built low-income housing," she said. "They have *so many* children, an average of three kids per unit. Now we're really going to have an English-as-a-Second-Language problem. And then, you know, once they're established here, they bring their cousins, their brothers and sisters, their uncles."

At the high school, the first football game of the season had been held on

Rosh Hashanah and the school-centered Community Fest on Yom Kippur. The choir's holiday concert made no concession to either Kwanza or Chanukah. And while the curriculum offered students the opportunity to study stress management, chemical awareness and strength training, it included no courses in French. Not one of the books the English department required students to read—over a three-year period—was written by an author who was not a white male. And while students were barred from wearing Budweiser T-shirts or Playboy Bunny attire, they were free to sport shirts reading, "Work Harder, Millions of People on Welfare Depend on You."

Until the arrival of TJ and Dwyne, the handful of minority students at Prior Lake had lived in social limbo, often social purgatory—with the exception of Scott Vig, whose wealth largely burnished his race. Scarred by his childhood experiences, Roger coped by rejecting his rejecters as forcibly as possible, walling himself off from any possibility that intolerance might mellow into polite acceptance. And the dozen or so Asian students had created their own society, a world almost apart from Prior Lake.

When Paul Yath, the American-born son of Cambodian refugees, transferred in from Mankato, a small city in southern Minnesota, just four months before TJ and Dwyne, the segregation startled him. "It's been a pretty big culture shock," he said. "In Mankato, we had kids from everywhere, Somalians and Africans and lots of other Asians, so this was a pretty big change. I try to be friends with everyone, you know, not separate myself. But when I first got here, kids made fun of the way I looked."

Like TJ and Dwyne, Paul's avenue to social prominence was performance—in his case, with a yo-yo and as break-dancer. He'd already won regional yo-yo championships and was headed to the world competition in July. But neither that skill, nor his membership in The Flying Noodles, a break-dancing troupe that performed at talent shows and pep fests, had conferred on him the panache of the two African-American newcomers. Asian with an attitude, after all, didn't have quite the same ring.

The substitute couldn't imagine how to respond to Tom Maust's Laker pride in the heterogeneity of the school. "What do you mean by diversity?" he inquired. Tom, who was at the top of his class, answered confidently, "You know, all the different groups we have."

•　　•　　•

Diversity, Prior Lake–style, was on display daily between 11:05 and 12:30 in the school cafeteria, where segregated seating was the social rule. For his Research Methods class, Justin Jorgenson had actually mapped the area— two separate rooms, in fact—dividing it not only by table, but by "comfort zone." His experiment in cartography was a virtual Fodor's Guide to the culture of Prior Lake High School. "As a student, you must know who it is socially acceptable to interact with," he wrote.

Justin's Region #1 belonged to those who cultivated a "distant attitude," which meant that Roger Murphy, Jayne Garrison, Marissa Clausen and Anna Bican gathered there. They would have preferred to eat lunch at an even greater distance from their classmates but, at the beginning of the year, they'd been barred from their chosen dining area, the floor in a secluded passageway.

No one entering the larger of the two dining rooms, the so-called "junior-senior cafeteria," could avoid going past their table. During the first week of school, one of the popular boys walked by and noticed a new face crowned by a Mohawk hairdo.

"Looks like we've got another freak," he said.

"I'm glad to know there's so much narrow-mindedness in this school," Anna Bican had replied.

"I'm not narrow-minded," the boy protested. "She IS a freak."

Until she reached middle school, Anna would have cringed rather than fought back against her own ostracism. Beginning in the third grade, she'd been the "chosen one," the kid singled out for merciless bullying. Anna was a perfect mark: she wore glasses, had no money for cool clothes and was willing to do "everything, anything to belong," she recalled. "I was so far down the social ladder that even the Nerds picked on me. The non-Nerds didn't even know I existed. For them, I wasn't worth picking on."

The one thing Anna had was a singing voice, an incredible, clear, crisp set of pipes, and an ear to match. But that won her no friends. "Stop singing, you're hurting other people's ears," her classmates complained when she was in the sixth grade. Anna had learned to keep her mouth shut at school.

But in the eighth grade, she began hanging out with Jayne Garrison, who had a different attitude toward the social pecking order. "Who wants to belong? They aren't worth belonging to." Sick of hating herself, Anna had followed Jayne's lead. "I stayed a Nerd, but became a Nerd with an attitude," she said, laughing.

Jayne was a one-woman anti-Jock crusade. She didn't just defend herself, she openly baited "those kids" with a fine, if heavy-handed, wit. Declared an outcast in the seventh grade—a lesbo, a weirdo—Jayne fought back. During her sophomore year, she'd slammed a boy in his testicles. By her senior year, however, her fights were more likely to be verbal. "Okay, you win, your penis is bigger than mine," was a classic Jayneism.

Staff members assumed that the weird Region #1 kids—the ones with Mohawks, blue hair, chains, spikes and safety pins—were the school's druggies. They were entirely wrong. Most of them had tried drugs, most having "indulged" when they were in middle school. Jayne, for one, had managed to run through pot, alcohol, Ritalin (stolen from kids with prescriptions), codeine and LSD. But by the time they reached high school, drugs and alcohol had become entirely too mainstream an activity for the group.

If drugs were too mainstream, so were academics. Most of Anna's friends practiced studied indifference to report cards. "I don't see it as affecting my future," Anna said. "Anyway, I'm having too much fun not caring." Her fun consisted of starring in virtually every school play, singing in the choir and winning state speech tournaments. Broadway was her dream, but she'd found little encouragement at Prior Lake, especially from adults other than her mother. "All through school they'd ask us what we wanted to do with our lives. If I told the truth, they'd smile nicely and say, 'Well, and if you can't do that, what would you like to do?' The message was pretty clear."

Anna's senior year was proving triumphant. She'd played Elizabeth Proctor in *The Crucible*, to standing ovations. She was the star of the choir and MadJazz. And, finally, Anna, who still saw herself as a goofy little girl with glasses rather than as a stunning young woman with extraordinary presence, had a boyfriend, Nick Olson.

The nearer a student sat to Anna and Jayne's group, the more likely he or she was to be a pariah. The Nerds strung themselves out among three or four tables, eating more as individuals than as a group. And the far end of that same row of tables belonged to the Drama Kids, bonded by hours of building sets and rehearsing together.

Those Special Ed kids who spent their days with aides at their sides, or who were visibly, seriously handicapped, created a no-man's land between the actresses and the Jocks, who seized the center of the room, the cheerleaders orbiting around them. The sole disabled student invited into the social mainstream, Nate Schweich was the only student to wander between the two.

In a peculiar juxtaposition, students from Friendship Church sat nearby. Under the leadership of their youth pastor, Mark Gold, Christy's dad, Friendship maintained the most active church teen outreach program in the area. Every Sunday morning, the church bused their middle and high school kids to the high school auditorium for their Extreme Uniquely Youth service, ninety minutes of worship, music and witnessing. While four bouncers circled the room like birds of prey, swooping down on anyone whose head nodded or who wiggled a little too much in his seat, kids raised their hands seeking special prayers ("for my Jewish grandfather that he comes to Christ," "for my sister, who has started to have sex"). One Sunday morning, a shapely woman told her own story, of accepting Christ during a slumber party when she was in seventh grade, then falling from grace and living as a "slut" until she found Jesus again. In the front row, Christy was riveted; such stories were her guideposts and her strength.

Mark Gold had taught the kids not to segregate themselves, even as they bore witness to their principles. But it wasn't easy for the religious kids to know how to respond when other students mocked "Fundies," or to cope with the swearing without succumbing to it. "I look at my lunchtime as a relaxing refreshing time when I can sit down with people who have generally the same point of view, tell them how I'm feeling and have them understand why I'm feeling that," explained Christy, a sophomore. "If I went up to a non-Christian and told him that I had a burden to pray for something, they wouldn't understand. Most kids would probably say, 'What's a burden?' But if I go to one of my Christian friends, they can support me and help me pray for that thing.

"It's pretty much the same thing with other kids. If you were a kid that lived on the reservation and all of a sudden you went bankrupt, other kids wouldn't understand. They would think that you meant that you only got two of the three cars you wanted for your birthday. Kids sit with kids that have things in common with them so they can sympathize with one another."

There was no gay and lesbian table in a cafeteria where words like "faggot" and "dyke" were bandied about, yelled out and flung across the room as the ordinary currency of both playful insult and studied derision. Jessica Furuli, Prior Lake's only publicly identified gay student—the only student, male or female, who risked being out—had graduated in December after a three-year blur of self-destruction that had landed her in a psych ward for drugs, panic attacks and self-mutilation. Weed and crank—which she'd traded for baby-sitting services—had taken the edge off the terror she felt every time she entered the school.

Until her final trimester, that terror had kept her locked firmly in the closet, emerging only at a center for gay teens in downtown Minneapolis. But she'd appeared in school in September of her final year wearing a rainbow bracelet, intent on demanding at least a shred of dignity with her diploma, hoping at least one of the other gay and lesbian students she'd spotted might join her over lunch or turn a one-student statement into an actual support group. She graduated disappointed.

Down from the Friendship group, on the same latitude, at least according to Justin's map, lay Chinatown, the home of the Asian Posse, AP, as Roger Murphy called it. Roger delighted in his skill as a cafeteria tour guide. "See there, in the center?" He pointed. "Those are the Ice Fairies, the hockey jocks. And behind them are the Oh My Gawd Kids, America's wet-dream kids who are perfect in every way."

Roger had a name for every group and drew the finest of distinctions. There were the yuppies—whom he called the Republican Yuppies, like Tom Maust—and the "Yuppie Throwbacks," the kids who "aren't good enough to hang out with the real Yuppies yet because they still haven't gotten their first SUV to drive to Starbucks." There were the Alpha Grade Jocks—team captains, kings of proms, homecoming dances and SnoBalls—Jock Lushes and Jock Throwbacks, the latter being athletes who loved sports more than popularity. Table by table, room by room, he pointed to Ravers and Burnouts, Nazi Wannabes and Wrenchheads, his name for rednecks.

Emily Rabin, a junior who belonged to the Raver tribe, the kids who lived for the semiunderground megaparties that were sweeping the nation, sliced the social pie less carefully. "Look at it," she said, "it's all about money. Being popular is about being wealthy. If you have the right clothes, the right look, you're popular." She was right on target.

"So, Roger, where are the other Chess Kids?"

Roger shook his head, as if puzzled that anyone could be so stupid. "They'd never eat in the cafeteria," he replied. "They're too busy playing chess in the physics room."

The chess fanatics weren't the only students to avoid the cafeteria entirely. Katie Cook, one of the Synergy students, would have been welcome at the table where the other soccer girls ruled. But by the winter of her senior year, she'd taken to eating lunch in Katie Hallberg's room. "I couldn't stand the cliquiness of the scene," she said. Every day, the number of students joining her, or simply avoiding the cafeteria, grew.

The students who skipped out on lunch entirely and hung out in the library, to the chagrin of the librarian, had dubbed themselves the school's self-styled SS, the "Social Snackers." "Lunch tables suck," said a member of that group, "and it never felt comfortable down there, especially if you're the type that doesn't fit into any of the categories."

The week after the SnoCapades, a group of sophomores entered the cafeteria fresh from a heated discussion in Mara Corey's English class. Intent on making the most of one of the few books juniors were assigned to read, in teaching *Huckleberry Finn*, she had staged a mock trial of the book, the charge being racism. The evidence was Huck's predilection for calling Old Jim a "nigger." Should it be banned from schools, as it had been in many districts around the country? Corey asked.

Dwyne—who was always unequivocally Dwyne and never caved in to social pressure—had testified that that word was perfectly acceptable. "Who cares?" he asked, standing in the food line with his hair in corn rows and a lollipop in his mouth. "That's just an old hang-up."

Most of the white students in the class had argued against banning *Huck Finn* on the grounds that doing so would violate the Constitution or create a dangerous precedent. "Every book has something in it that can offend someone," an Asian girl had insisted. "You can't ban the Bible and other books because you don't like the ideas in them."

Others refused to even engage in the discussion, agreeing with a boy named Nate, who just kept insisting, "It's just a friggin' book. It's just a friggin' book."

But Staci Bell, a small, quiet girl with silver barrettes in her hair and raggedy sneakers, had seconded Dwyne. "Nigger's not a bad word today," she proclaimed. "It's used in music. It's a friendly word."

The other students, all white, proved more reticent to rule on the acceptability of the word. Dwyne, then, had become the arbiter of good taste. "If the one African-American in the class says he's not offended, I think we can assume no African-Americans would be offended," interjected another white boy.

"It's not the place of a white person to be offended or not," said Tim Hodsdon, a fair-skinned blond boy who belonged on a travel poster for Denmark or Sweden. Tim's social status in his class made his a voice everyone listened to, even more so because he had been one of the first "cool" kids to hook up with Dwyne.

Dwyne, who remained as oblivious to his status as he did to the complicated currents that had lofted him into the social ionosphere, leaned out of his seat and pointed to Tim. "That's right," he said, still oblivious to his position. "Nigger's just a word. He says it to me, and I say it to him," he said, pointing to Tim.

"Who cares?"

Chapter Thirteen

11:30 A.M., Monday, March 13, 2000

Smoothly self-protective, Tony Lorenz practiced the most studied of indifference—lest anyone confuse him with someone actually interested in the opinions of others.

> *I am a pimp.*
> > *The ladies fight for my delight.*
> *I am humble.*
> > *Would these eyes lie?*
> *I am trustworthy.*
> > *Trust me!*
> *I am anything you want me to be.*
> > *What do you want?*
> *I am magical.*

> *Don't believe me . . . try me!*
> I am persuasive.
> > *Try to deny me!*
> I am everything.
> > *You name it, and I'll be that.*
> I am honest.
> > *What, you don't believe me?*
> I am arrogant.
> > *Wouldn't you be?*
> I am a role model.
> > *I can't help it.*
> I am sensitive.
> > *Hope you catch me on the right day.*
> I am willing to learn.
> > *But you better have something to teach me.*
> I am impatient.
> > *Can't you tell?*
> I am laid back.
> > *And I always will be.*
> I am my own person.
> > *Don't try to change me.*

During his three years at Prior Lake High School, Tony had refined that disdainful posture in the rest of his poetry, in his classes, in his every encounter with his teachers. And, delighting in the frustration it provoked in adults, he raised it to a high art in his approach to school. "It's no one's job to make me interested," he said. "Their job is to teach me if I'm interested. I refuse to rise to outside expectations."

Every trimester Tony chose a target grade point average—calculated to secure a "good student" insurance discount or to keep him eligible to play college sports—then decided what grade he should shoot for in each individual class. If he planned on a C, he set his sights on a 70. "Getting a high C is a waste of time since it's the same as a low C," he said, blithely, a smirk suggesting that he understood full well how infuriating that attitude was to those who sensed the depths of his talents.

"You just have to figure out what your goal is," he said, leaning back on an upholstered chair in his parents' living room in their home on a large wooded lot just a mile from the high school. "I do what I have to do to get by. And I haven't closed a single door I want opened."

How did he walk that exquisitely fine line? The rules, he said, were simple:

1. Show up for class and pay any semblance of attention.
2. Teachers almost always give you time to do your assignments in class, do them then.
3. If you can't bullshit 70 percent of the test, you have a problem.
4. If you have five classes, you can count on two being easy and two hard. Don't try to get an *A* or a *B* in the hard ones. Accept the *C*. Just get *As* in the easy ones.

That afternoon, Tony admitted that he had only read one book in his life, Dennis Rodman's *Bad as I Wanna Be.* He'd never done any homework unless he had a project. Even then, he'd bashed it out at a single session. In Creative Writing, he'd been expected to hand in a packet of poetry; he wrote it all in ninety minutes the night before it was due. For Economics, he'd been expected to maintain a trimester-long journal; he'd written the whole thing in one hour. Tony had finished the trimester with an 80.5 in that course, in which he'd been shooting for a *B*. "That .5 was a waste of my time," he declared.

"It's not hard," he said, his feet up on a table, a grin on his face. "You have to work to get an *F* at Prior Lake."

His girlfriend Lyndsay wasn't any more interested in learning than was Tony, but she was less immune to external pressure. She'd ended her sophomore year with a 2.5 without a qualm in the world. College—her only view of the future—felt too far away to provoke much concern. She'd been raised with too much security, and too shallow a notion of consequences, to engage in much long-term thinking. On the eve of her high school graduation, she still basked in that prolonged adolescence increasingly common to the scions of the upper middle class, utterly convinced that it would prove endless.

During her junior year, needled by her parents, Lyndsay had indulged in a few moments of worry about her grades, although that emotion hadn't translated into any meaningful change in her behavior. Entering her senior year, she'd meant to raise her GPA. But between cheerleading, peer counseling, student council, her part-time job as a waitress, her relationship with Tony, her girlfriends, her sister and the boat she adored racing around the lake, she never quite got around to studying.

She'd spent the fall trimester using Journalism assignments as an excuse to skip out of school so she and her friends could cook breakfast at each other's houses. The second trimester, she'd taken to cutting classes and napping in the peer counseling room, a cozy oversized closet—theoretically a safe space for kids who needed to talk in a hurry—that the student counselors had fixed up with couches and pillows, posters and music.

One week into her last term in high school, Lyndsay was vowing to bring home a report card with no grade below a *B* and, looking at her schedule, she smiled confidently. She'd managed to snare Schmidty for Math—"piece of cake, she's both easy and lenient," Lyndsay said. And she knew she could pull an *A* in Contemporary Fiction since Sara Strege graded on quantity, not quality, awarding grades according to the number of books a student read. "All I need for an *A* is a couple of extra novels and some short stories," said Lyndsay. "If I don't get around to them, I can get someone else to tell me about them."

Tony's pal Eric Prchal was playing for different stakes, which demanded a different strategy. Learning wasn't his object, any more than it was for Tony or Lyndsay. But Eric didn't want to go into the Marine Corps, or to study Interior Design at North Dakota State University, as did Lyndsay. At the age of seventeen, he was already a grown-up with eyes fixed firmly on financial success. His expectations seemed entirely appropriate. Comfortable and confident in adult circles, he worked a room with the ease and aplomb of a professional politician.

"My belief is that every part of life is a game," he said, without a trace of cynicism. "I even see it with my dad and his work. The question is: What can I get away with before it's a problem? At work, if I take a day off, will it be okay? And if it will be a problem, is the day off worth it? That's what the kids around here don't understand. You can't just leave and walk out of school. You can't just talk back. But can you tweak the system a bit? Sure. It's all a game and I'm playing the game right. It's not a tough game. Kids just make it hard for themselves."

Eric didn't crack many more books than Tony, but he spent more time working the teachers, pretending that he was engaged. He performed careful cost-benefit analyses and did only work likely to pay off in As. "I didn't take the time to learn what I was supposed to have learned," he said, looking back over his high school career. "I slid by. But, hey, I'll graduate with a 3.4 grade point average, and I had a hell of a lot of fun, so I must have played the game right."

In her approach to school, Tony's old friend Shannon McGinnis played no system whatsoever, unless sheer grit can be considered a system. After days spent in classes, at athletic practices, student council meetings, NHS events and concession stands, she often didn't get home until nine P.M. But focused on achieving her "personal best," the young woman, considered by most faculty and staff to be the school's most persistent over-achiever, still hit the books for four or five hours. "No way," other kids protested when Shannon explained how much time she dedicated to school work. The median amount of homework performed *weekly* by a Prior Lake student was between two and three hours.

Few of the other students at the top of the class were cut from that same cloth. Tom Maust also worked like a dog, but his best was never personal; it had to be public. "Second best is not good enough for me," he said earnestly, his pudgy cheeks giving him a boyish air. Organized, disciplined and goal-oriented, Tom performed every possible piece of extra-credit work and never broke or bent a single school rule. During his sophomore year, on a day when John Bennett was replaced by a substitute, Tom had hesitantly joined the other members of his Physical Education class in leaving the field early. When Bennett returned and learned about the students' behavior, he threatened the whole class with detention. Tom became hysterical. "I can't have that on my permanent record," he pleaded. "What can I do to make up for it?"

On the brink of his final trimester in high school, Tom was still frantic. "Any small flaw and I could lose everything I've worked for in three and a half years."

Most of the kids who ended up at the top of their class rankings, however, did so by accident, not design. Unlike Tom, they weren't looking for grades, or even, like Shannon, their "personal best." They wanted an education, and good grades were the fortuitous by-product. Reilly Liebhard lacked the genes to land him anywhere else. He wasn't just fiercely smart; he was too excited by ideas, information and concepts—a virtual vacuum cleaner of knowledge—to slack off. Unlike Tom, however, he never planned his schedule to guarantee himself high grades. Intrigued by Architecture, he'd signed up for the class knowing that he couldn't draw worth a damn, figuring, "What the heck, so I'll get a *B*."

Similarly, Jake Anderson hadn't plotted a stellar academic career. He worked hard when a subject interested him, and put forth a perfunctory amount of effort on everything else. He nonetheless managed to place among the top fifteen students in the school.

Jake and Reilly were among a handful—a small handful, a tiny handful—who worked to learn. Elsewhere, the philosophy driving education was capitalism in its purest form. Everything was about the reward, and the reward had to be delivered in the currency of teenage life: points and grades. Learning, students had been taught, was an exercise in venture capitalism and, like Eric and Tom, they expected a decent return. "How many points is this extra-credit question worth?" students badgered teachers who offered special questions at the end of some exams. "I haven't decided yet," a substitute once responded. "How can we know whether we want to do it then?" replied the students, clearly confounded.

"I studied for a whole hour, I better get an *A*," one boy announced in Social Studies. Spoken like a Prior Lake market analyst.

Amanda Halvorson went one step further in the January issue of the *Laker Times*, the student newspaper, suggesting that schools pay students for good grades. "The majority of students today said they don't try their hardest in classes because they feel there is no point," she wrote. "They also say these things to teachers all of the time: 'Why do we have to do this?' 'This is useless, and I will never actually use any of this in life.' One reason why kids don't try to do well in school is because they are not motivated." How can we motivate students? she asked. "Sending out a piece of paper that says 'honor roll' or 'student of the month' on it hardly qualifies as rewarding a student," one senior told her. "I mean, it is the 1990s, and kids need more than that."

In the absence of such monetary compensation, students were clear about the purpose of their education: "Grades are what school is about," they declared. And they received few signals that they were wrong. "Work hard, get good grades," their parents urged, not "Work hard, expand your horizons." Adults formed no Booster Clubs, as they did with athletics, to raise money for new lab equipment or more books for the library. Football and soccer banquets were lavish affairs; the induction ceremony for the National Honor Society was a dry ritual in the school auditorium. The school was festooned with banners urging kids not to drink alcohol, to feel good about themselves, to set goals. YOU ARE UNIQUE was the message, not KNOWLEDGE IS POWER, or A MIND IS A TERRIBLE THING TO WASTE.

What could students glean from the fact that during their sophomore through senior years, they were required to spend four trimesters in Phy Ed but not a single moment studying science? Or that Aerobics was worth the same amount of academic credit—and carried as much weight in class rankings—as Advanced Biology?

In the EdMart, where education was capital, if it didn't produce good grades, learning at least had to be perceived as "useful." Amanda was right, the most frequent gripe in the classroom was, "This is so stupid, I'll never need to know any of this." And bursting with self-confidence, few students conceded the possibility that they might lack the tools or omniscience to come to such a conclusion.

They were abetted in their disdain for "useless" knowledge by many teachers who openly acknowledged that much of the material in their curriculum had no practical application. In their after-school role as coaches, teachers told their athletes that lifting weights or running—hardly favorite tasks—was important to developing their prowess on the basketball court or the soccer field. So, every afternoon, the weight room was full and the sight of kids jogging was a familiar part of the landscape. But those same coaches, in their capacities as teachers, never explained that memorizing irregular verbs, or mastering trigonometry, was important because it stretched their intellectual capabilities, that the brain, like other organs, needed to be strengthened and stimulated.

The students, then, drifted, unsure what education was about beyond grades or a formula they might have to apply in job training. At the end of each year, administrators met with graduates-to-be and posed that question directly. "Preparation for life," was the rote response. But what did that mean? Was high school one long fraternity initiation rite, a college admissions academy, or a place to learn essential foundational knowledge and the basics of thinking?

The kids who'd chosen the bottom of the academic heap answered in unison by dropping out of a pledging ritual designed around grades. In other generations, the "alternative kids," beatniks and hippies, brandished their insecure superiority with academic and intellectual moxie. In recent years, however, academic achievement has been conceded to the athletes and student council kids. Student rebels, after all, were busy smashing the Corporate State; they were unwilling to trade in the currency of the educational commodities market by working for grades.

In fact, flaunting bad grades was their most powerful statement, an ironic pose of intellectual haughtiness. And students like Roger Murphy or Jayne Garrison chose academic ignominy with as much will and intentionality as Shannon or Tom achieved the opposite sort of notoriety.

Although they acted as if they were floating through school without any plan, almost every Prior Lake student was a fluent day trader with a clear-cut market strategy. During lunch, seated in the Honors Pass room, reserved for seniors with 2.8 GPAs and few disciplinary demerits, Jesse Rorvig, a passionate snowboarder, used that morning as an example of his approach to academics. During first hour, Economics, he did homework for another class. During the second, Precalculus, he'd gotten a library pass and chatted with his friends. The next hour was Journalism, and he'd used that time to hang out in the halls. Only during fourth hour, Physics, had he been expected to do any work.

A dozen students in the room joined the conversation. Remember: these were the good kids, the kids whose school work and personal behavior had won them Honors Passes. Homework: "Most of what we have to do is BS and you only have to do it half the time," the students agreed.

Angie Prindle, the president of the senior class, interrupted. "You can always do it in other classes while the teacher is talking." What about required readings and whole books for English classes? "*Cliff Notes* and *sparknotes.com*," they answered in unison. Tests? "Cram the night before." And if you don't get around to it? "Stay home," said Jesse.

Matt Brown played the dumb football player, and it worked like a charm, he insisted. "My teachers have always known that I didn't need any of the academic part, except to become eligible, so nobody has ever expected much of me." Others loaded their schedules with courses heavy in "group work" and befriended the smart kids, thus skating on their efforts. And cheating—at least by most adult definitions of cheating—was near universal. The year before, when a Physics teacher decided to crack down by making up two versions of his tests, students actually groused that he'd been unfair not to warn them.

In a world without much shame, students weren't ashamed of copying friends' work or pulling papers off the Internet. When Joe Goracke asked his Psychology students about the morality of the practice, they were candid and forthright.

"How many of you have *never* cheated?" he posed the question to his class that morning. Although Goracke was infamous for his toughness, his students seemed entirely relaxed and open in discussions.

In response to Goracke's question, one girl out of the group of twenty raised her hand. When her friends glared at her suspiciously, she lowered it halfway. "Well, I've never cheated on a test, just on worksheets," she said timidly.

"That doesn't count," the students declared unanimously.

"Why not?" Goracke pushed.

"That's just homework, it's different," they answered.

"What about tests, then?" inquired Goracke.

"I wouldn't plan to cheat on a test, but if the situation arose . . . ," one boy ventured.

"How does such a situation arise?" Goracke asked, smiling. He'd just finished teaching a unit on Kohlberg's stages of moral development, so his curiosity wasn't idle. "How do you cheat on a test?"

It's easy, the kids explained, excitedly detailing how they programmed their calculators with formulae or notes, left open notebooks on the floor, took bathroom breaks or told the person sitting in front of them to lean back frequently.

"What should happen if you get caught cheating?" Goracke kept at it, hoping that at least one student would make the connection to Kohlberg, or demonstrate that he had moved beyond Stage One (punishment and obedience) and Stage Two (self-gratification). Those hopes were dashed.

"Everyone deserves a second chance, so it depends," the students explained seriously. Goracke didn't let up. "Is that because you don't know in advance that cheating is wrong?" No, the students agreed. They knew they shouldn't cheat. But getting caught was lesson enough.

"What about the consequences at home, what would your parents do if you were caught cheating?" Goracke continued.

No one expected to be grounded or lose the keys to their cars. "That would be double jeopardy if we were punished at school, and that wouldn't be fair," one girl suggested. A dozen heads nodded in agreement.

"A couple of years back, two boys handed in worksheets that were identical, down to the spelling mistakes," said Goracke, trying to move the students in the direction of Kohlberg. "They weren't even smart enough to change that. I gave them both zeros and called their parents. The first mother said, 'Okay,' and left it at that. The second said, 'You can't do that. That wasn't cheating. That was cooperative learning.'"

Every face in the room looked puzzled, as if asking: And the point of that story was what, Mr. Goracke?

Craig Olson planted the bomb so quietly, so deftly, that no outsider would have sensed its presence. "My request is that teachers who share a course discuss the consistency of the grades they issue with the intention of eliminating inconsistencies that would be attributable to significant differences in teachers' expectations," he wrote in a memo to department chairs. Appended to that communiqué was a printout of the grade breakdowns for each teacher in their department, course by course.

Final exams were scheduled for the following week, so teachers were swamped with papers to grade, students begging to hand in work that was long overdue and examinations to prepare. But Olson couldn't have caught their attention more quickly if he'd unloaded a swarm of bees in the faculty lounge.

"I'm not going to lower my standards no matter what he says," one teacher huffed in his office.

By the entrance to the English department office, a male teacher leaned against one wall, repeatedly pawing the carpet with the ball of one foot, as if preparing to charge. "He needs to understand that not all classes are the same. I just had a really, really good group of kids. They deserved the grades they got and I'm not going to raise my standards just to make myself look good."

The teachers glared at one another suspiciously. "Does he think he's better than me because he handed out fewer *As?*"

"Could she think I'm a bad teacher because I gave so many bad grades?"

The tension was thick, verging on nasty.

"[I]f after preliminary discussion, you would like to involve me in a continued discussion," Olson had written, "I would be happy to do that." Not one department took him up on the offer.

The numbers told a clear story: In U.S. History, the grades given by one instructor averaged out to a 2.16, while the grades of another were 2.78. John Girtman, the head of the Social Studies department, had doled out *As* to 43 percent of his students, while Joe Goracke was at a miserly 19 percent. In English, Sara Strege, with ninety students in three classes, had handed out forty-six *As*, while one of her colleagues had awarded just two *As* —both *A*-minuses—to students in a class of thirty.

Olson's memo had been provoked by two parents who'd protested those disparities, particularly among the U.S. History teachers. It's "common knowledge," they told him, that a student's grade depended as much on which teacher he had as on his performance. Anyone who has spent any time in a high school probably would think, "Well, yes, everyone knows that." But when you're the principal of Prior Lake High School, the message was clear: Johnny got ripped off because he had Joe Goracke.

Goracke made no bones about being hard, although he didn't think that leaning a bit to the left side—the hard side—of the bell curve made him a tyrant. But the cumulative grade point average of the entire student body was running at just about a dead-on 3.0, a straight *B*, which put him pretty far out of the loop. He was losing no sleep over that imparity. In fact, if he was restless at night, the cause was more likely to be the abysmal performance of his students, and his absolute certainty that it was due to their own sloth. He'd just given his juniors a test on World War II, based on a study guide that led them through the test material. They'd read about the Holocaust, Kristallnacht, FDR and the A-bomb in their textbook. They'd discussed the definition of Fascism and the rise of the Nazis in class. All they had to do was go through the study questions, find the answers and memorize them, and they could not possibly do poorly.

Or so Goracke thought. But when he'd asked where Pearl Harbor was, students responded: Europe, Africa, Panama, Japan, Panama Canal, the United States, Denmark, Britain and Midway, with a few Hawaiis thrown into the mix. The other questions didn't yield much better results.

Goracke didn't take well to being bullied, which is how he responded to Olson's memo. Or perhaps he was hypersensitive because Boynton was complaining about the "poisoned atmosphere" in his class, her explanation for why a number of parents had specifically requested that their children be assigned to other History teachers. Joe wasn't buying that explanation. "As a parent with a child at a private university, I know that the difference between a 3.5 and a 3.8 could be $4,000 in scholarship money," he said. "So don't tell me this is about 'atmosphere.'"

"What do they want me to do, raise my grades? Ignore tardies and standards? Sometimes this place reminds me of Lake Wobegon, where all the children are above average."

John Girtman, whose grades fell at the opposite end of the spectrum, was equally defensive, insisting that Craig's comparisons were ludicrous since no two teachers had the same "mix" of students. "I have a different group of kids from Joe," Girtman said softly, skirting the unskirtable. "I'm not comfortable with anyone making these sorts of comparisons. I'm not comfortable with Olson's agenda."

Olson, of course, had studiously avoided announcing his agenda. A nudger, not a muscler, "a divergent thinker in a world of convergent ones," as he put it, Olson tended to ask questions, although he knew full well that teachers preferred answers they could then complain about. In his memo to the Social Studies department, he'd written, "At the present time . . . since I have no basis to do so, I would not care to take a position on whose grading standards I support and whose I might question." To anyone who asked, he said, "I don't know the answer. I just have numbers. My goal is dialogue."

The dialogue Olson had hoped to provoke never occurred. As a new teacher, Mike Carr had appreciated the comparisons, the chance to see how his standards stacked up. But when the members of his department met, they briskly moved past the topic, agreeing only to disagree about how to grade. The Math department, home to some of the most egregious disparities, never talked about the memo at all. Everyone knew that Schmidty and the other Math teachers didn't maintain Katie Hallberg's high standards in Geometry, and that students could skate through Algebra/Trigonometry with Buff Busselman—who bragged that he'd read only two books in his life, one about high school football, the other about Elvis Presley—so there was no reason to try to hash out the differences.

The memo provoked some discussion in the English department, although hardly of the sort Olson had been seeking. When the teachers of sophomore and junior English caucused on March 3, Chuck Lundstrom, the cochair, had seethed, "I refuse to be the only one with high standards, so I guess I'll have to lower them to avoid this mess." A polished, gracious teacher, Lundstrom was parsimonious with *A*s, except with his Honors students, and didn't hesitate to flunk kids who did no work. Yet his personal warmth seemed to blunt the edge of his grades; no one considered him to be an ogre.

When the full department met, Lundstrom tried to keep the controversy low-key, simply asking the faculty to think a bit more carefully about the number of *A*s they were handing out. But teachers tend to be touchy about invasions onto their private turf and, for many, passing around grade comparisons had crossed that line. Lynn Lally, the district Teacher of the Year for 1999–2000, was irate at Olson's "rudeness" and gave full vent to her fury, accusing the principal of patronizing teachers with his offer to meet with departments. An instructor of composition, Creative Writing and Contemporary Fiction, Lynn bestowed "Lally-money" on students who were particularly courteous or productive in her class. They could redeem their coupons for extra credit on tests.

No one was going to tell Sara Strege that an average grade of 3.2 was too high. "I just can't worry much about grades," she said. "I know there's grade inflation, but there's grade inflation everywhere, so it all evens out.

I try to grade on what students know and learn, but it's not fair not to give students credit for effort." And Jeff Hoeg protested that the implication that high grades meant low standards was personally insulting. "I believe that I'm better able to connect with the kids than some other teachers," he said. Young and hip—savvy about the language and culture of his students—Hoeg might well have been correct. "So I can get them to do more work. That's why they get high grades. They deserve them."

By then deeply estranged from her department, Mara Corey watched the angry mob in mounting confusion. Two weeks earlier, she'd spent hours grading the papers of her College Prep Composition students, trying to show them how to create more effective opening statements, how to build their arguments, how to sharpen their language, hammer home parallels and succeed when they got to college. But when she'd met with parents at midtrimester conferences, one mother had labeled her comments "cruel and damaging" to her daughter's self-esteem. "She's lost her will to live, and it's your fault," she'd said. A father had excoriated her for putting too much emphasis on "subjective" criteria like organization and reasoning rather than hard data like grammar and spelling.

"How can we raise standards with parents like that?" Corey asked.

Olson was the villain du jour, but he was really just the nearest, the handiest, target of teacher wrath. For years, teachers across the country had been enduring waves of scrutiny and attack by politicians, journalists, researchers, parents and school board members, the not-so-veiled suggestion being that they weren't doing their job, or that they could do it a hell of a lot better if they would only listen to whomever happened to be telling them what they were doing wrong on a given day.

Suddenly, everyone had become an expert on education, from the local newspaper columnist to the truck driver who sent letters to the editor, from politicians who'd never spent five minutes as students in public schools to bureaucrats who hadn't been in a classroom for three decades. By the end of the millennium, then, teachers had become sensitive to assaults on their professionalism.

They'd been drubbed by conservatives for the content of their curriculum, and by liberals for the same crime. Republicans were demanding that all teachers be tested regularly and, although they declared that teachers needed to be treated more like professionals, prominent Democrats like Al Gore had begun to jump on the bandwagon. They were being pounded for social promotion and for racism, for grade inflation and assigning too much homework, for overconcern with children's self-esteem, underconcern with children's self-esteem, teaching to Basic Skills tests, not teaching students enough basic skills, neglecting young people's need for electives, and insufficient emphasis on core courses—frequently by the same person in a single day.

In Minnesota, politicians and bureaucrats had actually drafted a new curriculum, mandated how it should be taught and decreed how student work should be graded—all the while proclaiming their abiding respect for teachers. In Prior Lake, Biology teachers had warded off attempts by members of Friendship Church to insert creationism into their curriculum, but Ron Lachelt remained wary every time he mentioned evolution. The English department, which had long brought a Holocaust survivor to speak to students, had come under fire from a Holocaust denier who'd demanded "equal time" for his position.

And teachers who'd been at the school during the flailing of Lynn Lauer, the Sex Ed instructor, tiptoed carefully around any matter related to sex. Five years before, members of Friendship Church had accused Lynn of encouraging immorality in an elective course dealing with relationships and sexual health. An investigation ensued, complete with a public hearing at which all of Lynn's teaching materials were carefully examined. Ultimately, she was found to have behaved entirely appropriately. But few could forget the mini-witch hunt that she'd been forced to endure.

And then Olson weighed in on grading disparities.

Needless to say, teachers were feeling frazzled. "I like controversy," said Chuck Lundstrom. "I think it is good and healthy. I just don't like controversy in a dark alley with no escape."

Prior Lake's teachers were caught in one of the trickiest moments in the history of American education, a time of public clamor for change, a moment of utter confusion about precisely what that change should be. "You're doing everything wrong," the public seemed to shout while demanding vouchers, charter schools, smaller classes and more testing. But in suburbia, at least, no two parents could agree on precisely what wrongs they wanted to right.

Basic Skills testing had just been phased in, as it had been in virtually every state in the country. But in thirty-six states, parents convinced that proficiency tests would hurt their children were already suing and lobbying against them. In neighboring Wisconsin, the legislature was swinging wildly back and forth on the question, one year mandating a standardized test for graduation by the year 2003, the next rolling it back entirely. And state after state had responded to low scores on tests allegedly designed to raise standards by lowering the standard for passing.

In Minnesota, grass-roots activists had lined up on the opposite side of the battle lines. State education bureaucrats were attempting to pull back on their own "high standards," by lowering the passing score on Basic Skills tests from 80 to 75 percent, and the Maple River Education Coalition was in a frenzy. "The Basic Standards test is intended to certify the minimum competency level for graduation in mathematics, reading and writing," testified Julie Quist, the group's vice president, at a public hearing on the issue. "Since this minimum competency level is so low already (sixth-grade level work for high school graduation), why lower it even further? Is it because the state believes that our schools are so inept that they are unable to achieve even sixth-grade level standards?"

Younger teachers, for the most part, found the ferment exhilarating. "All the discussion is important," said Corey. "It makes you feel like you're at the center of something significant." But veteran teachers, who'd been riding the education roller-coaster for two decades, were tired of the chaos.

Bill Bond had just exited the classroom for a position helping to train new staff. After thirty years in the district, the impish former English teacher had rewritten his course standards, redesigned his approach to teaching poetry and revamped his grading enough times. But he admitted that much of the chaos was of teachers' own making.

Bond had arrived at Prior Lake in 1969 from Crosby, North Dakota, "where the antelope actually roamed," he said, just as the high school was being opened. In those days, before the mainstreaming of special education students, before tracking had been declared racist and the standard curriculum an educational disaster, the district had adhered to old-fashioned standards, about behavior, core courses and grouping students by ability. "But by the '70s, we dumped all that," said Bond. In Prior Lake, as in districts all across the nation, teachers had heeded Grace Slick's battle cry, "Tear down the walls, motherfucker," and swept away all the dry old material like ancient history, grammar, *The Red Badge of Courage*, algebra, discipline and rigorous grading in an exuberant new vision of education. No more authority dynamic. No more tracking, which allegedly fostered elitism and what Bond called "dumb shitism." No more dry memorization or courses without relevance. Rather, teachers and students would band together in a thrilling and stimulating learning community.

"It was an exciting, vibrant time," Bill Bond recalled, laughing at the memory of himself, the kid from North Dakota, who didn't trim his beard for eight years, until he wound up looking like ZZ Top. During that period, Bond and the other members of Prior Lake's English department threw out their required curriculum, replacing standard grammar, composition and literature courses with electives like the Literature of Motion, the Literature of Adventure, Contemporary Humor, Poetry and Science Fiction.

"God, it was fun," Bond recalled, laughing at his old naiveté. "In Contemporary Poetry, kids did skits and presentations. We'd go to the auditorium where they'd play music and talk about music as poetry. That was just after Woodstock and, on the day I was being observed, the kids did the Fish Cheer," he said, referring to the "adult" version of the refrain from Country Joe and the Fish's "I Feel Like I'm Fixin' to Die Rag." "The observer thought I was doing a great job because the kids were engaged."

Educators assumed that being engaged equaled learning, which proved to be a major fallacy. By the 1980s, reality had begun to smack New Age educators squarely in the face. National test scores in reading, writing, math and content areas had plummeted. The utopian community of young, energized learners was wreaking havoc in the schools, interpreting teachers' antipathy toward grading as a reason not to care about doing any work. The new emphasis on group learning had become an excuse for the lazy and disinterested to ride the coattails of the motivated. Grade point averages soared so high that calculating who was class valedictorian became an exercise in advanced mathematics. And the best and the brightest went off to college and came back crying, "I got robbed. I can't read and write."

Grudgingly, in many cases, teachers acknowledged that the noble experiment had failed. But a generation of teachers who'd rejected the old ways could not face going back. Young, idealistic and as arrogant as baby boomers in any other profession, they refused to believe themselves incapable of inventing something better, something more vital than the system which had educated them. There had to be a way to excite and teach every single student, and they determined to discover it. Thus began a merry-go-round of education fads, each well-intentioned program promising the utopia that the former had failed to produce.

Phonics became "whole language" and then transmogrified back into phonics after students emerged from the new reading program unable to comprehend the new versions of Dick and Jane. The Old Math—that tedious series of fractions and equations that demanded memorization— became the New Math, with its emphasis on process, then the New New Math, pretty much the Old New Math in multicultural drag. By 1996, U.S. eighth graders ranked twenty-eighth worldwide in mathematical skills, which would hardly have surprised anyone who'd watched Prior Lake seniors try to perform simple multiplication problems without calculators. Higher-order thinking, Outcomes-Based Education, block scheduling, modular scheduling, open classroom, assertive discipline—veteran teachers had survived them all, each time with a bit less idealism and a few more unspoken questions about whether suburban education had really been broken when they'd started dismantling it in the first place.

By 2000, they had arrived at what Lori Boynton believed was the solid middle ground between the tyranny of the old and the anarchy of the new, and Prior Lake students' test scores seemed to have had certified its success. By every measure, the kids were outperforming their peers, both in Minnesota and nationwide. In 1998, 84 percent of eighth graders in the district had passed the state Basic Skills test in math and 78 percent the Basic Skills reading test, well above the statewide averages of 71 and 69 percent, respectively. Since the reading scores of Minnesota's kids were bested only by those of students in Maine, Boynton felt pretty cocky about how her charges stacked up. The results of their tenth-grade reading tests reinforced that confidence: a 92 percent pass rate, 33 percentage points above the city of Minneapolis. While a handful of the most affluent districts posted higher scores—Minnetonka at 95 percent and Edina at 97 percent—Prior Lake's pass rate put it among the metro-area elite.

More than a third of the seniors took Advanced Placement examinations in 1999—in Calculus, Statistics, Literature and Composition. And while nationally fewer than 15 percent of those who took the AP Calc exam scored perfect fives, 41 percent of Prior Lake students aced the test. On the PSATs, the practice exam for the Scholastic Achievement Test, more than a third of Prior Lake students scored above the 80th percentile, with only 9 percent falling below the 20th. Their mean composite ACT score was 22.4, against a national mean of 21. "Look at these results," Boynton declared proudly. "We must be doing something right to produce them."

But those scores offered wan reassurance to many on the faculty. "The standards have gotten so low, I just couldn't take it anymore," said Bill Bond, explaining why he'd left the classroom. Three times a year, the local newspaper devoted almost a full page to the names of the students—half the students in the school—on the "Honor Roll." The district's Board Scholars, students with 3.8 GPAs, regularly included 10 percent of each class. "The kids are not being forced to think. We don't have any academic agenda, we have an anti-intellectual one."

Just six months into her teaching career, Mara Corey was more candid still. "Excuse me if I don't find those numbers comforting," she said. "It just means that our kids are less dumb than the rest of the kids."

To Corey and many of the other teachers, international comparisons were more compelling—as testimony to a shameful saga of low standards. The bottom line was this: The longer American kids stayed in school, the more they fell behind their peers overseas. In elementary school, they regularly outperformed children from every country in the world, but by the time they graduated from high school, they were far behind students from across the globe in virtually every area.

Corey, then, didn't put much stock in the test results that were Boynton's point of pride. Her sophomores had just taken their statewide writing test, which consisted of an essay on "one thing you would like to change about yourself." They were given two hours to complete the assignment and told upfront that "minor errors" in grammar were permitted as long as they did not "detract from the overall quality of the composition."

"Is that what they mean by standards?" Corey asked. "'Cause that's not what I mean by standards. These kids aren't expected to know half the English or History I was expected to know in high school, and I'm only ten years older than they are. It feels to me as if teachers have been worn down, that they've stopped being outraged at how little the kids know. The kids are spoon fed. Everything has to be fun. They whine if you give them homework every night. They're incredibly intellectually lazy. Then they complain, 'YOU didn't teach me.' Well, excuse me if I sound like a student, but 'Duh?'"

Observing the school from his new perch in the Guidance office, John Bennett called the result of three decades of reform "pass-everyone education," and that from a 1971 high school Honors graduate who admitted that, thanks to an experiment in block scheduling, he had barely attended class during his senior year.

But even the teachers who concurred with Bennett could not come to any consensus about what was causing the persistent lack of rigor. Sally Davis, whose classroom boasted a name plate below which she'd written, "Goddess of Knowledge," blamed the self-esteem movement. "They feel pretty darn good about themselves and they won't do anything on their own. Shame is disallowed. But shame is what teaches us not to do what we shouldn't."

Andy Franklin, a third-generation teacher and natural contrarian who shocked students with his admission that he'd partied with the best of them at Woodstock, attributed the academic malaise to experiential education. "We made classroom education less important than field trips and skit practices. I've started feeling like I should reward kids who show up. A lax attendance policy leads to a lack of responsibility, which leads to not turning in work, which leads to declining grades, which leads to compensatory measures like grade inflation."

Ron Lachelt's diagnosis was adult disrespect for students. "We don't expect much of them, so they give up on themselves. It's so unfair to the kids. We act as if they can't do what we did, so we're dumbing them down." He pointed to the treatment of kids who fell under the rubric of Special Education as a case in point. "Obviously we need to make allowances for kids with problems, of whatever sort, but why aren't we allowed to push them to see how far they can go?" he asked, offering the tale of a student with Attention Deficit Disorder and Oppositional Defiance Disorder as a case in the point. The young man's federally mandated "academic plan" gave him the right to copies of Lachelt's lecture notes. "But I watched him, and he followed me fine if he didn't have the notes. If he did have them, he slept through class. So I wanted to see how well he could do on his own, but his mother refused to let me try.

"Then, when it's time for a test, the Special Ed kids all leave with their aides and, guess what, they all come back with the same answers. I finally said to an aide, 'Just tell me what grades to give them.' What's the point if no one wants to let me teach them?"

Lachelt felt much the same way about his mainstream students. When he first began teaching, in 1987, he expected his Advanced Biology students to memorize the muscles of the chest. "They'd kill me if I expected that of them today," he said. "Memorization has become a dirty word. We act as if we have to choose between information and process, so we wind up putting the cart before the horse. It takes knowledge to get knowledge."

Lachelt, who worked hard to keep himself centered, maintaining a shade garden in his unusual Japanese-style home, had carved out an approach to standards which left him with just enough conscience intact. He'd raised his passing grade from 60 percent to 65 and was edging up toward 72. But he'd given up on homework, at least more than what students could do in study hall. "It's an alien concept to them and, between work, sports and their social lives, most don't get home until ten P.M. at night." If a student put forth some effort, he accepted late work for partial credit, and he tried to smile when kids drifted into class three minutes after the bell. "For my colleagues, control is a big thing, so they sweat stuff like tardies and late work. I can't be that kind of guy."

Veterans like Lachelt, Franklin and Goracke were convinced they knew how to turn the system around, how to raise standards and, in the process, teach students how far they could actually go. That prescription included none of the elements politicians babbled on about in their search for the "education" vote—reducing class size, statewide testing or wiring all the classrooms to the Internet. These approaches might have made sense in the inner city, but universalizing from the urban experience helped neither the children of poverty nor suburban kids.

Their remedy was the academic equivalent of Nancy Reagan's antidrug crusade: "Just Say No." Say no to allowing students who refused to do their regular work to submit extra-credit work to pull up their grades, to tardies, sloppy grammar, ridiculous excuses for absences, late work, low expectations and skit practices that replaced classes. "Academics is like learning to lift weights," said Ron Lachelt, who shared that philosophy with Reilly Liebhard. "You need discipline and rigor to achieve. No pain, no gain."

But every attempt to codify such standards with consistent policies around tardies, late work, cheating—not to mention grading—was stonewalled by other teachers. In the English department, the Journalism teacher accepted late work until the last day of the trimester, while Chuck Lundstrom kept the door open for only two days beyond the due date. Franklin adhered to the tried-and-true grading system in which 90 was an A–. Mel Johnson of the Math department passed students with scores of 50. Sara Strege insisted on keeping her classroom "fun." That concept was anathema to Joe Goracke, who believed that sugarcoating education had sent the message that learning was a bitter pill.

Corey wanted to raise the bar on homework, but John Girtman worried that such an imposition would force his Focus kids to give up and drop out. And, as the father of an active and academically gifted student, he wasn't convinced loading kids down with homework was in the best interest of the best and the brightest either. "My son would have to give up something—his music, athletics or leadership work—and he shouldn't have to do that."

Day after day, over lunch in the teachers' lounge, at faculty meetings and in private conversations, Olson listened to teachers tussle over their differences. From time to time, he dropped in a question. But he was learning to keep his opinions to himself. "Why bother trying to push the teachers where they are not willing to go?" he said. "Academic freedom, after all, is sacrosanct."

Chapter Fourteen

5:00 P.M., Thursday,
April 20, 2000

The four senior boys had been almost giddy when they coasted their pick-up trucks and old cars down their driveways lest the grinding of starter motors or sputtering mufflers pierce the hush that was Prior Lake at 3:45 A.M. Eyes glued to their speedometers to avoid calling attention to their predawn journey, they wound through neighborhoods where street lights and security lamps shimmered in the rainy fog until they rounded the last corner to their friend's sleek suburban rancher. Peeking out of a curtained window, he cautiously opened a side door and ushered them into his basement bedroom, a finger across his lips cautioning them to silence. Rap music played ironically softly. The boys emptied their bags on the bed, slapped each other on the back, almost dancing with titillation, barely suppressing their excitement. They'd been planning this day for three weeks, plotting, strategizing, counting the hours. April 20 had arrived. They gazed at their

contraband, then looked at each other and laughed. They were finally
ready . . .

It wasn't yet seven A.M., and the attendance phone was already ringing.
The night before, parents had swamped Mary Wenner, the attendance secretary, with calls to her home about the rumors sweeping the community,
and her answering machine was blinking like crazy with early-morning
messages. Wenner was usually curt, if polite, to parents excusing their kids
from school—for trips to the doctor ("What, they can't go to the doctor at
three P.M.?"), visits to their grandmothers ("Isn't that what weekends are
for?"), or family vacations ("Does Mexico close down during Christmas
or summer break?") But, as a mother of two, the oldest a senior at Prior
Lake High School, Wenner empathized with the raw fear gripping mothers and fathers faced with the prospect of sending their children to high
school—especially to high schools like Prior Lake in communities eerily
similar to Littleton, Colorado—on the first anniversary of Dylan Klebold
and Eric Harris's assault on suburban illusions.

For more than a week, the nation had been reliving the disaster of the
previous spring. News channels were broadcasting special reports, and newspapers and magazines were reviewing every heart-wrenching detail. Bill
Clinton had flown to Colorado to continue his crusade against guns. And in
their quest for a four-year stay on Pennsylvania Avenue, both Al Gore and
George W. Bush were invoking the memory of the Columbine dead. The
politicians and pundits were well-intentioned. "Lest We Forget" was laced
heavily through their speeches. But in the mind of a nutcase, those intentions
could pave the way to anniversary hell. Or at least that was the fear.

The sudden appearance of 4/20, 4:20 or 420 graffiti spray-painted or
scrawled in school bathrooms and walls and in flyers plastered up at malls
and on lampposts, fed the terror of a replay of the devastation. So, in
Aurora, Colorado, the principal of Hinkley High closed his school when a
vague rumor of a bomb threat reached his office. At Epping High School
in New Hampshire, classes were canceled when a note about 420 was
found inked on a bathroom wall.

Closer to home, at Stillwater High School, nothing untoward had occurred. But the school had been evacuated the previous spring after a post-Columbine bomb threat, so eighty-five parent volunteers had been enlisted to patrol the building and monitor the doors. In nearby Hudson, Wisconsin, as a preventive measure, April 20 had been declared a teacher-training day. And the school system in Barron, Wisconsin, had been shut down when mysterious 4/20 scribblings appeared around town.

But Craig Olson and Lori Boynton were standing firm. No matter how many parents panicked, they would not cancel classes, assuming that doing so would convert a tragedy into a permanent holiday. Nor would they bring in police or special security. That would just encourage trouble. They mentioned nothing to the students, for whom that bloodbath had already become old news. But Boynton sent a memo to the faculty addressing the mounting concerns. "The advice we are receiving from police and the district office is to go about the normal business of education on Thursday," she'd written. "They feel this is the best method of making the hype/hysteria of Columbine go away.

"We all need to be extra vigilant in a nonalarming manner . . . Please be tuned into kids, and each other. We would also encourage you to be very visible, be out and about, and in the hallways . . . Craig, Dan, Goldy and I will all be out and about frequently that day as well—we plan on wearing our comfortable shoes!"

Normalcy, then, was the watchword, aggressively monitored normalcy. At least that was the original plan. But the Friday before the anniversary, Katie Hallberg had discovered an ugly bit of graffiti printed in bold block letters in a girls' bathroom. "MS. COREY IS A FAT BITCH. SHE WILL DIE ON 4/20," it read. Hallberg had called a janitor to paint it over and said nothing to Corey. When a student passed along the news that Hallberg had hoped to hide, Corey had dismissed it as a stupid prank, a childish attempt to frighten her. During the previous trimester, six girls had been overheard whispering in the library about their evil English teacher and how they planned to "get" her. Assuming they were the culprits, Corey vowed not to be intimidated.

On Monday, however, the graffiti artist had struck again, with "MRS. COREY'S GONNA DIE. 4/20." Lori Boynton had been too overwhelmed to focus on the threat. That morning, two flyers for X-Fest, a mini-

Woodstock encampment sponsored by a Twin Cities radio station, complete with music and forty thousand young people wallowing in the mud on drugs, had landed on her desk. The author, Prior Lake's own Jerry Garcia fanatic, had reserved a camp site for the long weekend and printed leaflets instructing all interested students to show up ready to party, with at least two six-packs of beer. Boynton was beside herself. "His mother will be so upset," she said as she picked up the phone to call her.

Then Boynton had gotten into an argument with the editor of the *Prior Lake American* over the school's policy on allowing a photographer to capture images of students on school grounds. The school's relationship with the newspaper had long been contentious since the editor thought like a newswoman, and Boynton, Olson and Haugen considered the paper a sort of weekly booster rag. Haugen and the editor had repeatedly locked horns over the paper's selections of Athlete of the Week, picks made by the paper's sports reporters. Haugen, who insisted that "not all good athletes deserve recognition," had demanded veto power.

The next day, just 48 hours before the Columbine anniversary, Boynton couldn't avoid taking the threat seriously because Paula Gaffney found a third bit of anti-Corey graffiti in the same bathroom, on the same wall. "What did it say?" Corey asked Boynton when the assistant principal called her into the office. "It doesn't matter," Boynton replied. It mattered to Corey, of course. It read "MRS. COREY, YOU'VE GOT TWO DAYS TO LIVE."

"My goal is to make sure the kids feel safe," Boynton added. Corey's eyes flared. As she walked out of the office, she mumbled, "What about making me feel safe?"

Standing by the staff mailboxes, Corey's department head, Chuck Lundstrom, dismissed the incidents, subtly suggesting that Corey had somehow provoked them. "After all, why would any student threaten a teacher?" he asked. "That's just silly." To Katie Hallberg, lounging nearby, Lundstrom's plaint sounded like willful naiveté. A teacher in Montgomery County, Maryland, had just been subjected to a gruelingly humiliating police investigation after a group of students had spread a rumor that he'd molested several girls. The kids ultimately recanted and admitted that they'd been on a vendetta, but the teacher's name had been dragged through the mud, a cloud of permanent suspicion cast over his life.

Several years earlier at Prior Lake, a boy had plotted revenge against a young Social Studies teacher he'd deemed unfair. The student and his friends spread scuttlebutt about the teacher being gay and having an affair with a student. Things got so ugly that the student in question had dropped out of school. The teacher left Prior Lake at the end of the year.

Hallberg couldn't forget the student who once had driven her to real fear. He'd screamed at her repeatedly, foaming in rage, until she was so terrified that the police were called in to assist her. Overhearing the conversation, Joe Goracke remembered his own agony after a student yelled, "I know where you live and I'm gonna get a gun and kill you and your kids."

Sara Strege had taken Corey aside to offer her advice. "You shouldn't come to school on Thursday," she counseled the increasingly anxious young woman. The night before, Corey had had that same conversation with her husband, Matt. Passionate about her teaching—about picking out each kid's strengths and weakness so she could guide them individually—and about mentoring students, she was shaken to the core by the ugliness. But fiercely protective of her self-image, as much as public perception of her, she had insisted to Strege that she most certainly should show up and spend the day teaching, as usual.

That afternoon, Goldy opened a police file on the incidents and questioned Corey about which students might hate her. Whom had she recently flunked? Who was angry about a grade? She recounted the story of the kids overheard plotting against her in the library, as told by a friendly student. She ran through her mental catalogue of pupils she'd nailed for plagiarism, the girl whom she'd forced to rewrite a research paper again and again, or the one who'd accused her of losing a test. The only student she could cross off her list was the latter girl. The day before, she'd picked a fight with a friend, who'd responded by throwing her through a plate-glass window. Injured, she hadn't been in school that morning.

When Boynton pulled into the parking lot the following morning, her heart had skipped a half dozen beats. The day before, the rock had been painted to resemble a softball. Now, a bold "4/20" glared off one face, an anarchist symbol off another, "Support Education, Boycott School" off a third and a provocative "Support Gay Rights" off the fourth. The rock was advertised as a freedom-of-expression zone, but nobody was fooled. If the expression crossed Boynton or Olson's unwritten line, Jerry, the janitor, was sent to wield his trusty paint can. That morning, Boynton's first task was to find Jerry.

Inside, everything looked perfectly normal, as the members of the girls' softball team filtered into school dressed in pajamas to call attention to that night's game. But just after seven A.M., a student raced to Boynton's office to report that yet another threat against Corey had appeared in the bathroom. This one read: "MRS. COREY, YOU'RE GONNA DIE, TOMORROW."

Corey's cheeks lost their usual glow. She'd tried to convince herself that a single student had been to blame, but this final threat appeared in cursive, while the others had been block-printed. The first had called her "Ms." In the last three, she was Mrs. Her eyes welled up with tears mixed with relief and frustration when Boynton announced that the superintendent had decreed that she should be given a "professional day" and told to stay home.

Dozens of students rallied around her in sympathy, handing her homemade cards, stopping by to say "I'm sorry this is happening to you," or "We love you." Her colleagues in the English department were markedly less supportive. Behind Corey's back, they scoffed at her predicament, which became a focus for their open dislike of their newest colleague. Building her penchant for exaggeration and her dramatic flair into a pathological need for attention, they concluded, albeit without a shred of evidence, that the young woman was penning the threats herself. "Do you remember the teacher out West who blew herself up to call attention to herself?" they asked. "That's Corey."

Roger Murphy and a classmate had begun the day by trading loud jokes about leaving school early to buy guns for 4/20. At lunchtime, a rumor flew through the cafeteria that stray bullets had been found in a boys' bathroom. Then the buzz turned to a map allegedly circulating around school with bomb sites clearly marked. Finally the talk moved on to a hit list and pictures of explosives drawn on school walls.

"I'm not gonna sit in some classroom, follow their stupid plan and get blown up," one boy boldly asserted. "Isn't it time to close school?" Lyndsay Schumacher asked. "Everywhere else they're either closing or giving kids excused absences. I have to talk to my mom." Dozens of kids pumped up the hearsay, certain it would win them a day of freedom.

Finally, Boynton went on the PA system to stop the rumormongering and reinstate calm. There's no map of the school, no hit list, she said. Two students had been caught drawing explosives on a wall and they would be dealt with. "Treat tomorrow like any other day, any normal day," she urged. "We are ensuring your safety."

That message left students even more confounded. Dozens of them had seen the map in question, which a Focus boy had drawn the week before. And Boynton hadn't mentioned the threats against Corey, which scores of girls had seen with their own eyes. So Roger Murphy, in his standard uniform of combat boots and fatigue pants, shook his head all through the announcement. "Why is she lying to us?" he asked. "Does she think we're stupid, or is there something she doesn't want us to know?"

Shortly after midnight, during a lull in the rain that washed in April 20, Travis Reddinger, a punk-rocker wannabe, wiped the rock in front of the school dry, hoping his paint would set before another downpour could erase his work. His creation of the night before had been slathered with gray paint, but Travis was nothing if not persistent. His message for the new day was "Spread Love Not Hate," decorated with a circled A, the anarchy symbol and a swastika with a line drawn through it. By the time students pulled up to school, however, it was virtually invisible. The janitor had expunged it just after five A.M.

Two hours later, Goldy climbed onto the roof of the building, balanced a portable video camera on a ledge overlooking the student parking lot and checked to make sure the tape was rolling. Police patrols would swing by the school all day. The superintendent planned to make his presence felt. Mostly, the staff held its collective breath. After the shootings in Colorado, hundreds of copycat threats and rumors had paralyzed American schools. Through it all, Prior Lake had enjoyed blissful quiet—which only made everyone more tense on the anniversary, as if a huge "It's Our Turn" was hanging over their heads.

The school felt almost empty, as if the 120 absent students had sucked all the air out of the building. "My boys are sick and won't be in school," one mother reported. "Sick? What's the matter?" Nancy Jans, the secretary who had taken the call, inquired. "They're not sick," the mother shot back angrily. "I'll tell you why they're not coming to school. I'm very upset that the school's not doing enough to protect the kids. I'm praying for you."

Every hour, the vacuum felt more profound as more students were called home by parents who'd finally realized what day it was. Just after nine A.M., a father phoned Mary Wenner in outrage that the school had remained open. "I called the police and they said they wouldn't send their kids to school," he yelled. As usual, Mary checked. The police had received no such call.

Jayne's friend Anna Bican stayed home at her mother's demand, which was a relief to a member of the group that had suffered the most after Columbine. As the anniversary approached, Anna and Jayne Garrison had both flashed back to the day after the massacre, when they'd heard other kids whispering about them and watched them move aside to avoid bumping up against "those weirdos." Ironically, in a sea of blond hair and blue eyes, those weirdos were uniformly dark. "I bet that Anna Bican would do that if she had a gun," a group of boys had muttered. Her counselor had suggested that Anna take off her emblematic hooded sweatshirt.

Jayne, somewhat of an antigun fanatic, was tormented as "Satan," or, for those unable to conceive of the devil as female, "Satan's concubine." Pete Williams, Roger's closest companion, hadn't been in school for fifteen minutes when he was called to the office. "Are you all right? Are you being ridiculed by the other students?" Wow, Pete had responded, why the sudden concern? "They weren't worried about my welfare," he said. "They were checking me out."

Ironically, Roger had been given freer rein after the bombing. "It was hysterical," he recalled. "Could I look less like the Columbine shooters? But they were so worried about me that I could have done almost anything and no one would have dared stop me for fear that I would see it as provocation."

On the anniversary, Roger was more amused than concerned about the prospect of the special scrutiny he knew he'd receive. When he noticed the video camera mounted above the door to the cafeteria, he smiled for the lens, the same smile he offered Boynton and Goldy when they checked out his black shirt half-covered by a two-thirds-length jacket, fatigue pants, half-gloves and combat boots with spiked anklets.

Columbine jokes filled the air, as students released their fear or took advantage of the moment. One sophomore boy handed a pass to his Social Studies teacher for a signature; he'd listed his destination as "Death Room." Assigned to help clean up the cafeteria as a punishment for throwing food, a senior boy asked another teacher, "Can I get out of it because it's 4/20? Remember what happened to kids who spent too long in the cafeteria at Columbine."

But a serious young woman, a senior, rushing into school late, asked the secretaries plaintively, "Are we going to die today?"

Jeff Hoeg opted against normalcy, choosing to devote his sophomore Honors English class to a discussion of Columbine. "According to the paper, kids today aren't thinking much about Columbine, they're either uninterested or self-absorbed. Is that true?" he asked. Their honor challenged, a dozen voices competed for attention. "That may be true of some, but lots of us still think."

"Yesterday the rumors and threats were the only thing people were talking about."

"The media has made too big a deal about it," a girl with long sandy-colored hair protested. "If no one had mentioned it, I wouldn't have remembered the date." The class broke out in full laughter. "How could you forget 4/20?" a boy in the corner asked coyly.

The building was utterly serene. Even between classes—generally a raucous five minutes of slamming lockers and boastful high-fiving—students giggled in small groups rather than screaming down the corridors. When the school store opened after first hour, the line, usually six or seven students–long, reached almost to the Media Center, a good two hundred feet, but everyone in it was docile when the teachers nudged them along to their classrooms, never noticing that the boy selling doughnuts was winking and muttering, "Holiday today." Students appeared spacy, glazed-eyed and more apt to nod off in class. But that was a relief from the usual frenzy, especially at such a strained moment.

Throughout the day, Goldy and other staff members monitored the news. Nothing yet. Nowhere in the nation. Not a single bomb scare. Not a single death threat. Inside Prior Lake, there hadn't been even one suspiciously long trenchcoat or oversized backpack.

By one P.M., you could almost taste the relief. After six hours keeping watch over every byway of the school, Boynton, Olson and Les Sonnabend, the superintendent, actually sat down to eat lunch. Goldy still leaned against the wall by the entrance to the Guidance office in his classic position, but his body was no longer rigid. "The kids have been really wonderful today," he said. "They've been really appropriate, quiet and respectful of what the day is."

What we had there was Prior Lake's version of the famed "failure to communicate" line Strother Martin immortalized in *Cool Hand Luke*. The students weren't being respectful. They were stoned. The early-morning foray through the streets of Prior Lake had been one of a dozen small 4:20 A.M. smoke-ins. A larger gathering had been held in the PDQ parking lot at seven A.M. A few puffs in the parking lot, a quick toke or two in the bathroom, had been the rule of the day. Even Tom Maust, the school's straightest arrow, admitted that half the seniors were operating "under the influence." His classmates laughed at the estimate. "Eighty-five percent would be more like it," one girl said.

For adults, 4/20 conjured up memories of the bloodshed in Colorado. For teenagers, it meant something different—Smokers' New Year, the international pot holiday. Whether Klebold and Harris chose the date for that reason is unknowable; it was not mentioned in the diaries and videotapes they left behind, and none of the copious journalism devoted to their rampage as much as probed a possible connection. Whatever the case, on that Thursday, while the adults of Prior Lake commemorated the anniversary of the carnage with dread, the teenagers celebrated *their* 4/20 with sheer delight.

Smokers' New Year had been held at the same modest gray house with red trim in Savage for three years running, and after school let out, a long parade of cars, trucks, vans and SUVs lined the quiet street where preschoolers played in small backyards behind rows of tract homes. No one inside denied that Prior Lake could turn into Columbine, but when you're packed in a living room with fifty-four other teenagers taking hits off a dozen pipes and four oversized bongs, the prospect that the guys sitting next to you in homeroom might blow up your school becomes either a massive joke or a theoretical possibility in a universe of theoretical possibilities about which you can discourse endlessly.

The kids—whose names are better left to their discretion—knew that they were part of a movement, a single unit in an immense international underground celebration that somehow had managed to elude adult radar. Legend had it that the date commemorated a California police call code for "pot smoking in progress," although Section 420 of the California Penal Code addresses the use of public land for private purposes, not marijuana. Others insisted that April 20 honored the 420 molecules in THC, which made sense only to chemistry illiterates.

The editor of *High Times* magazine claimed that 420 had originated at a high school in California, where a dozen phreaks who called themselves the Waldos met daily at 4:20 p.m. by a campus statue of Louis Pasteur to smoke pot. The number was their code for "Got any weed?" or "Do you want to get high?" and it spread through the hemp culture with the help of the Grateful Dead and their dedicated cohort of stoned fellow travelers.

"There's something fantastic about getting ripped at 4:20, when you know your brothers and sisters all over the country are tokin' up right along with you," read a flyer passed around at a Dead show in Oakland, California in 1990. "Now there's even something more grand than getting baked at 4:20. We're talking about the day of celebration, the real time to get high, the grand master of all holidays: 4/20, or April 20th."

The Prior Lake students didn't care where or how the term originated, just that the 420 Hemp Fest was in full swing on Mt. Tamalpais in Marin County, California; that across the Golden Gate Bridge in San Francisco, the Cannabis Action Network was sponsoring its second annual 4/20 celebration at Maritime Hall; that the Hash Bash was underway in Ann Arbor, Michigan; and, in Kalamazoo, Club Soda was holding a 4:20 ball. 420 was everywhere—in parks and on college campuses, in suburban living rooms and in the legendary center of pot culture, Amsterdam. The fact that adults mistook the reference as to Columbine only increased the delight.

How could they be so lame? On April 20th the year before, *The*

Simpsons had paid tribute to the holiday, airing at a special time, noting that Barney's birthday was on 4/20, flashing a jackpot sign reading $420,000. Clocks in Quentin Tarantino's hit film *Pulp Fiction* had been set to 4:20. The Oakland-based punk-funk band Puzzlefish had titled their first album *4:20*, which they then used as the name of their record label. The Internet offered hundreds of 420 links—to 420 Tours, 10-10-420 (a directory of pot links), to head shops, T-shirt designers, handmade bong specialists and drug reform law activists. "It's like 'Miller Time' for hippies," one head shop owner explained. But forget hippies. It was Miller Time for half of suburban America.

"Did you see Goldy watching Roger, Jayne and that whole group and totally ignoring us?" one girl asked, passing a small straight pipe to a late arrival. Each student had appeared at the celebration with his favorite smoking implement—a hand-blown glass bong, a straight pipe, a classic pipe, a designer pipe. One boy had even brought a gas mask modified to connect to a bong. "Gee, they really know a lot about drugs," someone responded. Everyone was almost too ripped to laugh. Kine bud—$40 for an eighth-ounce—had dulled the sense of hilarity. But few things excite teenagers more than getting over on grown-ups, and they'd just pulled off another whopper.

A boy asked if anyone had noticed one of their female classmates' eyes during Carr's class. "They looked like a fire engine," he said. The girl sitting next to him on the couch didn't even acknowledge the question. Her foot tapping to the beat of Puff Daddy, she was playing with a doll she'd snatched off the shelf above her. Five minutes earlier, she'd been equally engrossed in the vacuum cleaner.

Cell phones rang constantly as friends across town checked in. Was it worth dropping by? Five cats purred in shy confusion. Every few minutes, a wave of fresh air wafted through the room as cigarette smokers paraded in and out the front door. Nicotine was banned from the house. The only smoke penetrating the walls was laced with THC. It had rained the night before, and the teenagers, suburban to the core, were careful to leave their muddy shoes at the entry to avoid tracking dirt on the wall-to-wall carpet.

Kids were everywhere—clustered outside puffing on cigarettes, seated around the dining room table, leaning against the counters in the kitchen.

Every chair and sofa in the living room was filled, and newcomers had to climb over the gaggle seated on the floor. Not a single can of beer was in evidence; water, Dr. Pepper and Mountain Dew soothed the cotton mouth. Jeans and white socks were the uniform, although one particularly sexy girl sported white toreador pants and bare feet, which showed off her toe ring. A scattering of tie-dye marked the occasion, as did a fake UPS T-shirt that read, "Why Drink and Drive When You Can Smoke and Fly."

The party-goers weren't Prior Lake's serious druggies, the dozen or so kids who'd been in and out of drug rehab, or should have been. Most of the revelers routinely brought home above-average grades. They played in the band or sang in the choir, took to the field wearing the uniform of school athletic teams, worked with the student council and were elected as royalty for formal dances. They dreamed of getting married and raising kids in Prior Lake, just like their parents had done.

Sure, there were a couple of notorious potheads in the group. But most were mainstream kids who did as much homework as everyone else in the school, worked part-time jobs, got along with their parents and showed up at church on the occasional Sunday. According to the most recent survey of Prior Lake seniors, 27 percent smoked cigarettes habitually, more than a third regularly downed five or more drinks, almost half smoked pot and 26 percent had tried drugs like acid, methamphetamines or MDMA. "Coke is a dying fad," Ryan Sauer, the school drug expert, explained. "And there's no real crack or heroin. People here like their drugs to be socially clean." The group celebrating 4/20 defined that social cleanliness.

The smoke-in was the third event of the illicit Senior Season. The official, school-sponsored season would begin the following week with the prom, followed by the junior-senior barbecue, senior recognition banquet, graduation, the lock-in party and scores of private open houses. But *their* season—sponsored by and for Prior Lake seniors by the "cool" kids in the school—had begun on Friday, March 24, the Friday before Spring Break, with the annual wearing of the senior T-shirt, and they planned to keep it going nonstop straight through to graduation. The T-shirt wasn't the authorized brand, of course, which could be ordered from student council members in the cafeteria, but the off-brand, a custom which Lori Boynton had been trying to eradicate for as long as they could remember. One year the T-shirt had bragged, "Third in the Nation, First in the State," Prior Lake's rumored rankings in teen drug and alcohol consumption. The infamous Class of '98 had reached a new high when they'd emblazoned theirs with the slogan, "Sex Is Fine, Beer Is Great, We're the Class of '98."

Tina Farrell's friend Tana had outdone that clever rhyme with "The Cops Are Here, We Gotta Go, We're the Class of '00," printed on a white T-shirt illustrated with a drawing showing a Prior Lake police officer arresting a student draped over a blue-and-gold keg marked PL, for Prior Lake. According to tradition, seniors sporting the illicit garb entered the building en masse were nailed by Boynton and ordered to turn the offensive T-shirt inside out. Tana had upped the ante: The Class of '00 T-shirt was printed on both sides.

On the appointed T-shirt day, a senior boy who lived on the fringes of popularity, always striving for attention from the Scott Vigs, hadn't waited for the full group to gather in the parking lot. He'd sauntered up the stairs alone at 7:15 A.M. and been nabbed by Boynton and Olson, who were waiting for the arrival of the intrepid. "Turn it inside out," Olson told him. His tone was not quite an order, but the boy was anxious to comply. Boynton froze at the message on the inside of his shirt. "Boynton Bust 2000," it read.

"I could file a libel suit against you," she said, her voice trembling. "Whatever," the boy said, the classic nonresponse of Prior Lake teens. He didn't know much about libel law. But since when was the truth libelous?

Sent home to change his clothes, he had waited in the cafeteria for the full crew to gather. The mood was buoyant as they marched upstairs in groups of twelve to fifteen. Later, Boynton insisted to the local newspaper that no more than three dozen students had participated in the minirebellion. The number was closer to seventy—student council members and athletes, Honors students and near dropouts from a dozen different cliques.

Lyndsay Schumacher knew that her appearance in the T-shirt would infuriate Mary Haugen. She could recite the stern reprimand that she, as a student council member, would receive well before it was delivered. "She'll make me feel like shit," Lyndsay said, "but I thought about it and realized, what difference does it make? All she can do is take away my letter in student council, but so what? It's already on my transcript. I want to have fun and prove to my friends that I'm not a goody-goody." Her boyfriend, Tony, who'd just enlisted in the Marine Corps, had no such concerns. "I don't give a shit what they think of me," he said nonchalantly. "I'm doing what I want to do."

Seeking the thrill of defiance without the consequences, Zach Moses, one of the football captains, and Melody Donovan, Prior Lake's top female pop vocalist, had it both ways. Zach wore the T-shirt, but with a sweat-shirt covering it for most of the day. Mel kept her coat on when she was outside her classrooms. Eric Prchal wasn't willing to run even that much risk. He'd ordered a T-shirt, which Tony had dropped by his house the night before. But by the morning, he couldn't find it in the chaos of his room, or at least that was his story. He'd decided that the rush he'd get from defying the authorities probably wouldn't be worth angering Boynton and Haugen, whose respect he'd carefully nurtured.

Boynton and Olson sent the T-shirt wearers home to change, warning them to be back by the final bell. One by one, they assembled by the pic-nic tables just outside the cafeteria, Goldy standing watch, laughing at the mischief. Tinged with just a dollop of defiance, the prank lacked any hint of real rebellion, a distinction not lost on Goldy. Teachers and administrators bemoaned the kids' "childish" acts of defiance. But if they'd mutinied in "adult" ways, they would have been kicked out of school. Few were independent enough to run that risk. They liked their consequences to be predictable so they could devise solid risk-benefit equations, and the adults around them had dutifully complied.

As they raced toward their cars that morning, away from Boynton's instruction to return promptly, Olson pursued them. "I want them to make the right decision," he said. Most didn't stop to hear him out. They had agreed to meet at Perkins for breakfast. They knew precisely what their pun-ishment would be: a day's confinement in ISS. They were right on the mark.

The second event in Senior Season—a collective declaration of inde-pendence from rules, regulations and adult expectations—had occurred far from school property, although Olson and Boynton had still embroiled themselves in it. For five or more years, Prior Lake students had joined thousands of other American teenagers for a week of nonstop partying—read that as nonstop drinking—on the beaches of Cancún, and the Class of '00 had not broken with that tradition.

Like other school administrators around the Twin Cities and the nation, Boynton and Olson waged annual war against that weeklong Spring Break party, barraging parents with letters about the nature of the trip, which presupposed that parents were naive about what teenagers did when they were away from home and in a country with no real drinking age. "Yeah, they tell them it's a week of drugs, sex and alcohol," explained Tina Farrell. "What do they think goes on weekends in Prior Lake?"

Suburban teenagers have been plotting wild Spring Breaks since 1960, when George Hamilton, Yvette Mimieux and Connie Francis romanticized the concept by partying in Florida in *Where the Boys Are*. But Cancún— where each year, a hundred thousand American kids dedicate themselves to beach, booze and boogying—bore little resemblance to tame 1950s surf-side parties. Fort Lauderdale à la 1970, where students seized control over Route A1A, was a church picnic by comparison. So sixty Prior Lake seniors paid $878.75 each for a chartered flight and seven nights in triple rooms at the Continental Plaza Hotel to join the postmodern version of Beach Blanket Bingo.

No one came home disappointed. During what little the kids saw of the day, since few awoke before noon, they lazed by the pool or the beach, ordering Dos Equis beer or fruit daiquiris from waiters who had no concept of "drinking age." The only break in the sun- and alcohol-drenched routine had nothing to do with the nearby Mayan ruins at Tulum and Chichén Itzá. It was a day-long Booze Cruise, the most memorable scenery being the male gams displayed during the Sexy Legs competition.

Cancún was about the nights, about the dozens of clubs that occupied the infamous Drunk Zone. The Lakers started off at the Baja Beach Club, where Scott Vig handed a wad of cash to the Whistle Shot lady, who sauntered through the press, pouring tequila down willing throats. The second night, they discovered Hurricanes, the dark-rum and passion-fruit-syrup specialty at Pat O'Brien's. Then they moved on to LaBoom, a huge, happening club with a light-and-laser show and a boxing ring for the dance floor. There was free body-painting and Glo-sticks at the Myth, endless shots of tequila and buckets of water thrown over partiers at Liquid. One night, Scott's girlfriend got so drunk that she fell off the bar at the Baja. On another, a Prior Lake student wandered back to his hotel and, accidentally, into a stranger's room, where he kicked the resident girl out of bed and woke up only when her boyfriend emerged from the bathroom and started beating the hell out of him.

Home alone in Prior Lake, Ashlee Altenbach, who'd dreamed of such glorious moments for three years, had sunk into depression. Her court date, stemming from the day she'd stolen clothes from her employer, had been scheduled for the worst possible week. Ashlee didn't dare ask her parents to help change it. After her arrest, her mother had made her promise to stop drinking, at least until after her sentencing. Within weeks, she'd come home plastered. She'd tried to elude her mother, who'd been preparing for a Super Bowl party. She'd tried to control her nausea. But when her mother walked into her room, the shade of green on Ashlee's face had been a dead giveaway. She'd lost her car and been ordered to leave home after her eighteenth birthday. Predictably, Ashlee had projected enough remorse to regain her parents' graces. But she'd skated so close to the edge that she knew better than to push it.

Ashlee wasn't the only Cancún absentee. Scores of parents hesitant about the jaunt to Mexico had refused to allow their kids to join the group, although most offered them consolation prizes—chaperoned trips to Mazatlán, family vacations to Jamaica. Eric Prchal's parents had whisked him off to Hawaii for two weeks. Intent on protecting their older daughter from a week of alcohol pickling, Lyndsay's parents had sent her to the Cayman Islands with a friend—seemingly without checking the drinking age on that island. Even Mark Gold, youth pastor at Friendship Church, had planned something special for his kids, who would never have dared seek permission to go to Cancún in any event. While their classmates were plying themselves with tequila, Christy Gold and her friends were working in a clinic in rural Haiti, learning about poverty firsthand.

Having heard her sister's stories about Cancún, Shannon McGinnis had opted out and flown to Hawaii with her girlfriends. Since the notion of a week drinking and partying with the In crowd held little attraction for Jake Anderson and Justin Jorgenson, they and their friends went to Montana for a glorious week of snowboarding. And Nick Busse, Jayne Garrison and Roger Murphy went nowhere. Not born to a family that jetted off to Hawaii or Mexico, Nick Busse had spent the week at work, arranging fruit in the produce department at County Market. Roger's time had become freer since he and Marissa had broken up. He slept late every day and vented his aggression chopping wood for the bonfires he and Nick Olson built every night to entertain themselves.

By 4:15 P.M., every eye at the smoke-in, at least those that could still focus, was peeled on a watch. Two girls tried to organize a countdown, New Year's Eve–style, but the energy was all wrong for a group activity. Bowls and bongs were packed for the Big 4:20 hit, but no watches were synchronized. The great moment passed a dozen times, according to a dozen different clocks.

By 4:30, the house was deserted. One girl raced off to a family birthday party, another to her job as a waitress. The cook at a local country club was already two hours late behind the grill. And the lifeguard at the local health club knew his boss would be wondering what was keeping him. The cars pulled out in a line, as if forming up for a parade or a funeral cortege.

"Happy 420," they honked and yelled to one another. The neighbors glanced at the curious sight, then turned back to their lawns and their children. "Happy 420?"

Chapter Fifteen

4:30 P.M., Friday, April 28, 2000

The prom wasn't scheduled to begin for four hours, but Lyndsay Schumacher's updo was already starting to wilt. The tile walls of the cafeteria were grimy enough after seven months of fried chicken and pizza to pose a danger to her baby-blue outfit—a long skirt and top that left her midriff entirely bare. And her makeup, perfect for the evening, looked harsh in the bright sunlight.

But there could be no prom without Grand March, and Grand March was nothing without parents and grandparents, brothers, sisters, aunts, uncles and family friends, stacked into the bleachers in the Gold Gym, videocameras, digital cameras, instant print cameras and multilensed Nikons at the ready. So there they were at 4:30 P.M.—two hundred couples in slinky dresses and tuxedos, fairy princess ballgowns, top hats and canes—waiting in line in the cafeteria. A familiar phalanx of teachers sat behind desks to check them in, explain their places in the march order, then guide them to the professional photographers, who'd set up their "environments" in the sophomore cafeteria and, finally, to the corridor just outside the boys' locker room, to wait for their names to be called. The setup made a Ford assembly line look disorganized.

For weeks, the students had scurried around making plans for the formal—shopping for dresses, negotiating dinner plans, juggling one prospective date against another, hopefully better, option. Just two weeks earlier, four girls had spent a full study hall period sitting on the carpet outside Mike Carr's room trying to help a sophomore out of a *serious dilemma*. She'd longed to go to the dance with a cute red-haired senior, but he'd shown no signs of inviting her. Terrified lest she be left dateless, she'd accepted an invitation from a different guy, and then—"isn't that just like boys"—her dream date had finally approached her. She'd readily agreed but couldn't figure out how to get rid of Bachelor #1. Could they find someone else for the first boy and somehow hook them up?

Her primary confidante, a buxom cheerleader, had problems of her own. She'd set her sights on going to the dance with Dave Busselman, a certified football hero, and, since he hadn't gotten around to asking her, she'd resolved to ask him herself. But every time she screwed up her courage, he was surrounded by friends. That was a potential exercise in humiliation, the girls agreed, so she'd just have to keep following him around school until she could corner him alone.

Some things still hadn't changed even after a generation of feminism.

What had changed was the sweetness of some of the boys. Adam Heany, for example, had skipped out of school during his seventh hour study hall to arrange a special prom invitation for a girl with whom he'd spent lazy afternoons on a Mazatlán beach over Spring Break. Clutching a poster made from a photograph taken during that trip, Adam had snuck into her house, where he tacked the poster and a poem on her bedroom wall. Finally, he'd left a trail of flower petals from the front door to the poster for his hoped-for date to follow. Although his disciplinary record was whistle-clean, John Bennett had awarded Adam a full day of ISS for that stunt. "He said I needed the experience," explained Adam, laughing. "It was the most boring experience of my high school career. But I got the date, so it was worth it."

Prom was a minority affair; just a third of the school swooned at the prospect of dancing the night away with the principal standing watch. And being part of school life didn't come cheap. Tickets ran $50 a couple, tuxedo rental another $75, as a minimum. Garters with engraved hearts cost $24 a pop; flowers, a good $40; dinner, at least $50. And then there were the girls' expenses. Gowns, gloves, shoes, tanning, hair, nails and a boutonniere for their dates routinely added up to more than $500. Unless your parents were shelling out the bucks, you had to care, really care, to spend that kind of money.

Many might have cared, in theory, but had already overdosed on authorized social events. The National Honor Society had kicked off the year with an informal dance after the first football game, and the student council had sponsored Sadie's—the Sadie Hawkins Dance, another party without high heels or flowers. Then there was Homecoming, the first fancy affair of the year, the first donning of strapless formals and suits and, in midwinter, the formal SnoBall. At both events, the formal had swiftly dissolved into the casual. Spike heels had been traded in for bedroom slippers or bare feet within minutes of arrival, the boys' jackets were swiftly jettisoned, and some girls even changed into jeans the minute the professional photographers, set up in special palm tree–bedecked photo areas, had captured their elegance.

But prom was, well . . . prom. A rite of passage. A ritual woven into popular culture. One of those "Oh, dear, you can't miss *that*, you'll regret it for the rest of your life" activities that adults assiduously promoted. While scores of seniors managed to reject that advice, on the afternoon of the great event, the remainder waited through almost two hours of the Grand March, where each couple was formally presented, in the spirit of the Miss America Pageant. "Lyndsay Schumacher, escorted by Tony Lorenz," Ron Lachelt read down the list. (Insert the emergence of the couple through a spotlit arbor on stage and the flashing of cameras by the appropriate families.) "Katie Miller escorted by Eric Prchal." (More flashing of cameras.) Ladies first, in all cases, even if the lady in question was not a Prior Lake student. With each introduction, the gymnasium emptied, as families rushed off to the soccer games and piano lessons of their younger children. By the time Jill Krinke and Clay Hunter, the 216th couple, were introduced, the room was virtually vacant.

•   •   •

The members of the audience found nothing strange about the ladies-before-gentlemen introductions, which Prior Lake had used for as long as anyone could remember, and Tim Keough, Katie's younger brother, was the only student who seemed to object to such lingering sexism. "High school is still about very traditional roles," he said. "The boy still has to ask the girl out, to court her, to buy her nice gifts. After two months or so, it becomes a relationship and the guy is expected to call every day." His friend Anna Bican blushed at the description. "It's true. Every girl wants to be equal, but she also wants to be pursued by a boy, to have him call her, buy her presents and open doors for her."

Old-fashioned in matters romantic, Prior Lake students veered toward the traditional even in matters sexual, at least by the standards of their parents' sexual revolution. "We're not having nearly as much sex as people think," said Emily Cook, seated at Lakers' Restaurant with a group of Prior Lake's most popular girls. "Well," several others interrupted, "some people aren't." Everyone laughed, unsure whether that relative lack of sexual experience should be a badge of pride or shame.

They'd all entered high school with the "romantic fantasy," as they dubbed it, of "saving themselves" for marriage, or at least for the perfect partner. Love, then, was the sine qua non of sex, except oral sex, which wasn't sex, by their definition, because it carried no risk of pregnancy. But by the end of their sophomore years, they explained, that fantasy had begun to dissolve in a sea of pheromones. "Adults think everything's about social pressure, but adults are wrong," said one of the most popular girls in the school. "It's about hormones. Where there's pressure, mostly, it's pressure you put on yourself. You think, 'Get it over with or you'll be the last one left who hasn't had sex.'"

Most of those girls had lost their virginity to older boys, to prominent juniors or seniors whom they had hoped to win as boyfriends. Ashlee Altenbach was the sole exception. She'd jumped at sex at the first realistic opportunity. "I wanted to be the first girl I knew to have it," she said, her face turning beet-red. None of them had emerged from their first experiences with either their enthusiasm or romanticism intact. "You start off saying, 'I want to be able to look back on my first sexual experience without regret,'" Tina Farrell added. "Then you wind up, a senior in high school, regretting almost every sexual experience you've had."

The regrets weren't just of the emotional variety. Few sexually active students practiced regular birth control, although most of the girls had been offered birth control pills or some other form of contraception by their mothers. Pills, they insisted, bloated them, and condoms felt "yucky." So, month after month, faith in their invulnerability their only protection, they played Russian roulette, regularly boosting the profits of early-pregnancy-testing companies. That year alone, at least nine Prior Lake girls had lost the game. All but one—Hillary, Pete Williams's girlfriend—chose abortion over carrying the pregnancy to term.

That was a difficult decision for suburban teens who'd been shown sonogram photographs of fetuses since they were in junior high school, and finding an abortion provider was a veritable nightmare. Pregnant by a sophomore who was even more clueless than she, one young woman unwittingly called the first entree under Abortion Services in the local Yellow Pages. Alpha Women's Center lured her in, then offered not practical advice but a videotape about the horrors of abortion, narrated by women talking about the pain and heartache of the procedure.

Terrified of talking with her mother, that young woman, a perky senior, had looked around school for someone who might help her, but feared there was no one there she could trust. She had no way of knowing how many female staff members would have quietly helped, or that the high school had once been sued for guiding a student to Planned Parenthood. The girl wound up at that same clinic on her own, but by the time of her first visit, she was sixteen weeks pregnant, which required a two-day, $1,300 procedure.

That student, however, was lucky, at least compared with her friends. When another young woman sought an abortion early in her pregnancy, she was turned away because she was just seventeen. Unwilling to ask her parents or a judge for permission, she'd been forced to wait until her birthday, which fell on the last day of her first trimester. She celebrated her adulthood, then, on a cold metal table in a sterile clinic in downtown Minneapolis.

While the girls worried about pregnancy when they first became sexually active, what the boys worried most about was the experience of their partners. "I didn't want to start having sex with some girl who'd already lost her virginity," said one boy, clearly not a Dustin Hoffman wannabe longing for an Anne Bancroft. "I wanted it to be as special for her as it was for me." The boys vehemently denied the possibility that any twinge of performance anxiety might have contributed to that attitude.

•   •   •

On prom night, sex, of course, was dessert, at least for the half of the students who were sexually active. As Anna said, first the girls needed to be courted. That began with dinner, which couldn't be a burger at McDonald's. The boys made reservations at the area's fanciest restaurants, although one group that had planned such an elegant culinary experience wound up eating pizza after they waited for their table at the Festival restaurant at the Radisson Hotel for almost two hours.

Eric Prchal didn't see the point of shelling out that kind of money, especially since his date was Katie Miller, a close friend, not a romantic partner. In fact, he wasn't sure that he saw the point of prom altogether. As a member of student council, he'd pressed for converting all formal dances but prom into casual ones so that the finale would regain its luster. But he'd been outvoted by the girls on the committee. So he, Tony and Jordan pooled their resources and arranged for one of Eric's neighbors, a professional chef, to prepare them a gourmet repast at home.

In 1999, prom had been held at a night club in nearby Golden Valley. But the officers of the class of 2000 had chosen something more unusual: a dance cruise down the Mississippi River. Two party barges, the side-wheeler *Anson Northrup* and the larger *Betsey Northrup*, both studies in faux New Orleans, with white iron grillwork and tin ceilings adorned with decorative molding, were coupled together for the evening. The downstairs of the *Betsey* was set aside for the DJ and the serious dancers, the open area above it for quieter, more intimate moments. The rear boat was a floating version of the Prior Lake cafeteria with the same sort of fake wooden tables and glaring lighting. The only unfamiliar note was the bar, but the Michelob tap had been conspicuously shut off for the occasion.

Promgoers had been warned to be at Padelford Landing in Boom Island Park no later than 9:45 P.M., but one large group got lost and almost missed the sailing. Another went to the wrong dock and actually didn't make it. A few ran down the plank in the opposite direction the minute the departure whistle sounded, unwilling to be trapped midriver without any . . . refreshment.

Olson stood at the dock as they arrived in limousines and Winnebagos, buses, cars, trucks and vans. He'd fought back the temptation to show up at the prom in jeans and a T-shirt, a desire he squelched annually, anticipating the horror he might provoke in parents. But, in quiet rebellion against conspicuous consumption, the son of a different era had carefully chosen pants and a jacket that he'd purchased secondhand in a local thrift store.

Children of the age of postmodern materialism, where money was the most popular antidepressant, the students had no such compunctions against consumption. So Shannon McGinnis glided in wearing a $1,200 beaded dress she'd purchased for the Miss Teen Minneapolis pageant, while Lisa Gilbert wore a black beaded gown, the back cut out like a spider web. In his white tuxedo, Zach Moses, a cocaptain of the football team, showed off his girlfriend, who wore a brilliant-blue sequined strapless number.

Slits, plunging necklines and open midriffs displayed taut, youthful skin. Ashlee Altenbach eschewed the vampish look and played the innocent, a fairy princess dressed in baby blue with long gloves. Katie Keough, in a shimmering white gown, had woven a garland of flowers for her hair.

The boys weren't easily outdone in an age of socially acceptable male vanity. A junior drew as much attention for his white top hat as his date, who was draped in silvery spandex. Eric, Tony and Jordan had decided to wow their peers by renting pale blue, lavender and pink 1960s tuxedos. Lyndsay had preapproved the look, although she'd reconsidered when she saw how much attention the three were attracting. But the hit of the evening was a couple sporting Harley colors, the girl's gown black Spandex, her platform shoes and over-the-elbow gloves the trademark orange.

High school dances aren't about actual dancing, about packing into the crowd where the DJ blared a careful mix of techno, pop, rap and punk calculated to entice every partier into shaking a limb, at least for a few minutes. The only Prior Lake student who spent the entire evening on the dance floor at Homecoming or SnoBall was Nate Schweich, whose friends and protectors on the football team pulled him into every circle, every line, as the girls in the group flirted openly with him. No one dared exclude Nate from a dance. One girl had tried, at the opening party of the year after a male friend suggested that she take Nate for a spin. "But, but, he's a retard," she'd replied. That remark had turned her into a social pariah.

At Homecoming, students milled around the harsh fluorescent lights of the sophomore cafeteria, more bored than festive. Few seniors stayed longer than an hour, since how much fun can a teenager have at a dance when the school cop is standing by the door with a portable Breathalyzer on the table, and the orange plastic refreshment container actually dribbles out H_2O?

During Homecoming, Jayne Garrison had peeked into the gym and emerged within twelve seconds. "I have to maintain some dignity," she'd said, explaining her abrupt about-face. The DJ was playing Britney Spears, which was a tad tame for a girl with a multihued Mohawk. "I can't be in there with that swill they call music."

But at prom, Jayne managed to ignore the music and stay on the dance floor with her ex-boyfriend, or at least that's how she and Randy defined their relationship despite the fact that they couldn't stop kissing. Something about the mood of the evening, about the mystique of prom, the lingering sense of the waning moments of life as they knew it, loosened the inhibitions and turned the dance floor, rocking with the swell of the river, into a roiling sea of writhing bodies—solo and in couples, in circles and in lines.

Lisa Gilbert, who invariably brought boys from preppier high schools like Wayzata or Edina to dances, grabbed the latest of her dates, this one with a cell phone on his hip, and joined the crush. Even Scott Vig, who usually confined his dancing to stunning performances of traditional Sioux hoop dances, broke a sweat on the dance floor, although, unwilling to be stranded onboard until 11:15, he was down the gangplank and on solid ground before the boat pulled away from its mooring.

First the boys' jackets came off, then their shirts, until most were left in tuxedo pants and vests, while their dates turned their bow ties into necklaces. Jordan Culver sent a chill through the room when he stripped down to his T-shirt, the illicit class shirt that he had never dared wear to school. None of the chaperones noticed the insubordination; if they did, none cared enough to confront it. Tom Maust alone remained fully clothed.

A dozen teachers and chaperones hugged the periphery, trying not to cast a pall over the party. Jan Hofman, the drug-and-violence-prevention coordinator, seethed not altogether silently. Goldy had been unable to come and his replacement, an off-duty Minneapolis police officer, had forgotten—at least that was his story—to bring a Breathalyzer. Hofman was certain she smelled alcohol on one student's breath, but that boy told the cop that the odor was emanating from his tongue, which had been pierced that afternoon—and he displayed the newly adorned organ as an offer of proof.

She was also convinced that a girl in a sexy black dress was tripping and that three or more others were stoned. In fact, virtually everyone had had something to drink before boarding the boat, and scores of students had taken quick hits off their pipes in the parking lot.

"I thought about bringing cups in for urine testing," Hofman said. "And I should have."

Overhearing her, Reilly Liebhard, who'd been dancing, couldn't resist commenting. "If this were 1936, the idea of demanding urine samples would be worthy of inclusion in *Triumph of the Will*. Holy shit. I'm not the kind to advocate drunkenness, especially of the teenage variety, but we all know the real issues behind teenage drinking, like living in a yuppie suburb which abandons its kids to the whims of consumer culture, then wonders what the hell is going on when they turn out utterly short on substance and personality, then overcorrects the situation by losing all faith in everyone who's not a football player and, as a result, enacts a mini–totalitarian government.

"We are talking about people who are eighteen now. For better or worse, most of their value systems are almost fully established. They have made their drinking decisions, and should they run into consequences, legal or otherwise, they will have to deal with them on their own. Instead of realizing this, the school runs around thinking that it can still do its Vulcan mind-meld on people who are about to enter the adult world, and they practice illusory, 'substance-free' scare tactics, pun intended. It's sick."

Reilly was having a wonderful time, despite the tameness of the music, which tended toward Backstreet Boys club mixes rather than techno, the Sex Pistols, Fragma, or "music for more experienced club-goers," as he put it. Prom wasn't Reilly's usual sort of pastime. "I hate to admit it," he said, "but I came because it was one of those things. You know, 'It's your senior prom, you should go.'" But even a political wonk like Reilly loved to dance. And there was something about the setting, about the bond of music, about being so close to the end of school that broke down the barriers between "the Stupid Jock vs. Punk vs. Stoner vs. Farmer vs. Hunter vs. Motorhead vs. Geek vs. Thespian bullshit."

When a Limp Bizkit song began blaring from the four-foot speakers, Travis Reddinger, the would-be punk, formed a mini–mosh pit with the same boys he'd been ready to strangle during endless discussions of gay rights in Mike Carr's class. Lyndsay found herself in a dance line with a girl in an elegant black evening gown with spaghetti straps—Jayne Garrison, a classmate she'd feared for a year. Emboldened by having his first girlfriend, a lanky redhead soccer player and another of Prior Lake's serious intellects, Jake Anderson, who'd avoided all school dances except Homecoming of his senior year, looked relaxed, as if he felt he belonged. And even Nick Olson showed up in a classic tuxedo, escorting Anna Bican, stunning in a deep turquoise dress, the costume of a medieval wench she'd bought on eBay.

"I think some of us finally might have broken out a little and learned to love and respect real differences and reject all that bullshit about making everyone into a round peg for a round hole," observed Reilly. "Even if it is only for one night."

Andy Ottoson, the dean of the student drama crowd, had not been swept up into that magic, into the pageant billed as the culmination of the social drama of high school. The meaning of the event eluded him. Prom no longer served as the middle class's answer to high society's debutante balls. These days, "coming out" parties provoke more puzzlement than envy among the middle class. Anyway, by the age of eighteen, most suburban kids have already been "out" for years: out to formal dances, fancy dinners, fabulous vacations. The mystique of the affair—planted in American popular culture in the days of Gidget—felt like an outdated ritual, a rite of passage that was the detritus of another generation.

Andy had carefully calculated the money spent on the prom—on tickets, tuxedo rentals, dinner, limousines and dresses—and came up with a conservative figure of $90,000. "If we could have gotten 1,840 hours of community service (four hours each from 460 people), plus $90,000 in charitable donations— man oh man, what we could have potentially done with that night.

"I could not, in good conscience, participate," he said. Instead, Andy deliberately scheduled himself for a shift at the movie theater where he worked in the box office. His tuxedo came courtesy of the Muller Family Theaters.

Chapter Sixteen

8:30 P.M., Tuesday, May 23, 2000

Les Sonnabend refused to get up. Planted behind the receptionist's desk at the Prior Lake–Savage Schools district office, he simply wouldn't budge—not to share his angst with the members of the school board who were milling about, not to grab a slice of the pizza congealing on the table in the board room, not even to go to the bathroom. It was as if a mantra was playing in the superintendent's head: If I don't move until the results come in, the news will be good. If I just stay here, the referendum curse will be broken.

That curse had lasted for eighteen years, and Sonnabend, who'd run the district for eleven of them, recalled every demoralizing moment. It had been eighteen years since Savage and Prior Lake voters had passed a school bond referendum the first time out. So Sonnabend, a 6'7" former basketball player—a hall-of-famer at Mankato State University—stayed glued to the receptionist's chair, rolled back from the desk to stretch out his lanky frame and prayed for a new high school.

There was no getting around it. Prior Lake needed a new school. One of the ten fastest-growing school districts in the Twin Cities metropolitan area, they had opened the 1996–97 school year with 1,220 students in a structure designed for a maximum of 1,050. The following fall, they'd relieved the pressure by sending the ninth grade over to Hidden Oaks Middle School. But that was a temporary measure, at best. Student enrollment was rising inexorably, 6.1 percent in 1998, 5.3 percent in 1999. They would reach critical mass again in less than two years, and all forecasts suggested that the student population wouldn't peak before 2010. Where could they possibly put the projected 2,000 high school kids the district would have by that time?

Sonnabend, Olson and the school board had met with architects, state officials and planners to consider alternatives to a new building. They'd performed theoretical shifts of students from building to building, played with grade configurations, and still didn't have the space. To maintain a student-teacher ratio of twenty-five to one, they would need thirty-one new high school classrooms. An addition to the current school was out of the question; it sat on too little land to satisfy the state. Olson had designed a scheme for combining HOMS and the high school into a single campus by constructing a skyway building over the road between them to house the ninth graders. But it proved nearly as expensive as a new building.

The answer was clear. But Sonnabend knew that the answer had been clear before and had still failed to sway Prior Lake and Savage voters.

In fact, voters all over the country were refusing to be swayed by public schools' entreaties for more money. Al Gore and the Democrats blamed stingy old folks and nonparents, assuming they were indifferent to the plight of the nation's schoolchildren. But parents, too, seemed skeptical that they were getting much bang for their educational buck at a time when the nation's schools were spending record sums per child, even adjusted for inflation. "This is not the 1950s when everyone trusted the government and school districts to do what was right," Lee Ann Schutz, the editor of the *Prior Lake American*, wrote in an editorial. So even in an era where "children are our most important priority" had become the staple refrain of public life, even in an affluent community like Prior Lake, Sonnabend and the school board struggled, year after year, to raise money.

In September 1994, they'd asked taxpayers to float a $20.2 million bond issue for a new elementary school, an addition to the middle school, computer technology and renovations to the older buildings. As it would be six years later, the need had been self-evident: the elementary schools were bulging with students, the district's handful of computers were already two generations out of date and the twenty-five-year-old high school, built for a community that had refused to see itself as growing into a suburb, was a mess. Olson's office was jammed with school records, the overflow from his tiny storage room; the guidance offices were so small that counselors could meet with parents and children together only in the greatest of intimacy; six computers and three printers were squeezed into a 7-by-12 foot closet; and they were already operating above the building's capacity.

Yet the voters rejected their request by ninety-four votes.

Sonnabend was nothing if not persistent, so he'd gone back to the public five months later, on Valentine's Day of 1995, with the same result. He'd launched a third campaign for the money like a general, with a full year of planning and public education. A special school booster group, Citizens Allied for Schools and Education, had flooded the community with mailings and plastered signs all over both towns. And Sonnabend had dealt a few powerful rhetorical cards: Without more space, students will have to study on split shifts, some starting their day as early as six A.M., he'd explained. Class sizes will rise to thirty-five, maybe up to forty. The only alternative, he added, would be year-round schooling.

It was never clear whether that bleak vision turned the tide, or whether Sonnabend had just worn the voters down. But the third time out, the referendum passed with 59 percent of the vote.

At that point, Sonnabend knew that he needed to give voters a rest and mend some fences. But he also knew that even with the referendum money, he was still woefully short on technology. And he couldn't stop thinking about his high school, already bursting at the seams.

Sonnabend was trained as an educator, as a teacher, not a politician. "As an assistant principal, I couldn't have cared less about politics or making ends meet," he said. "I had no idea." Once he moved into administration, Sonnabend had still managed to remain out of the bull's eye of public scrutiny; his specialty was curriculum development. Being clueless about the politics of public education probably would have caused Sonnabend no difficulties if he'd risen to superintendent in the old days, the days before multimillion-dollar budgets, taxpayer revolts and the public belief that government officials were profligate spenders. But those days were ancient history, especially in Minnesota.

Proud of its progressive social policies, Minnesota had been one of the first states to address perhaps the trickiest problem in modern education: equity in school funding. Raising money for schools through local proper-ty taxes, long a standard practice in American education, inevitably meant that school districts dense with expensive homes and large commercial cen-ters—with hefty tax bases—could raise huge sums and still keep their tax rates low, while rural and inner-city districts, even with high tax rates, could never keep up. Why should children who happened to live in tax-poor dis-tricts receive unequal educations? advocates for the underclasses asked. "Share the wealth" became the new demand of educational reformers.

Minnesota had responded by centralizing education funding in state hands, with every school in the state receiving a fixed amount of money per student, according to a typically arcane and complicated formula. But as a sop to districts that had long spent more than that sum on education, the state contravened its own equity objective by permitting districts that wanted additional funds—for so-called excess levies to cover ordinary operating expenses or for bond issues to pay for buildings or equipment— to appeal to their local taxpayers for the extra dollars. The state matched a portion of the excess, depending on the wealth of the district.

In the most affluent and commercially developed districts, convincing voters to support excess levies was no problem. But men and women in positions like Sonnabend's, superintendents in districts with more meager tax bases, were condemned to life on a merry-go-round of appeals for excess levies to already overburdened taxpayers.

Before Sonnabend could mend his tattered fences or think about a new high school, he faced a budget crunch caused by those levies. A five-year excess levy authority he'd received was due to expire in 1998 and, with it, $1.4 million from his budget. Olson was already operating with less money per student than almost any high school principal in the region. In fact, only five of the fifty-five districts in the metro area operated with less, and Minneapolis's premier high school, Edina, received more than $6,800 per pupil unit, as schools measure their budgets, while Olson was given just over $5,800. Olson knew how to stretch a dollar, but his instructional budget was a mere $104 per student. Joel Volm, who taught astronomy, had been reduced to setting up his own in-school corner store, the Volm-Mart, to raise money for a new telescope. Departmental copying budgets were so low that the student council had been forced to bail out the English department, which had run out of cash halfway through the year.

To make things even worse, every year, the state tacked on more mandates—for new types of door knobs, security planning, special education and drug counseling—without offering to pay for them. And with the rising number of students in the district, Sonnabend needed more teachers—in Math and Science, Languages and electives. Should he shelve plans for new technology and a new high school and go back to voters just to renew the levy, or should he fold all his needs into a single referendum?

In August 1997, the school board held a special workshop to address that question. No one seemed anxious to go back to the public year after year, to waste time, money and good will on separate requests. They decided, then, to hold a single referendum, a megareferendum, in November and ask taxpayers to extend the old excess levy, to add a second levy to raise the school budget by $200 per child, and to fund $5.9 million in bonds, half to buy 110 acres of land for a new school, the other half for instructional and technology support.

Neither Sonnabend nor the board expected much problem with the levies. Extending the old one wouldn't raise property taxes; it would simply maintain them. And the additional levy would increase taxes by only $131 on a $300,000 house. Furthermore, the state would more than match those funds. They deluded themselves into believing that no one could reasonably object to the purchase of the land since land prices were skyrocketing, and everybody knew that a new school was inevitable. And technology? Well, that was a no-brainer with both the president and vice president singing the praises of computers in education.

When the public disagreed, voting down the bundled request, Sonnabend was left stunned, muttering, "It was so unexpected." He warned of budget cuts of \$1.5 to \$2 million. Hiring freezes. Reductions in transportation and extracurricular activities. Huge class sizes. The full monty. Then he announced that he would go back to voters again to ask for that same technology money, along with an even greater excess levy than he'd sought a year earlier.

The 1999 campaign began well, with a citizens' task force formed to endorse the technology recommendations and a new citizen's group, the Stand By Me committee, launched to raise a \$20,000 war chest for the struggle. Then, John Maher entered the fray. A retired college professor, the former chair of the School of Business at Southern Connecticut State University, John had lived in Prior Lake for just three years. But he'd worked in the schools as a substitute teacher and was appalled by what he had seen: middle school students who didn't know when the Civil War was fought, eighth graders who refused to sit down, courses based on films and tapes. Technology? That's not the problem, he concluded. The kids need teachers, really good teachers, and a solid, serious core curriculum.

Maher launched a counteroffensive against the school board's \$3.9 million plan. At every public meeting, Maher was there. In every issue of the newspaper, John's letters appeared. He rarely strayed from a single message: "We need reading, writing and arithmetic more than computers." Back to the basics with a longer school day, more-focused textbooks and teachers certified in their disciplines. After that, we can talk about computers.

This time, each section of the referendum request was separate, and when the election results were tallied, the results were mixed. Maher won on the technology issue, while Sonnabend and the board received their excess levy authority. The price for that victory had been high. After months of charges and countercharges, threatened lawsuits and vitriolic letters to the editor, the town was sorely divided, fraught with distrust of the district, which still needed to ask voters for a new high school.

No wonder, then, Sonnabend was nervous in the hours after the polls had closed on the day of *that* referendum.

He and the board had run the special election like a crusade. Eight months earlier, they'd begun soliciting public input about the growth problem, about whether to build a new high school or a new elementary school, although the board had already agreed on the answer. They'd inundated the newspaper with information about their record enrollments and the difficulty of playing musical chairs by moving whole grades from one school to another. Savvy to the power of the issue, they beat the class-size drumbeat loudly and persistently. They even drafted the chairwoman of the Stand By Me committee from the previous year to run Stand By Me 2000.

The full plan had been released to the public in March. The district would request money to buy land for a new high school, build the school, renovate the existing high school for use as an elementary school, upgrade the other buildings and improve their technology. The price tag: $68 million—a bargain in an era of $60-million high schools.

The public rationale was strong, the choice presented, stark. We need a new high school. The longer we wait, the more we will pay. And Sonnabend, the board, and Stand By Me members churned out enrollment projections, comparisons between Prior Lake's school spending and that of surrounding communities, tax impact studies, economic forecasts of the districts' growing tax base and projections of the rising price of land to bolster their case.

As the campaign moved into high gear, Sonnabend had no way of telling whether that message was getting through, or being accepted. Attendance at public meetings on the proposal was sparse, the questions almost entirely self-centered. "Will the auditorium be big enough for an orchestra?" the mother of two elementary-school children asked at one meeting. "I think my daughter would really benefit from an orchestra."

"Gymnastics shouldn't have to share space," said another parent at that same meeting. "My daughter says they spend too much time moving around equipment. I want to be sure that if we get a new high school, this changes."

"I hope you're planning on air-conditioning," a father interrupted. "My kids can't concentrate by the end of the year."

Tellingly, not one question about academics was proffered.

Sonnabend smiled, trying to be pleasant. Every meeting, every referendum, was the same. Nothing but the best for *my* children, with a heavy emphasis on the *my*. Move the bus route so *my* child doesn't have to cross the street. Change your program to accommodate the interests of *my* child—no matter the cost.

Opposing voices were faint against the tattoo struck by Sonnabend and the board. A few parents wondered aloud, Are they just threatening us with talk about two shifts? A few more asked: Are they planning to build the Taj Mahal?

The single misstep by referendum activists was the public release of an artist's rendering of a possible design. The building had not been designed. Olson had combed the area for an acceptable model and still hadn't found one that came close. But the school board had wanted to show the public something, and that something had included an archery range and a golf driving range. A citizen named Ron Peters fumed. "Are we building an institution for learning or a sports entertainment complex?" he asked in a letter to the editor. "Do we have to entertain our children with sports and other nonacademic activities to get them to go to school? What happened to 'learning is for fun?'" Fortunately for the school board, John Maher was off teaching in China.

By election day, bright-yellow Stand By Me 2000 posters were more ubiquitous than Christmas lights in December. Lines of vehicles drove up to the eleven polling places, the turnout extraordinarily high. At Lydia School out in Spring Lake Township at the far end of the district, it was battered old farm trucks and sensible, American-made sedans, although more than one Ford Expedition pulled up, the driver, always a newcomer to the community, carrying a cell phone. "We don't need fancy," voters said. "We had plain and we did all right." One man disagreed. "Do it now before it gets even higher," he said. "You know they'll keep coming back and back, so we might as well get it over with now."

At Glendale Elementary School in Savage, it was Lexuses, Windstars, and Range Rovers, the vehicles of choice for soccer moms, who most decidedly wanted fancy. "Our children deserve the finest of everything," said one young woman pushing a baby stroller. "How could anyone possibly vote against this referendum?"

In town, a white-haired woman walked slowly to St. Michael's Church to vote. "It's not that I don't care about children," she said. "That's how they make you feel. But I live on a fixed income. Every year they say, 'Oh, it's not very much money,' and, every year, my taxes go up. It's never very much money, until you add it up at the end of the decade."

Given freedom to leave school in order to exercise their civic obligation, which they might have fulfilled after the last bell of the day, Prior Lake seniors cast their ballots in droves. Several student council members ran over to Minnesota Valley Community Church during study hall to vote for the first time, a firm yes for a new high school. Four boys followed shortly after. Four solid nos. "We won't be around to see the improvements," they said.

Working all day, Sonnabend overheard none of the conversations. He'd been told that the vote was going his way, but he was afraid to hope. By 8:30 P.M., the watch had begun in the district office. With Sonnabend by the phone, Martha Hoover, Dick Booth and Diane Zieman from the school board gathered with Olson in the boardroom. "I don't need fancy and the kids don't either," said Olson, wiping a dollop of pizza cheese from his beard. A blusher, he would have turned red if he'd known how much he sounded just like the farmers in Spring Lake Township. "What I want is for people to look at the new high school and think, 'How the hell did you do that so cheaply?'"

Every time the telephone rang in the foyer, Sonnabend bolted for the receiver. "Prior Lake–Savage School District," he answered, his voice shaking. "Any news yet?" disembodied voices asked. Sonnabend shook his head, and went back to his mantra. Had they asked for too much all at once? Would it have been safer to seek money just for the high school? Would the technology request scuttle the entire referendum? Would the childless and elderly ruin his plans? Would he ever have time to be creative in his job, to concentrate on issues like flexible scheduling, year-round school or new start times?

Sonnabend's angst was not entirely selfless. Unlike teachers, he had no tenure, and his predecessor had been pushed out because he'd failed to convince the voters of the need for more money.

The Savage and Prior Lake town polling places were the first to report. "Holy Trinity, 398 yes, 321 no. Minnesota Valley, 480 yes, 258 no." Nobody moved. The news was too good. "Harriet Bishop Elementary School, 196 yes, 52 no. Glendale Elementary, 428 yes, 194 no." Dick Booth burst out into laughter: "Not even close." Sonnabend still would not leave his desk. Olson began to smile. "If we get Lydia, I'll go door-to-door naked to thank the voters," he said with soft cockiness. "Credit River Township, 283 yes, 252 no." Olson's eyes snapped wide open. Credit River, like Lydia, was Old Prior Lake, the country. They never voted yes on referenda. Ten minutes later, Lydia finally called in. "Spring Lake Township, 254 yes, 292 no," Sonnabend announced, finally giving up his post. An enigmatic smile flitted across Olson's face. He seemed almost . . . disappointed.

The final tally was 3,325 to 2,210. According to the polls, nonparents had voted more overwhelmingly for the bond than had parents with children in the schools.

"Well," Sonnabend said, resting against the side of the table, the remains of eight pizzas sitting in a pool of hardened grease. "I guess we better start thinking about a new levy. We can't open a new building with double the space without more operating funds."

Chapter Seventeen

Noon, Monday,
May 29, 2000—seven
days and counting

Lori Boynton's memo landed in Ron Lachelt's mailbox on the wrong day, at the wrong time.

SUBJECT: END OF YEAR VIGILANCE
1. PLEASE: Limit passes! Too many kids are wandering!
2. Get out of your "Comfort Zone." Feel free to wander around in the hall and confront kids about their destination.
3. The results of the exit interviews we conducted with the seniors will be in your POs ASAP. The kids have all repeated their belief that teachers need to be tougher on attendance, tardies and expectations in general. So do them a favor and be tough!

Like hell, Lachelt said. "Tough on attendance? What attendance? Why don't we just stop pretending and cancel May? There aren't any kids in school anyway."

Lachelt was not given to hyperbole. It was late spring, and during late spring, Prior Lake High School gave new meaning to the expression "Field Trip High." The first week of May hadn't been all that bad. On Monday, Lachelt had lost just a few kids when members of the track team were excused early for a meet. But on Wednesday, his classes had been thrown into chaos because 122 Outdoor Education students had left to play golf. On Friday morning, he'd had to make do without any of the kids enrolled in Spanish because they'd had a special breakfast during the first two hours of the day, and the student counselors were gone all seven periods for a special seminar.

On Tuesday, May 9, the track team had left school early, again; twenty-three members of the Death Education class had spent the day walking through a cemetery and watching an embalming at a funeral home; and the student council had held its annual elections and asked that the kids be allowed to leave class to vote. On Wednesday, another thirty Death Ed students had gone off on the same field trip, and fifty-five other students had been locked up in the media center to take the AP Literature and Composition and the AP Statistics exams. Those didn't last the entire day, of course, but the teachers had thrown the students parties after the arduous tests, so scratch Advanced Biology. On Thursday and Friday, his classes had been relatively full; only the Calculus students were gone the first day, and the golf team, the junior class officers and half the baseball team the second.

But the following Monday, all eighty Physics students were at Valley Fair, a local amusement park, for the park's annual citywide Physics Day, when hundreds of students bopped around in T-shirts with slogans like "Mind Over Matter—If You Have a Mind, It Doesn't Matter" while measuring the velocity of the roller coaster and calculating centrifugal force on the Scrambler. Since the twenty-eight members of Rosalie Schaefer's Fashion class were off doing research on whatever fashion students research, teaching had pretty much come to a standstill. Tuesday had also been an utter waste, with the Outdoor Ed students climbing ropes at the YMCA, the

Synergy and Honors English kids at the Guthrie Theater, and the High Mileage auto class gone for two days at Brainerd International Raceway. Wednesday and Thursday had been bearable but, on Friday, a hush had fallen over the school. All the Focus families were cavorting at Valley Fair, the choir director had called a half-day rehearsal for his hundred and twenty-six singers, twenty-six students were on a field trip to the zoo and sixteen baseball players had an early game.

And that didn't count individual absences, which were running high. The Friday before Memorial Day weekend, sixty kids were excused from school—twenty on vacation or out of town, sixteen for medical appointments and the remainder for drivers' tests, college visits, college placement exams, illness or a state synchronized-swimming tournament.

And Boynton was lecturing the teachers about being tough on attendance?

"Somebody's got to do something about this," Lachelt said, to no one in particular. The teachers around him stared. They all knew that that "someone" would not be Craig Olson. The principal believed in "experiential" education, although what golf games, track meets and jaunts to Valley Fair had to do with "experiential" education, no one fully understood. All the faculty knew was that most of the field trips were for nonacademic purposes, and that every time a student was excused from class, they had to help him make up the work. Missed the first lecture on DNA? Don't worry, I'll type up my notes for you. Oh, you didn't take the exam because you were golfing? No problem. I'll just write a new one for you. You need to complete the lab experiment we did while you were at the theater? Sure, I'll come in at six-thirty tomorrow morning and set it up especially for you.

No slouch, Lachelt wasn't simply complaining about the extra work. "It gets some kids so far behind that they simply give up," he said, and encouraging students not to give up was Lachelt's singular obsession. "When kids give up on themselves, they decide they can't or won't do the work. That's dangerous." Lachelt did virtually anything to avert surrender. If students fell behind because of field trips and couldn't find time to make up quizzes because they had jazz band before school, sports in the afternoon and no study halls, he gave them the points rather than risk demoralizing them.

During the second trimester, when Biology students dissected pigs, three girls had become hysterical, declaring themselves unable to face the task ahead. "I led them through it," said Lachelt. "They did it and, more importantly, they learned they could do something they thought they couldn't do. Does it make a difference? I don't know. I like to think so. I have to think so."

The teachers' frustration went well beyond field trips and parents cavalierly pulling kids out of school for vacation. The school year was winding down the way it was supposed to, with an endless round of barbecues and banquets where students were fêted for jobs well done and Most Valuables were awarded, where coaches were politely applauded and parents spent yet another evening beaming with pride. At the band banquet, held at Mystic Lake Casino, the seniors were actually roasted, with baby pictures projected onto a huge screen.

The sole group advisor to reject bestowing honors on students with food, Tom Hassig had staged a two-hour salute instead, a showcase of Laker talent that packed the auditorium. One of Mike Carr's Focus students slicked back his hair, swiveled his hip and belted out "Jailhouse Rock" in a perfect imitation of Elvis, whom he'd never seen live. Reilly's closest friend donned bell-bottoms and a combat jacket for an acoustic guitar rendition of Don McLean's "American Pie" that drew every grownup in the room into a sing-along. The full concert choir, dressed in Hawaiian shirts and tossing beach balls, sang the best of the Beach Boys. And Anna Bican dazzled the audience with her tribute to *Grease*, "There Are Worse Things I Could Do."

But no matter the venue or its content, for the faculty, the finale added up to one bracing reality: Their students were too busy being celebrated to be taught.

Even when they weren't somewhere else, the seniors seemed to be on permanent vacation from school. Half of the students in Economics were barely passing, and few appeared interested in getting better than a *D*. What for? the seniors asked. They already had their college acceptances; overwhelmed by transcripts, the University of Minnesota didn't even want to see the final grades of their incoming freshmen. "Typically, grades start dropping off toward the end of the year, but I've never seen anything like this," said Lachelt. He'd run off a bar graph of the marks in Advanced

Biology. Of twenty-four students, six had *A*s, three had *B*s, four had maintained *C*s, but the rest were off on the far end of the chart, in a soaring tower of *F*s.

Joe Mestnick, one of Mike Carr's closest colleagues, struggled to remain calm. "I don't want to have a heart attack in the next five days," he said, sitting in the lounge with the principal and the usual members of the faculty. The other Joe in the department, Joe Goracke, had no talent for calm, and that morning, his patience had been seriously tried by a mother who'd called to discuss why her child was not doing very well in his class. "It's your fault for ignoring his ADHD," she'd chastised him. "I'm not ignoring it," Goracke responded. "But his problem doesn't appear to be ADHD. In fact, he's quite mellow, too mellow. He sleeps in class and he's only handed in one-sixth of the assignments." The mother persisted. "Yeah, that's the other problem. When you wake him up in class, it's humiliating."

Olson laughed. When he was still teaching, he'd never awakened sleeping students. Instead, he'd built book towers around them that would collapse the moment that they stirred. Sally Davis of the Spanish department preferred a less risky approach in today's litigious age: she drew Magic Marker mustaches on sleeping students' faces, or taped their heads to their desks.

Usually the first to throw in a story, or pose a question, Corey sat quietly at the table like an outsider. The day after the Columbine anniversary, Olson had called her in for an "update" and, in the course of a long discussion, shared with her his "concerns" about her relationship with the other members of the English Department. The message rang through the sugarcoating with icy clarity: Your colleagues consider you to be a braggart, an abrasive teacher and a pathological liar.

Before she could begin to recover from being told what she'd already suspected, Boynton started calling her in, once or twice a week, to confront her with a new rumor, a new story she'd picked up. One morning it was about Corey's lacing her classes with sexual innuendo. Corey was puzzled; Boynton was talking about an incident that had occurred during the first trimester, almost six months earlier, when students had been nagging her about their ungraded papers. "I was grading last night, but my husband came home and he deserves some time, too," she'd explained. "Oh, getting it on?" one boy had joked. Corey had ended the conversation, but it came back to haunt her.

Then Boynton had demanded to know why Corey was scaring students by telling them that she had a fatal disease and was going to die, probably before the end of year. Was it worth trying to explain that in driving home a point about taking care of themselves, she'd mentioned, in passing, that she had serious asthma that could kill her if she didn't watch her health? Next Boynton accused her of defaming the teacher she'd replaced. Three days later, the problem was her bragging about her ability to speak French. The barrage didn't stop. A loop had been woven between teachers who'd disliked Corey from day one and students who resented her sarcastic sense of humor and tough standards. Every move she made, every statement she uttered was twisted and perverted. As in the old game, Whispering Down the Lane, by the time an incident was described to Corey, usually by Boynton, it bore little resemblance to reality.

With some tame prodding from Olson, Corey had finally cried "uncle" and resigned. Devastated and humiliated, she struggled to maintain face during the final weeks of school, but the response from students was straining the ease of her departure. As word of her surrender spread, notes and poems and buttons from fervent admirers littered her desk. "I'm thankful to have had an incredible teaching machine that cares so much for every student!" wrote one junior. "The truly great teachers make every student, maybe for only one tri, enjoy learning."

One boy whom she'd worked with during hours of her free time, said, "I cannot possibly thank you enough for the teacher, mentor and friend that you have been to me. I swear to you that I have never learned more in any classroom, and not simply English and writing. And I thank you for . . . ripping me from my safety zone and showing me so, so, so much." One of the stars of the school, a serious and talented young man she'd pushed hard despite his initial resistance, finally brought her to tears. "Though many kids didn't like you, I feel it was because you were a good teacher and they hadn't had one before," he wrote. "I learned so much this year . . . and I am NOT just saying. Because of you I am a better writer and for the first year, I actually enjoyed English. Other than being an excellent teacher, you were an excellent friend. A thousand thanks DOESN'T say it . . . you will be missed."

Even parents rallied to her side. "I can't believe they're letting her leave," said one mother. "We need more Mara Coreys at Prior Lake, not less."

Mike Carr was hanging on, although barely. Some time during the first part of the trimester, Mr. Mellow had forgotten about calm; his face had turned the eerie red of a sedentary and obese sixty-year-old with high blood pressure.

He'd given up on his Focus students one morning, when he'd looked out over his class as they worked on a project due the following Monday and realized, in a burst of clarity, that he'd be lucky if one of the sixteen submitted the final version on time. Chilled by the prospect of another year of arguments, of putting students on contract, he'd quietly informed John Girtman, the senior Focus teacher, that he preferred to stick with mainstream kids in the future. Girtman was stunned; Carr's departure would leave him as the only male teacher in Focus.

Carr stood firm. "What are we doing here, baby-sitting them so they can get high school diplomas?" he asked. "These kids expect to get pampered, to be bribed with special treats. They get too many second chances and too little education. We pretend they are learning what the other kids are learning, but it's a lie. We've set a ten-foot hoop at four feet for them and pretend that they're playing on the same court as the rest of the players. Is so much compassion really compassionate?"

Ashlee Altenbach still couldn't control herself for more than five minutes at a stretch, and didn't seem inclined to as much as attempt to learn self-control. Jayne Garrison and her old boyfriend had decided to give love another try, so Jayne was too busy mooning to finish any school work. And Ryan Langhorst was living in suspended animation as hearing after hearing passed with no resolution of the legal problems that resulted from his Halloween stunt. His trial had been scheduled to commence in late April, but the judge had suppressed his confession and, rather than cutting a deal with Ryan, the district attorney had appealed that decision, which would delay any resolution until well into the fall.

Roger remained Carr's single Focus triumph, although he, too, was getting on Carr's nerves. "Let's have a Roger-Carr switch day," he'd suggested. "I can't come to school looking like you," answered Carr, horrified at the prospect. "YOU shouldn't come to school looking like you. You'd look so nice if you'd, you know, wear different clothes." Roger still hadn't admitted defeat and had enlisted his classmates in a full lobbying effort. "Come on, Mr. Carr, it would be fun." "Gee, Mr. Carr, lighten up." The whimpering had grated like a fingernail scratched across a blackboard.

At the other end of the spectrum, Carr's Honors Sociology class had deteriorated into anarchy. Six of the twenty-four students had solid As, but the remainder were floundering. Carr tried. God knows, he racked his brain, combed magazines and begged every teacher around him for ideas to make the class exciting and stimulating. He'd taught gender roles using children's books, television and the movies *Tootsie, Trading Places* and *The Truman Show.* Hoping to engender a heated discussion about deviant behavior, drug use and teen sexuality, he'd even risked parental wrath by showing a PBS series about an epidemic of syphilis among teenagers in Conyers, Georgia, the result of group sex and rampant drug use.

But it made no difference. Every discussion disintegrated into silence or childish squabbling. The kids seemed immune to even the most provocative material. When Carr tried to lead them through a new version of the classic "which-people-get-to-remain-in-the-lifeboat" values-clarification exercise, a girl named Jessie Wenner whined, "What if I don't want to choose?" Most weeks, she and a girlfriend sat whispering or muttering from their seats on the sidelines.

Another afternoon, a loudmouthed boy refused to stay in his seat and Carr finally yelled, a full-bodied, furious holler. The boy yelled back, spitting out, "This is fuckin' bullshit." Carr resorted to the ultimate weapon in a teacher's arsenal: He ordered the student to leave the room. The boy did not budge. Carr was helpless. Five dozen adults can keep a thousand teenagers under control only if their charges obey instinctively. In the face of passive aggression, Carr was left with no option but to ignore the insubordination or call in the campus cop.

Furious and distraught, Carr just couldn't pick up the telephone and call Goldy. Carr's powerlessness unveiled, even generally respectful students went wild, turning his class into pandemonium. Some days, the students from Synergy—Katie Keough, Jake Anderson and Andy Ottoson, the counterculture coterie—allowed him the illusion that the class was having an organized discussion. Mostly, however, they sat in the far row of desks, looking disgusted. Only Tom Maust, the student council president, and a German exchange student dutifully submitted their homework and responded to Carr's questions.

Finally, Carr simply lost it. "You guys act like you're in second grade," he screamed to an audience that included the top students in the school. "I try and give you leeway, but I feel like I'm being walked all over. I give up. That's it. If you don't behave, I'm going to kick you out of class."

Cringing in a corner with a migraine headache, Katie Keough yawned. "He won't do anything, he never does," she said with a clarity that Carr himself—too young and too unrebellious as a teenager—could not grasp. "He's completely lost control of the class. First, he let us know that he wanted to be our friend, which was really stupid. Second, he asked us what we thought, like after a test. Of course we were going to say, 'Oh, it was really hard, Mr. Carr,' although it was unbelievably easy, because we're seniors and we don't want to do any work. After three years in high school, we're experts at manipulation. So he got easier and easier until we got bored. Finally, he tried to control us by saying things like, 'You're seniors in high school.' Yeah, we are. Who cares? We still don't want to do anything."

Jake Anderson took issue with Katie's assessment of how Carr had lost control. "You can't lose something you never had in the first place," he said.

"Control" was the watchword all over the school, but as the seniors moved inexorably toward graduation, the strings teachers and administrators ordinarily pulled to keep them in line were unraveling. The school roiled with hormonally charged energy. All spring, Boynton, incensed that a particularly mouthy senior boy had made it through the first two periods of a day flaunting a "Will Work for Weed" T-Shirt, had conducted a one-woman dress-code crusade. But seniors came to school in "Just Say Yes" T-shirts and beer bandannas, begging their teachers to chastise them. When Tana Sappington showed up wearing a lime-green shirt with skimpy straps and an open back, Boynton ordered her never to appear in a backless blouse again. The next day, Tana and her friends Tina Farrell and Ashlee Altenbach arrived in the skimpiest possible tank tops. The day after, Tana donned a blue strapless shirt that covered much of her back, but that showed at least three inches of her midriff.

Zach Moses, a basketball and football player, had been privately raging against Mary Haugen for weeks for interfering in his relationship with his girlfriend, whose mother was trying to cool down the ardor between the young lovers. The mother had called Haugen for advice and, unable to resist involvement, Haugen had lectured the young woman about letting Zach, a touchy kind of guy, hold her hand during school, massage her neck or give her a kiss. Zach held his tongue until the end of basketball season, knowing that Haugen could bench him. The minute the season ended, however, he flew into her office and, well, "ripped her a new asshole" was how he described it.

Tony Lorenz envied Zach's blow for freedom. He would have liked nothing better than to have given Sara Strege a similar verbal lashing, but lacking two credits in English, two credits only Strege could give him, he was forced into uncommon restraint. Tony and Strege were plaid and checks, an impossible combination. There was nothing that Strege hated more than cocky young men, and she took open delight in knocking the wind out of Tony's sails. There was nothing that Tony hated more than people who wielded power over him, and he mocked that power with willful, if measured, precision.

The two had a long history that began with Tony's older sister, Shannon, Strege's pet student. Shannon had been the "mother figure" of CLASS, the drug- and alcohol-free student group that Strege sponsored. Created as a social home for students who wanted to have fun without alcohol, under Shannon's leadership, CLASS had evolved into something of a cult that closed itself off, creating a zeitgeist that sent a sharp message, "If you're not in CLASS, you must be a drinker." Worried about their reputations, or trying to prove something to their parents, scores of students, including dozens of drinkers, flocked to the group.

Tony was not one of them, which Strege interpreted as a proalcohol statement, sowing the seeds of a not-so-cold war between the teacher and the student. Tony, in turn, copped an equally hostile attitude toward Strege for her cavalier attitude toward males, toward her penchant for ragging on boys, for lecturing them on the natural inferiority of the male gender. Strege was never shy about her disdain for males, even when accused of sexism. "Of course I'm sexist," Strege responded, laughing, when a boy protested her constant mocking of the boys.

"Imagine what would happen if a male teacher talked to female students that way," Tony said. "She thinks she redefines cool. I'm embarrassed for her. Can't she behave like an adult?"

Tony knew he wasn't the only student who was finding Strege's sense of humor unacceptable. When Brita Pagels resigned from the CLASS executive board, Strege had joked to her friends, "Oh, Brita couldn't stay on the board, she's pregnant." When Brita caught wind of the comment, she stormed into the peer counseling room, fuming. Tim Keough, another member of the CLASS board, was equally uncomfortable when Strege called him a "hottie," or kidded, "You're so cute, come spend the weekend with me at the Day's Inn." He knew she wasn't serious. But there was something . . . Tim couldn't summon up the word. "Unseemly" was the sentiment he was trying to capture.

For scores of students, Strege was the epitome of hip. But many, boys in particular, preferred more traditional teachers. "Yeah, she's fun, I guess, but I prefer Mr. Lundstrom," said one senior. "Sure, he's hard, but hard's not the point. There's no game-playing. You don't have to kiss his ass like you do with Strege. He's fair."

Tony's first formal run-in with Strege occurred during the second trimester, shortly after he handed in a packet of work for her Creative Writing class. Seated in the computer lab working on a paper, he looked up to find Strege behind him, motioning him into her room. "Who wrote this for you?" she challenged him. Tony did not take well to affronts to his honor. "Give me a piece of paper, a pen and a topic, and we'll see if I can't write like that," Tony responded. Strege backed off, but she never forgot his sassy retort. And Tony never forgot Strege's accusation.

But it was in Strege's third trimester Public Speaking course that the two came closest to blows. The students in Tony's section were a rowdy bunch, and Strege tried to contain them with easy humor. One afternoon, she turned a bit curt. "This class has the potential to be such a great Speech class, if you guys would only cut it out." Leaning back, half out of his desk, Tony raised his hand. "You've got the potential to be a really great teacher but some days you fall short, too."

Tony kept it up, baiting Strege daily. Then came the lip-synching unit, the self-consciously, strenuously fun-loving teacher's rather unusual method for making kids more comfortable in front of an audience. The requirements were to choose any song, learn the words, lip-synch them at the front of the classroom and keep it clean, or at least reasonably clean, in accordance with Strege's ambiguously defined and curiously shifting standards. The students were warned that the inclusion of more than four swear words in any song selection meant a loss of points. Their overall grade, she announced, would be based on how well and precisely they moved their lips.

In several instances, however, she could not even see their mouths. One boy, the son of another English teacher, enhanced the atmospherics of his act by performing under a black light. Strege might have objected, but she was too busy giggling and hooting. "Don't excite us!" she teased the student. It felt like an exercise in titillation, not learning, and she recorded it all with a video camera, faithfully taping his every utterance and gyration.

The next students to perform offered a lascivious rendition of the rapper Sir Mix-a-Lot's "Baby Got Back." *I like big butts and I cannot lie. You other brothers can't deny that when a girl walks in with an itty bitty waist and a round thing in your face you get sprung, wanna pull out your tongue cuz you notice that butt was stuffed deep in the jeans she's wearing.* Crouched among the students, Strege and Schmidty, who was sitting in on the class, roared along with the students as the two boys performing the song bumped and ground and mouthed the lyrics: *I gotta be straight when I say I wanna (uh) til the break of dawn, baby got it goin on. A lot of pimps won't like this song cuz them punks like to hit it and quit it. But I'd rather stay and play cuz I'm long and I'm strong and I'm down to get the friction on.*

At last it was Tony's turn, and he could not imagine that anything he was about to do would break the boundaries of what had already been done. He grabbed a life-size blow-up doll that he'd stashed behind Strege's desk, clutched it to his chest, hiked up his baggy jeans and hit the play button. *I wanna freek you*, came the lyrics, which the rapper Jodeci sang and Tony mimed. *Every time I close my eyes I wake up feelin' so horny I can't get you outta my mind.* The effect was less raunchy than ridiculous, and deliberately so, because the inflated paramour in Tony's embrace was a far cry from anatomically correct, lacking the proper protuberances and orifices. Tony fondled and humped it and pretended to croon: *I don't give a damn about nothin' else, freek'n you is all I need.*

Strege blew up. "That's too pornographic," she fumed, and to punctuate her point, she not only turned off the video camera but rewound the tape to erase all evidence of Tony's transgressions. Tony was genuinely flabbergasted. Was anything he had done any more pornographic than a declaration that *I Like Big Butts?*

Even so, he knew he couldn't afford a confrontation. His graduation from high school depended on passing this course, so he raced to his locker, scavenged for something relatively innocuous, returned to the classroom and loaded a new tape into the cassette deck. The change of pace could not have been more dramatic. *One boy, one girl, two hearts beating wildly*, he lip synched the sweet love song, pulling Eric Prchal out of the audience. He and Eric had played this kind of game so many times that it came easily and naturally to them, and they gazed adoringly into each other's eyes as the lyrics explained, *To put it mildly, it was love at first sight.*

Strege visibly relaxed, video camera rolling, as the song continued. *He smiled, she smiled. They knew right away this was the day they had waited for all their lives.* Tony danced with Eric and managed to dip him, even though Eric was a good ten inches taller. It was a transcendently and hilariously awkward sight. Then the boys took their mock seduction a step farther: Tony straddled Eric, thrusting wildly. Strege abruptly swung her camera toward the ceiling and kept it pointed in that direction until Tony and Eric disengaged.

Tony noticed the gesture and suspected that it might not be the end of Strege's protest. The performance by the next group of students, however, easily upped the ante on what was permissible, on what Strege was willing to abide. The song was "Date Rape," by the punk band Sublime. The lyrics started with a boy meeting a girl in a bar. They go outside, where the girl is forced to fight off the boy's advances. *She said let go, he said "No way! C'mon babe, it's your lucky day. Shut your mouth, we're gonna do it my way.*

C'mon baby, don't be afraid. If it wasn't for date rape, I'd never get laid."
Familiar with the words, the students sang along. *C'mon party people, won't
you listen to me: Date rape's nightly!* Strege lent her own cheery voice to the
chorus, and laughed along with the crowd at the song's conclusion.

As the students filtered out of her classroom, she motioned Tony over
to her desk. "That was entirely inappropriate," she said. "You really put
your grade in jeopardy."

"Inappropriate?" he asked softly. Tony almost always spoke softly
when he was angry. "More inappropriate than singing about date rape?"
He left the classroom without uttering so much as a syllable of contrition,
and Strege was left to mutter, "I'm gonna get Tony Lorenz, he's such a
wiener." She made good on her promise the very next day, hauling Tony
into the principal's office for a lecture. It omitted any mention of the kind
of material the other students had selected.

Boynton expected petty confrontations with the Tony Lorenzes. But the restlessness of the "good" kids, students whom she'd counted on never to defy
authority, caught her off-guard. Eric Prchal had simply stopped working. His
grades were solid; his basketball scholarship to Morehead State University
was signed and sealed; and his reputation was so secure that he could risk
pushing the envelope. That push came on his birthday, when he, Tony,
Jordan and two other boys decided to celebrate Eric's eighteenth birthday
with a trip to a strip club in the warehouse district of Minneapolis. Aside
from voting and registering for the draft, entering strip joints and casinos
were the only privileges teenagers gained when they turned eighteen, and the
boys planned to take full advantage of their newfound liberty.

They decided to spice up their adventure by taking Tom Maust along on
their journey, knowing that he'd be alternately horrified and titillated by the
invitation. Tom didn't drink. He never partied. Being "bad" just wasn't part
of the social vocabulary of a boy whose life was organized around his studies, helping his parents and polishing his image as a leader in the school. For
Tom, success was inexorably linked to maintaining the approval of adults
in authority. Mary Haugen, his mentor and heroine, would hardly approve
of a night out with the boys. But did she have to know?

The most clean-cut of the group, Eric extended the invitation. Tom begged off, offering a pile of homework as an excuse. "Come on, Tom, don't be a wuss," Eric pressed. Tom, who wasn't included in many social outings with "cool" kids, folded. The boys drove downtown and landed at Choice, a not-quite-sleazy joint with a $9 cover charge. It was early evening, so the small club wasn't quite full. But twenty nude girls—young, pretty girls who could have been cheerleaders at Prior Lake—were dancing and waiting for marks. Jordan's jaw sagged, his mouth open. A beatific glow lit Eric's face. Tony played Mr. Cool. And Tom, well, Tom was speechless, virtually catatonic as the dancers displayed their bodies inches from his face.

The boys grabbed a table, ordered soft drinks and scoped out the situation. The deal was simple: $5 for a personal lap dance at the stage, $15 for the full treatment. Eric called over a buxom blonde, handed her $15 and pointed to Tom. Startled, Tom wasn't sure what to do. The young woman led him to a couch in the rear of the club and pulled out all the stops, rubbing and pumping her body against his, shaking her breasts centimeters from his lips, wrapping her legs around his neck. Tom's friends roared with delight. Intent on the moment, Tom sat like a rock. When the music ended, he stood hesitantly and walked back to his friends, red-faced with noticeable tumescence.

Prchal chose a tiny girl for himself, then, one by one, the other boys walked to the couch, or dangled money for personal lap dances. In awe, Jordan wasn't content with one full lap dance; he emptied his wallet purchasing a much-needed second. By 11:45, they were all broke. "It was the best time I ever had in high school," Eric declared. "I could live there," Jordan added. Tom said nothing. At school, he told no one what he'd done. When word got around, he vociferously denied the vicious rumor.

It wasn't just Eric. Jake Anderson showed his parents what a report-card *F* looked like, his first grade below a *B+*, delivered midterm by Mike Carr because Jake hadn't handed in any work.

When the Physics teacher posted grades two weeks before the end of the trimester to show his students what they'd receive if they did not hand in their final projects, most of the class breathed a sigh of relief and opted out of the added work. "I wish I could be that way," said Shannon McGinnis when she saw her *B+*. "But I can't."

Then, during the spring play, Agatha Christie's *Appointment with Death*, a minirebellion broke out in the unlikeliest quarter, among the drama students. The improbable leader was Andy Ottoson, the son of the AP Literature teacher, one of the most easy-going kids in the school. Andy had been born with "greasepaint in his blood," as his mother, Carol, put it. If not born, he'd been infected as a child, since his mother, the principal theatrical director in the school, dragged him along to rehearsals, set-construction evenings and performances. Andy had started helping her out with the lights when he was still in middle school, and had become the master of the Prior Lake lighting booth.

Andy had considered passing on designing the lights for the final play of his high school career because he had a long history of clashes with the co-directors, Tom Hassig and Mette Forster, a middle school teacher. Every time he worked with them, he wound up feeling used and patronized. During one season, Forster had ordered the student director of a play to pick up her laundry. During another, she'd given a student actor ISS for saying "bastard" on stage. And Hassig, well, Hassig was a control freak set on doing things the *right* way. So was Andy, although his definition of right, needless to say, differed from Hassig's.

But Andy couldn't resist the chance to play with his brand-new lighting system, installed in the late fall, one more time. Forget the past, Andy—Paco, as his friends called him—told himself. Let's just make this work. He bit his tongue when Hassig and Forster barred the crew from rehearsals, claiming that they were making too much noise, and instructed them not to mingle with the cast on performance dates. He remained silent too when they tried to quash the Prior Lake ritual of nightly cast parties, arguing that partying left them too tired to perform.

But by the opening day of the play, Andy—a top student, an Eagle Scout, a kid who'd never spent one minute in detention, ISS or OSS in his life—was rambling around school asking anyone willing to listen, "Do you believe in justifiable homicide?" He'd hung his lights according to the plan Hassig had approved. But, at final rehearsals, Hassig had instructed him to change the design. Andy had been through such last-minute changes with Hassig before and bitterly resented the last-minute work. "There are only three ways this play could be worse," Andy continued prattling. "One, if Mr. Hassig designed the lights himself. Two, if Mr. Hassig or Miss Forster stepped in and took over the acting roles. Three, if the school was blown up."

He could never have anticipated what else might happen. Exuberant about their children's accomplishments, Prior Lake drama parents have a habit of throwing flowers onto the stage during curtain calls. On opening night, one mother went a bit overboard with the number of blooms. Forster was not pleased, and as the auditorium emptied, she thrust a broom at the crew, demanding that someone clean up the stage. When the mother in question grabbed it herself, the room crackled with tension. The students knew they hadn't heard the last word about flowers.

The next day, at a full-cast-and-crew meeting called in the choir room, Forster denounced the tradition and ordered that no flowers be thrown onto the stage for the remainder of the run. It's a health and safety hazard, she insisted, since thorns or stems might poke someone in the eye, or provoke an allergic reaction.

The students watched her performance with glazed eyes. "What a stupid bitch," one said. For most, the harangue fell into the "not my problem" category. After all, *they* hadn't thrown any flowers.

That night, two students in the audience tossed blooms during curtain calls. Hassig and Forster ordered Andy to bring down the stage lights. Then, on Saturday night, the third night of the show, just before the Act III curtain was raised, Hassig walked onto the stage and announced that the play would end without a curtain call, due to the heat in the auditorium. That excuse fooled no one. It wasn't *that* hot in the building. Two mothers pulled Hassig outside and read him the riot act. He relented, but the die had already been cast.

"You can do a lot to strong-minded intelligent teenagers like those of the drama department," Andy said. "You can pull out truly incredible work from them. You can help them do incredible things. You can lead them down new paths of discovery. But you can never, ever, EVER, control them, which is exactly what they tried to do that night."

The following Monday, a flyer was passed around school, reading "CONGRATULATIONS CAST AND CREW: THANKS TO YOUR HARD WORK, FLOWER-RELATED INJURIES ARE DOWN 100%." Two female cast members bought dozens of black T-shirts and had that message printed across them. The entire cast and crew agreed to appear in school on Friday wearing their new garb.

"You don't want to ruin your reputation by doing something stupid three weeks before graduation," Boynton, who'd discovered the plot, told Andy on Thursday afternoon. A scene from *L.A. Confidential* flitted through Andy's brain, the moment when Jack Vincennes warns Edmund Exley how damaging reopening the Nite Owl case might be to his career. *Are you really willing to destroy everything you've built?* Vincennes asks. *I've gotta wrecking ball,* Exley responds. *Wanna help me swing it?*

On Friday morning the drama kids caucused at Laker's Restaurant, just down the street from the high school. By then, Andy had decided that Vincennes was right, that wearing the T-shirts would be pointless. Boynton would be waiting for them to enter the building. She'd order them to turn the shirts inside out, and slap them with a day in ISS. "I have no problem with getting a day off in ISS," Andy argued. "But what's the point if nobody ever sees the T-shirts?"

Persuaded by Andy, who can be very persuasive, the students devised plan B, which was to wear their new T-shirts during curtain call that night instead. But as they laid their plot, they ignored the fact that a dozen teachers were sitting at a table nearby. Within two hours of his arrival at school, Andy was called into Mary Haugen's office. The collective protest collapsed under Haugen's promise to mediate the ongoing problems with Forster and Hassig. But drama kids sported the T-shirts for the rest of the semester. Even amidst the end-of-the-year excitement, the bitterness did not dissipate easily.

Threats to order were coming from every quarter, and Boynton held her breath each morning as she pulled into the parking lot and confronted the Rock. It was just a hulking hunk of granite, perhaps thigh-high. But it had become a battleground for student expression. The Rock had originally stood in a pasture across the street from the high school, and students took to painting it to announce the victories of their sports team. At one point, the old superintendent had vowed to bury it, which, inevitably, turned the Rock into sacred ground. When the pasture became Hidden Oaks, the

Rock had even been moved to its prominent spot directly in front of the high school's administrative entrance.

Joking that the Rock had begun as a pebble, its increase in mass a result of thousands of coats of paint, Mary Haugen liked to think of it as a booster for class spirit, a place where students could express their pride in victory, their sadness in defeat. She loved the way seniors painted their class names and slept by the Rock the night before graduation, lest juniors try to steal their final thunder. But she and the rest of the administrators ignored its potential as a place for different sorts of expression, at least until the spring of 2000.

One Friday night, just after midnight, Nick Busse and a friend seized control over the hunk of granite and decorated it as an advertisement for Jello Biafra and the punk movement. As they put the finishing touches on the logo of Alternative Tentacles, a punk music label, friends cruised by and stopped to visit. "Good old smokin' and paintin' the Rock," they'd joked, puffing on cigarettes and admiring their handiwork. PRAISE THE LARD, the most public face of the Rock announced the following morning to a community unfamiliar with Jello's band. In a classic case of culture clash, adults assumed the boys were committing sacrilege since they had painted the Rock on Good Friday.

Another morning, toward the end of the year, an even more disturbing message appeared that sent Boynton into a rage against the school's most serious partiers. On the side of the Rock that faced the street was the message:

> We
> Each
> Earned
> Diplomas

The message on the other decreed:

> Because
> Everyone
> Enjoyed
> Running

Boynton never learned the truth, but the partiers were not to blame. Josh Albright, the class valedictorian, and his friends had crafted that message.

Reilly Liebhard had been eyeing the Rock for months, looking for a new approach to its mass. Could he split it? No, he concluded, granite is simply too hard. What about moving it? Justin Jorgenson, who worked summers with his father as an excavator, assured him it could be done with carefully placed BobCats. After performing careful calculations, Reilly dismissed that notion out of hand.

"Dr. O, what are the rules about the Rock?" he finally asked the principal one morning. "Can I see them?" The regulations were not written down at all, Olson informed him. He and Boynton exercised their discretion in determining what was too "offensive" to remain. Something of a First Amendment absolutist, Reilly was incensed. "What if 'Soccer Rules' offends me?" Reilly wondered. "Would they paint it over in that case?"

Reilly had a rich fantasy life, and he indulged it for weeks about the surface of the Rock and other creative mischief. "What about 'Haugen Rules'? Would anybody get the irony?" he asked one afternoon. He was wearing a T-shirt reading, "At Least Nixon Resigned." Reilly's mind sped too quickly to dwell on the Rock for too long, so he moved on to devising a method for seizing control over the school's public address system. "Imagine what we could do. We could blast the 'Communist International' throughout the school, or 'Solidarity Forever.'" He didn't notice that the students he was talking to were unfamiliar with both songs.

Reilly hadn't slacked off academically. Offered the chance to write a one- or two-page extra-credit paper for U.S. History, although he already had a solid *A*, Reilly submitted a fifteen-page study of the massacre at Kent State, complete with illustrations. But being treated like a child was getting to him. One morning, he ran afoul of John Girtman, who was on the lookout for students avoiding an early assembly. Racing to a Mathematical Modeling competition, Reilly was headed in the opposite direction, which drew Girtman's wrath. Reilly snapped back at the teacher, complaining, "He treated me as if I were another stupid little drunk."

Toward the end of May, Reilly was sitting in the computer lab working on a paper during his study hall, a diligent student, not one of the slackers goofing off in the media center. "Where's your pass?" the computer lab supervisor asked. "I don't need a pass, I have an Honors pass," Reilly responded. "You still need a note from your teacher," the supervisor informed him brusquely. Reilly offered up a little brusqueness of his own before storming off. "Jeez, you'd think that I was building a bomb instead of doing my homework," he said.

The next morning, as Reilly was hustling down the hall to have his yearbook photo taken, Sara Strege stopped him and demanded a pass. "I don't have a pass," he explained. "I just got paged to go for my photo. You can have a DNA sample if you want." Strege, who'd been in the midst of a confrontation with Ashlee Altenbach, who had no destination, legitimate or otherwise, patted Reilly on the head. "You're cute so I'll let you go. But if you were homely, I'd kick your ass."

As Reilly stomped and fumed, his mother asked, "Why are you so angry?" Reilly wasn't really angry. Filled with energy and ideas, he was like a bird with clipped wings, flapping and frustrated. "The motto of Prior Lake High School is *Bibo ergo sum*, I drink therefore I am," he said. "I want a T-shirt that reads, 'I'm Pissed Off Therefore I Am.' How would you say that in Latin?"

But Reilly couldn't act out. He was congenitally incapable of being the asshole he often dreamed of being. After his testiness with the computer lab supervisor, he actually reported himself to Boynton and apologized for his tone. Faced with Strege's patronizing comment, he just walked away.

On the surface, the school looked perfectly normal: rambunctious kids, dedicated teachers, one big happy family. The building was wallpapered with signs for student council elections.

> "Want $10? . . . . Scott wants $10
> Want a New Car. . . . Scott Wants One Too. Vote Scott
> He Wants What You Want.

> For a Sr. year you'll
> never forget...
> Vote for Tara

Blue Collar Workers
Vote Alana

Vote for the Popular People
Conform!
Conform!!!
CONFORM!!!!
-moo

In one of the regular fund-raising drives—and one seemed always to be going on, for one student group or another—the National Honor Society was auctioning its members off to those willing to pay at least $5 for someone to wash your car, bring you a homemade lunch or organize your locker. And a Spanish teacher had plastered the faculty lounge with a flyer about Mary Kay cosmetics, one of the endless fund-raising drives by faculty who could barely pay their mortgages on their salaries.

At 6:30 A.M. on Thursday mornings, kids still gathered in the classroom of an English teacher, a Promisekeeper, for Bible study, as they had all year long. The teacher did not supervise. This was student time, and Scott Whitmore or Christy Gold from Friendship Church led discussions of Bible verses over juice and doughnuts, or shared their doubts and fears. They worked hard to stay centered. "If there's one hypocrite among us, we're all branded," Scott explained. "You have to know who you are." Matt Brown, a member of the Friendship Youth Group, knew exactly who he was. "I live by the four Fs," he said, "family, friends, football, and fun." He never appeared for Bible study. "Even Jesus doesn't get up that early," he explained.

But appearances tend to deceive, so Olson and Boynton didn't delude themselves that the worst had already come. Having been around high schools for decades, they knew they still had to survive senior pranks. The class of 1975, led by Nate Schweich's father, had unleashed a greased pig in the school, a caper revived by the class of 1985. In 1986, seniors had released a flock of pigeons inside the building, and the birds had committed mass suicide against the plate-glass window looking out on the parking lot. One Social Studies teacher fondly remembered how his senior class had hauled in concrete blocks to spell out '89. And after they turned the tassels on their mortarboards, Andy Franklin and his fellow 1969 graduates had pulled joints, real or simulated, out of their clothing and lit up.

No one mentioned what would happen to Prior Lake students who pulled any of those stunts.

With the Class of 1999, the most "pliable" in recent memory, the previous year had ended with a whimper. But the Class of 2000 was reminding Boynton and Olson of the Class of 1998. They were set to watch it end, then, with the same sort of a bang.

Prior Lake seniors had long held graduation parties—some might say illicit graduation parties—over the two days between the end of the school year and graduation. The Class of 1998 had continued that tradition and, within two hours of the final bell of their high school careers, 150 seniors had crammed into cars loaded with tents and sleeping bags, boom boxes, vodka and food, headed for a campground along a slimy creek in Wisconsin called the Apple River. The campsite had been reserved in the name of the Prior Lake Christian Youth Group.

The party was hardly a secret. Scores of parents knew where the kids were going. "Don't let the mosquitoes bite you," Ron Lachelt had joked as they'd headed to the parking lot. "Be safe," a Physical Education instructor had added.

It was a cold night in June, and the students gathered around a huge campfire, grilling burgers, drinking some beers, dancing to the music blasting from a camper. Every hour, more cars drove up. By the time dusk dissolved into full darkness, only the baseball team had yet to arrive. A campground security guard was the only adult intruder, but he strolled by casually, no apparent threat to the fun. When he noticed a girl who'd hit her head on a rock in a drunken fall, he even offered to show her the way to a hospital.

An hour later, the party was in full swing. The senior class song, Green Day's "Good Riddance" had energized the group.

> It's not a question but a lesson learned in time
> It's something unpredictable but in the end is right
> I hope you had the time of your life

Matt Selinske—a student council member, a peer counselor and athlete—had moved to the side of the crowd when he noticed two trucks drive up, their headlights off. The music was still blaring, *I hope you had the time of your life,* when he saw four police cars, vans and a paddywagon race up behind them. He was already sprinting across the field toward the woods when he heard a voice echo out of a bullhorn, "STAY WHERE YOU ARE." He didn't look back as forty friends scattered, the rest of them, nailed. One by one, the Lakers were lined up and Breathalyzed while police searched the woods perfunctorily by flashlight. When they finally left the campground, with all the alcohol they'd spotted in tow, more than eighty-two Prior Lake students had received tickets for minor consumption of alcohol.

Too drunk or shaken to drive home, most of the students remained and kept partying. After all, the police hadn't searched their cars for beer, or their bodies for drugs. "That fucking Boynton," the students muttered. Everyone assumed that the assistant principal had gotten wind of their plan and called the cops in herself. No one considered that innocuous-looking guard who was upset about the stumbling-drunk girl with a bleeding head.

By the time the seniors returned to Prior Lake, the administration had received word that more than one-third of the senior class had been cited by the police. Reporters were phoning, parents were hysterical and Mary Haugen had called a student council meeting for just before graduation rehearsal breakfast. Matt Selinske refused to go. "Fuck it," he said. "She's nothing to me any more." He walked into that breakfast flaunting his senior T-shirt, "Third in the Nation, First in the State."

Matt had barely set foot in the door before Haugen grabbed him. "We have to talk about Apple River," she said. At the meeting that morning, she'd handed each senior student council member a form to fill out: Had they attended the party? Had they been drinking? Most had refused to answer the second question, acknowledging only whether they had received a citation from the police. "I don't want to know if the police arrested you for minor consumption," Haugen told Matt. "I want to know if you were drinking. I already know, so you might as well be honest."

Matt was unabashed, and not surprised that Haugen's pets had self-protectively ratted out their fellow students. "I was drinking and I ran like hell when the cops came," he said. He did not voice the "and it's none of your business" that was running through his head.

The faculty and administration decided that it *was* their business, as the students discovered when they were called into the auditorium after breakfast for a thorough dressing-down. Their teachers were seated on the stage, their faces stern and unforgiving. You've disappointed us badly, Ron Lachelt said. You've disgraced the entire community, Olson declared. The students were stunned. What's the big deal? Seniors party every year. The only difference is that we got caught. "I'm an alcoholic and this scares me," Sally Davis announced, weeping. "Her alcoholism has nothing to do with us," Matt whispered to a friend.

That morning, in the *St. Paul Pioneer Press*, Boynton had been quoted as saying, "We are embarrassed, disgusted, ashamed of them."

The student scheduled to speak at graduation lost the right to do so, although she delivered her remarks to a group of her classmates at an ad hoc ceremony held by the Rock. Seniors who'd been cited or forced to admit that they'd been drinking lost the honors due them as members of the National Honor Society or class officers. And Olson inserted a letter in the program and delivered almost identical remarks from the podium.

> [T]he day after the last day of school for our seniors, we received word that over thirty percent of the members of this graduating class had been ticketed and are being charged with minor consumption of alcohol or resisting arrest or obstructing justice. They had chosen to attend what has, unfortunately become a tradition among our senior classes, a huge unsupervised party in Somerset, Wisconsin.
>
> We are angry. We are disappointed. We are ashamed and embarrassed. And we are scared. But we are not surprised. Apparently, lessons many of us have been attempting to teach have not been learned well.

We sincerely regret that the events of the past four days have drawn attention away from many members of the Class of 1998 who did not deserve to have their graduation week spoiled.

Ben Selinske and Katie Cook, both members of the Class of 2000, sat in the audience, stunned. Ben was Matt's younger brother, and Katie's brother Chris, who had not been implicated in the drinking, was also waiting to receive his diploma. "My grandparents and uncle had all flown in from California to share in a joyful time in my brother's life, and left the ceremony as angry as all the rest of us," Katie said. "Graduation ceremonies are supposed to celebrate the culmination of twelve years of schooling. Instead, Dr. O made it into a criticism session."

Her mother was even more furious. "They tried to erase every one of these kids' accomplishments," said Pam Cook. "This was graduation. How could he have ruined it that way? They better not try anything like that when it's Katie's turn."

After the '98 ceremony ended, Mary Haugen pulled Matt Selinske out of the crowd of graduates and well-wishers. "I still think you're a good person," she said, offering him a hug. Almost two years later, on the eve of his brother's graduation, sitting in a coffee shop near the University of Minnesota, where he was a sophomore, Matt was still kicking himself for not responding honestly. "I wish I had said, 'Where the hell do you get off judging me this way, reducing me to one night in my life,'" he said. "Who did she think she was? It cast a pall over the entire year, the entire time I was at Prior Lake. When I think back to high school, I land on that moment. That is high school to me.

"I hope it ends better for Ben."

Chapter Eighteen

3:30 P.M., Monday,
June 5, 2000

The plasticized chain restaurant wedged between Best Buy and an Amoco station astride I-35 in Burnsville was an unlikely place for philosophy: Serious conversation over melted American cheese and machine-formed burgers ordered off one of those menus designed for the illiterate, or at least illiterates naive enough to believe that the salads would emerge from the kitchen looking as crisp and well-dressed as they did in the photographs.

But Nick Busse, Justin Jorgenson, Jake Anderson and Katie Keough were raised to fast food, to faux leather booths, lighting designed for people suffering from Seasonal Affective Disorder and cuisine for the risk-averse. Besides, food and ambiance weren't the point. They were hungry for conversation, and school had done nothing to sate their appetites.

Was the universe really infinite? Could infinity be captured by such a finite term? Was all organized religion a sham, as Nick insisted, or just the suburban churches where they'd been raised? Struggling with her relation-ship to Catholicism, Katie had more questions than answers. Jake, as usual, was ambivalent. Although his mother was a regular churchgoer, his father had recently given him books about Buddhism, which intrigued him, perhaps because he was uncomfortable with dogma or certainty in any guise. Justin couldn't resist parrying Nick's attacks on religion. He clung to the fundamentalist Christian faith of his parents as if it were the only solid ground in view.

Could the spoken word be disappearing, replaced by nonverbal com-munication? Justin asked, apropos of nothing. Nick's brow furrowed in silent puzzlement. Justin was not deterred. What else could explain the impoverishment of language over the past two generations?   More of Justin's random speculations, at least to Nick's concrete way of thinking. Justin was always off on a tangent, an existential journey to the improba-ble. Nick assumed that meant he was stoned most of the time.

Jake listened more than he talked, quiet, almost deferential to whomev-er was speaking. Pressed, he always offered a careful, usually tentative thought. But he ceded ground the moment he was interrupted, as if unsure that what he had to say was really important enough to take up time and space. It was never clear whether Jake was just gentle, or depressed. Some-thing roiled inside, but he rarely offered even a glimpse of the turmoil.

Like Nick, Katie lived in the here and now but, unlike him, she wasn't programmed for angst. The end of the familiar—finishing the assembly line of school, moving away from home, leaving her friends—had tied her in a thousand knots. She worried incessantly about her college choice, her summer plans, her brother Tim, her friends, homeless children, starvation and world peace. But she couldn't contain a natural exuberance that radi-ated optimism.

The four were not best friends. Even before he'd left to finish up at Normandale Community College, Nick had withdrawn from almost everyone and everything at Prior Lake High School and radiated hostility to his soon-to-be alma mater. Jake, on the other hand, had made his own peace with high school, closing himself into a tight circle of boys, a group that kept its social distance from campus. Early on, Katie had thrown her-self into high school with less reserve. But most of her friends had graduated in 1999; she was clearly lonely. And then there was Justin, who flitted from Jake's group in a dozen different directions, usually simultaneously. His life was a strange amalgam of disaffection from high school and an inexorable need to feel connected.

Most weeks Nick was disgusted with Justin, who tended to disappear for unexplained hours, and Justin railed at Nick for his bottomless negativity. Wanting to become part of Jake's inner circle, Katie felt sure that her gender had proven an insurmountable obstacle. And everyone missed spending more time with Jake, who was spending an increasing amount of his time with his girlfriend, Johanna.

But in the "don't worry, be happy" atmosphere of Prior Lake, conversation wasn't as cool as smoking pot, downing brewskies or shooting pool to a driving beat. So every week or so that spring, the four would set a date for dinner at Perkins and talk about school, parents, politics, destiny and sex. The boys' closest male friends had branded them the Culture Club, and the intent was not flattery.

The conversation moved in desultory circles as they warmed up for the "heavy shit."

"Are you always angry?" asked Katie, who was wrestling with Nick's tense fury. It was alien to her, too self-confident for a young woman who focused her anger inward as guilt. Having added Nick's obvious unhappiness to her list of things to worry about, Katie was trying to reach out and comfort her friend. But gentleness was not part of Nick's emotional vocabulary. He didn't know how to respond.

"Usually," said Nick, pouring himself another cup of coffee, his intensity out of place in Perkins, a searing wind in a chill environment. Nick's proclivity for rage puzzled everyone around him, but it wasn't the negativity of the emotion so much as the passion which confused them. It was so . . . uncontained in a culture of containment.

"I don't think I've ever been angry," Jake said, catching himself, as if not wanting to be *that* different. "Well, maybe a couple of times."

The conversation drifted as Katie and Jake told Justin and Nick about the PBS video that Mike Carr had shown to their Sociology class. A

Frontline investigation, it was the story of a syphilis cluster that developed in Conyers, Georgia, where students remarkably like the Lakers were immersed in a culture of drugs and group sex. The period had started with a boy racing into the room chanting, "Porno, porno, today is porno day." Real mature way to act, quipped Katie, disgusted. As the tape rolled, the students had squirmed in discomfort, giggling with embarrassment, blustering in macho bravado. Mostly, as they watched often-graphic images of the lives of their peers in the South, Katie's classmates had tried to distance themselves from the reality of sexually transmitted diseases and boys lining up to "gang bang" drunken girls.

"That would never happen here," Tina Farrell had asserted confidently. "Five girls would line up and pull her out, yelling, 'Wake up, girl, you're acting like a 'ho.'" The girls in the room who'd spent New Year's Eve at the most raucous party in town were less sanguine than Tina. That night, one drunken female student had spent half the night in a plush bathroom having sex with almost all comers—and no one had attempted to drag her out of her own humiliation.

The students weren't used to serious discussions about sex. Few had had any such discussions with their parents, and they rarely talked about it among themselves. Carr's questions—about oral and anal sex, about what sex meant, about what they would tell their children about sex—provoked profound discomfort.

"Oral sex isn't sex, that's ridiculous," Justin said, interrupting Katie's story about the class. He didn't expect much disagreement since he had never considered the possibility that anyone might count anything but intercourse as "sexual activity." Almost everyone he knew agreed with him, and they had all been puzzled during the Clinton impeachment drama, when they discovered that a whole lot of adults defined sex somewhat differently.

"Of course it's sex," Nick said abruptly. "Why are you distinguishing between one type of exchange of bodily fluids and another?"

Justin and Katie were stunned at the implication. "Kissing is sex," Nick pressed. "The problem is that everyone's trying to give themselves permission."

Nick hated to admit it—which means he did not—but he was naturally inclined toward the straight-laced, whether of the old-fashioned "discipline and hard work" variety, or straight-edge punk, a sort of postpunk punk, a philosophy and movement with all the noise and the anger of punk, but none of the nihilism. Straight-edgers rejected drugs, alcohol and promiscuous sex. Don't just go along to get along, they preached. Don't be manipulated by advertising and conformism. Don't waste yourself. Ian MacKaye, the lead singer of Minor Threat, had summed it up in a single line from his song "Out of Step": *[I] don't smoke, don't drink, don't fuck, at least I can fucking think.*

In unguarded moments, Nick sounded suspiciously like MacKaye, but being out of step was an expensive proposition for a suburban eighteen-year-old. Nick had paid for his rejection of drugs and alcohol with years of loneliness. In the months since he'd enrolled at Normandale, he still hadn't found a mooring and hung on the margins of Jake's tight circle of friends. The unstated price of full admission was a willingness to smoke some dope and drink some beer, rather than observe from the sidelines. He hated pot, so Nick had begun working on developing a taste for vodka.

With school ending, sex, however, was not the issue weighing heaviest on the minds of the Culture Club. Scott Vig and his friends were worrying about the arrangements for the senior class party, and Olson and Boynton about how well Prior Lake students had learned their alcohol lessons. But Nick, Katie, Justin and Jake were plagued by whether they had learned anything at all. Were they ready for the future? What kind of future? How would they create it? What did it mean to be an adult?

Nick and Katie had recently helped design a survey of what Prior Lake students had, and had not, learned. The questions were easy, at least they'd thought so when they were making them up. The results still nagged at their view of reality. Three-quarters of their classmates knew that Albert Einstein had come up with the formula $E=mc^2$, but it was unclear how many knew what that formula, or the Theory of Relativity, meant. An equal number could not muster up the name Betsy Ross when asked who'd sewn the original Stars and Stripes; "Is it Susan B. Anthony?" several had written tentatively. One in three believed that Shakespeare came from France, Germany or Italy, and a similar number were unable to name even one of the rights guaranteed by the First Amendment to the Constitution. Eighty percent couldn't multiple 567 by 937 correctly without a calculator, 60 percent thought that the vast majority of the world was Christian, two-thirds didn't know what "women's suffrage" meant, and only 6 percent could name Yorktown as the city where the British surrendered to the American colonists.

The Culture Club knew that they weren't quite that undereducated, but could the education that had produced those results possibly be adequate?

That afternoon's gathering was a brief meeting, a quick touching of bases sandwiched in between final projects, work and a dozen end-of-the-year activities. Jake had to rush off to the annual Senior Recognition Banquet in the gym, the final celebration of student achievement. The affair was Mary Haugen's favorite moment of the year, and she made sure that "her kids," the student council members, received full attention. But there would be something for almost everyone—for athletes and drama kids, chess players, antidrinking activists, yearbook writers and academic achievers—in a world ruled by an "everyone deserves an award" zeitgeist.

Jake had not been singled out for an individual award, despite Katie Hallberg's best efforts. When the members of the Math department had met to select a student to receive the year's departmental honors, she'd first suggested the name of Reilly Liebhard. "But he didn't take his Math here," the other teachers insisted, seemingly peeved that Reilly had completed six semesters of Math at the University of Minnesota instead. Katie pressed the issue, reminding them that Reilly had been active in Prior Lake's Math Club, that he'd participated as a Laker in the National Mathematical Modeling Competition, that he knew more math than any of them was ever likely to learn. But to no avail.

Succumbing to the collective opposition, she'd proposed Jake's name, then caught herself midsentence. Shit, she thought, my suggestion is the kiss of death. She was right. Jake was passed over. That night, he'd be honored as one of sixty-five students with a cumulative grade point average of 3.5 or above.

Katie Keough had expected to join Jake in that company and to receive a round of applause for being in the National Honor Society. But there'd been a mix-up with her ticket, she had a ton of work to do crashing out a final group project for Advanced Placement Literature and Composition, and she was a die-hard vegetarian. So she'd passed on the Kentucky Fried Chicken served in the gym. Nick's name would also be called, as one of the school's four National Merit Commended Scholars—not that he planned to be there to respond. Having received no honors, Justin, who nonetheless believed that he deserved recognition—although he could never quite put his finger on why—had made other plans.

The next afternoon, he and Jake were due to drive up to the senior party, the location of which had been kept a well-protected secret. Everyone had been told that if they showed up at four P.M. in the parking lot at Dakotah Sports and Fitness, the gym and ice rink on the reservation, they'd be given maps to their final destination. Nick wasn't going. Even if he'd been tempted, he was broke and scheduled to work at the County Market. And Katie, well, Katie had already been to one drunken brawl that spring, and that was about all she needed for "at least another year or so."

School was almost out, and the Culture Club was splitting up, spreading out in four different geographical directions. Nick, the most desperate to get at least three thousand miles away from Prior Lake, was headed to the University of Minnesota in the fall, trapped near home by his finances. After months of agonizing, Jake had sent his deposit in to Boston University, although his friends still joked that, knowing Jake, who was perpetually unable to make up his mind, he might still be undecided.

Katie felt trapped by her college choices. Attracted to the possibility of close, personal relationships with her teachers, and urged by her parents to stay near home and get a Catholic education, she'd searched for a small, private Catholic school in the Midwest with a decent social work program. She'd narrowed her choices down to Clarke College in Dubuque, Iowa or Edgewood College in Madison, Wisconsin. By the time she'd received her acceptance letters, however, she hated the idea of being at a small school and couldn't have cared less about its religious affiliation, nor whether it was public or private. By then, of course, it was too late.

Her college problems weren't fodder for the Culture Club, but for conversations with her friend Jenny Reagan, who shared her conundrum.

Jenny and Katie looked like polar opposites. With a streak of electric-pink hair framing her face, and a high, soft voice, Katie looked wispy, an impression belied by a steely strength she had yet to understand. Jenny was all substance, with an intentionality to her mien that projected woman, not girl. She'd stopped "hanging out" in the ninth grade, ceased going to parties and trying to fit in. "I always felt I was different," she said, more puzzled than proud. "I'm not a chameleon. I don't compromise what I think." She was widely viewed as untouchable.

Jenny dreamed of singing opera, although she'd never seen a live performance. But the exactitude and rigor of opera tugged at her, and she trained with a private teacher, spent summers in vocal camps and breathed music even while she worked the appointments desk at HairMate, a Prior Lake beauty salon. Like most of her friends, Jenny had conducted a pretty blind search for a college. She knew she wanted to study music and that she didn't necessarily want to stay near home. But she was inundated with mail from schools she'd never heard of, and had no one to guide her. Her teachers sent her to the Career Center, which she found useless. The advice from counselors and other adults was pretty much confined to "Well, St. Thomas is a good school," or "So-and-so goes to Mankato and likes it." But no one really knew much about schools outside of what she called "the box" of Minnesota.

The University of Puget Sound had piqued her interest; she thought it might be an open environment with a vibrant opera community. But when she finally visited, she'd hated the campus, the city and the people. So she wound up with her "safe" school, Luther College in Iowa. "A pretty sorry way to choose a four-year learning atmosphere, I know, but I don't think that I'm the only one," she said.

The choir's trip to New York in February had been Jenny's epiphany. Walking the streets of the city, she had inhaled the energy. This is it, this is where I want to be, this is where I *need* to be, she told herself. During the group's tour of Lincoln Center, their guide had invited the aspiring singers to test out the acoustics on the stage of the Metropolitan Opera House. Jenny alone accepted the invitation. When she stood center stage, where Renee Fleming sang regularly, she blocked out her friends, her teachers, her guide. "I needed to be alone, to feel that moment," she said. Then she opened her mouth and belted out a piece of her favorite Italian aria.

Jenny's friends had snapped her photograph as she stood smack in the middle of Times Square, her scarf blowing in a frigid wind, so that she wouldn't forget. "I want to be bold, self-confident," she said, terrified that, like most people she knew, she would settle for less.

At the end of her senior year, Jenny was exhausted. She'd maintained a 3.8 GPA, sung in the student jazz ensemble, worked as president of the concert choir and kept up with CLASS and peer counseling. Outside of school, she was heavily involved in Catholic youth activities, as a group leader and a Eucharistic minister. In her free time, she tried to keep up with seven courses, including two advanced placement classes taught on a college level. "If I do my homework, I'm lucky to get six hours of sleep a night," she said.

"I thought I would be wasting my time if I didn't do all these things," she explained, the child of a world in which being busy conferred status. "Now I know it was too many activities, too many titles. What does it all mean? Yet I missed so much. I always wanted to go to a rave, but I felt that I couldn't because I was in CLASS. I never had time, time to . . . I don't know what. Maybe just to sleep, maybe to have real quality conversation. But I was always too busy."

In that lull between late lunchers and the dinner crowd, Perkins was mostly empty. Waitresses topped off the ketchup and salt, chatted with customers or caught a quick cigarette out back. The Culture Club had the place to themselves. As college hopes and fears flitted across the table, Justin played with his napkin and looked out the window. He never talked much about college.

Having racked up a record number of absences, he was still playing chicken with the administration, daring them to withhold the diploma of a gifted kid who'd placed 108th out of a field of fifteen thousand students nationwide in the WordMasters Challenge, a national reading analysis competition. He cut class to go turkey hunting with his father, to meander through the woods, or to sleep. By mid-May, he had missed nineteen days of the trimester and had three *F*s going into the final weeks of school. With no leeway to fail even one course, he'd negotiated a deal with his First Aid teacher about the three tests and ten worksheets he'd missed: if he completed the exams, one worksheet and all the final assignments, he would pass the class. He was skating by in Age of Majority, which he'd already flunked once, but he was in trouble in English 11, another repeat, because he'd missed a spelling test, as well as the deadline for making it up. He owed Carol Ottoson two journals on books he still hadn't read for English, and getting through Government was still touch-and-go.

"How do I handle you?" John Bennett, his counselor, had asked him. "I don't know, that's your job," Justin had replied. "It's my job to get in trouble. It's your job to fix it."

Things weren't much better at home. During the second trimester, Justin had brought home two *F*s, one *D*, a *C* and a single *A*, in band. His parents had hit the roof. When he followed up that insult by breaking curfew, his father took away the keys to his car. Furious, Justin stormed into his bedroom. His clothes were piled up on his bed, a clear invitation to leave. Once his parents fell asleep, he stole back his keys, threw all the things that were important to his "interior life" into his car and drove off.

"I love my parents, but it's not working out for me to live with them," he'd said. He needed time, he insisted, time and space to sort himself out. For ten days, Justin had been a vagabond, sleeping at Drew's, hanging out at Jake's, eating at Justin's, at Brad's, at Eric's. Finally, he'd slinked home. "I had to," he'd explained. "You need a place to go for down time, and I couldn't support myself."

After avoiding all thinking about college during the fall, Justin had finally started looking for some place—any place—that might be willing to admit a chronic underachiever. A list of colleges that admitted 100 percent of applicants, downloaded from the Internet, had included the University of Montana. The campus had disappointed him, but Justin announced that he planned to move to Missoula in the fall.

Nick, Jake and Katie were skeptical that he'd leave, despite Justin's insistence that he was desperate to strike out on his own. He had more than a little Peter Pan to him, as did most of their other classmates. In their parents' generation, teenagers had counted down the days until they could move out of the house, run off to college, throw futons on the floor of their own apartments. Loading up the VW Bug and driving across the country was the rite of passage of hundreds of thousands of American eighteen-year-olds.

But freedom and independence were the watchwords of a different generation. In Prior Lake, the seniors were ticking off the days until they finished high school, but abandoning the familiar for anonymity and uncertainty, the comfort of childhood for the perils of adulthood, was a different matter.

The four students gathered at Perkins had just attended their final Synergy meeting, where adulthood had been the topic of discussion.

"I want to stay a kid," Lisa Gilbert had said. "I don't feel any need to hurry up and become a grown-up. Everyone talks about 'starting my life.' I already have a life."

"My problem is that I don't want to grow up but I don't want to be treated like a kid," said Katie Cook. "Does that make sense? I guess I want it both ways, huh? It's just that I don't want to be my parents and, to me, that's what it means to be a grown-up."

For Katie Keough, the difficulty was that being an adult seemed to mean leaving behind all her hope and imagination. "Almost every adult I have ever met has told me that I am too naive and too much of a dreamer for the 'real world,'" she said. "That scares me. It scares me a lot. I don't EVER want to be the wife who works, cooks, cleans the house, takes the kids to daycare, watches the soccer games and gossips to the other moms about extravagant vacation plans and how they can't wait to get their kids out of the house, and tries to please her husband while talking to others about all his annoying problems.

"We are always told to enjoy the high school and college years because they are the greatest of our lives. With this idea instilled in our minds, why would we ever look forward to the future our elders have predicted for us?"

Growing up wasn't a distasteful prospect just to Lisa and the Katies. Adulthood seemed to be a decidedly unappealing concept among students of every social group, every social class, every background. Andy Ottoson suspected that the shift in outlook of suburban youth reflected the change in the nature of childhood as much as a collective distaste for the lives of their parents. "As children, we are put on a throne," he said. "We are given the divine right to do as we please—play video games instead of taking music lessons, masturbate instead of doing homework, get ploughed with friends instead of spending quality time with the family. We can do all this, provided we get passing grades and go to college, then get a diploma, AND THEN start to do something with our lives. Essentially, we are given a twenty-two-year vacation.

"So, if we're sitting home hung over and playing Nintendo while wanking, who's making the change in the world? Ah, that'd be the adults. Between the ages of twenty-two and sixty-five, you have to actually do stuff.

"So, given our choice (wanking vs. working), it's not much of a wonder that adulthood is not necessarily considered as divine as it once was. Why would we give up being waited on and allowed to slide by, and instead enter a world where we can try our hardest and get nowhere while the lucky ones suddenly become our bosses?"

Chapter Nineteen

3 P.M., Tuesday,
June 6, 2000

Not a single member of the Class of 2000 of Prior Lake High School aspired to become Craig Olson, or to become Dr. O, the principal. Scores of wannabe teachers and lawyers, engineers and social workers, athletes, writers, computer programmers, musicians and businessmen were about to don their caps and gowns. But not one wrote "high school principal" on his or her career-wish inventory.

Maybe nobody dreams of becoming a principal. Maybe principals are made, not born—which would hardly be surprising. If there was ever a maligned profession in need of a public relations makeover, it is principalship. Think about *Rock'N' Roll High School*'s evil, music-hating principal, Miss Toger, or Evelyn Doyle, who ruled *High School High* with the aplomb of Benito Mussolini. If they're not autocrats, they're bumbling idiots, like Principal Warneke in *Blackboard Jungle*, who had trouble admitting that the school had discipline problems, or Principal Flutie of *Buffy the Vampire Slayer*'s Sunnydale High, who tried to be friends with the kids and was eaten by hyena-possessed students.

"My predecessor, Mr. Flutie, may have gone in for all that touchy-feely relating nonsense," his replacement, Principal Snyder, announced. "You're in my world now. And Sunnydale has touched and felt for the last time. A lot of educators tell students, 'Think of your principal as your pal.' I say, 'Think of me as your judge, jury and executioner.'"

Craig Olson was neither a bumblingly clueless Warneke nor a fascist like Snyder. Pale, thin and all angles, he was the type of man who disappeared in crowds with stoop-shouldered reticence. His wispy hair managed to lie flat on the sides and in the back, but it defied gravity on top of his head. He was the school intellectual, a philosopher who would have been glad to dispense wisdom—if anyone had ever bothered to ask him.

The few who did were taken aback by his candor. Several years earlier, the mother of a chronic cutter, a boy with 0.8 GPA but high test scores, had lamented to Olson that she couldn't get her son to go to school. "I can," Olson answered quietly. The next morning, he appeared at her door and walked into "the incredibly messy room" where the young man lay in bed. "Do you want it hot or cold?" asked Olson, assuming that the still form was, in fact, awake. Eliciting no response, Olson sent the mother for a spaghetti pot, filled it with lukewarm water and poured it over the boy's head. The student got out of bed, threw on some clothes and went to school. "I can't do that," the mother whimpered. "Well," responded Olson, "I only do this once, but this is how it's done."

At Prior Lake, Olson served more as the mayor of a small town than as the commandant of a POW camp, although he joked that he wanted a sign in office reading, "This Is Not a Democracy. This Is a Benevolent Dictatorship." But, ultimately, he lacked any inclination to dictatorship, no matter how benevolent. "I have three emotions," he explained, "anger, amusement and, at times, amorousness." The second reigned over Prior Lake High School.

Although he hid them well, Olson suffered from crippling headaches, and none of the nerves firing in his brain was ignited by the myriad educational crises politicians were talking about. Overcrowding, the teacher shortage and class size might have been serious problems in urban schools. But in suburbia, at least in Olson's corner of it, the headache provokers were less amenable to easy political rhetoric.

What do you do with the school's most notorious cheater, a young man under relentless parental pressure to bring home straight *A*s, but so inept at plagiarism that he'd become the joke of the school? Carol Ottoson had flunked a boy for submitting a paper copied off the Internet. His father, however, had stormed into Olson's office, protesting that the document had been downloaded as a "resource," and threatened to carry the case to the U.S. Supreme Court.

How do you handle the girl who asked for a schedule change so that she could start her part-time job before the end of the school day? Olson had denied the request, but the girl had kept nagging. "If I go to work earlier, I can get home earlier to study," she pleaded. The answer was still no. "Please, Dr. O." No. "That's so unfair, Dr. O." No. "But I need the money, Dr. O." No. "Are you getting annoyed with me, Dr. O?" No. Olson laughed at that point in his telling of the story. "I had to say no, she was testing me," he explained. "She was hoping I would say yes."

Olson informed her that he would change her schedule only if her employer certified that his business would collapse without her early presence. "He'll say that," the girl replied. "Where do you work?" Olson asked. "Victoria's Secret." The girl was right, the employer penned her the requisite letter.

How do you cope with the state's requirement that you bar from class any student whose parents had not sent in proof of current vaccinations or boosters against measles, mumps, rubella, polio, diphtheria, tetanus and pertussis? Every year, Olson was expected to fill out the state's forms certifying his compliance. Every year, he mailed back those forms, along with a letter explaining that it would be much more sensible to set up an electronic recording system through the public health offices and that he had not worried overmuch about diphtheria, tetanus, pertussis or polio, but had insured that all students were vaccinated against infectious agents that could lead to actual epidemics.

How do you deal with teachers who complained and complained and complained but refused to enforce school rules? "We've failed to teach things that we can teach, like punctuality. But how do we do it if the staff won't cooperate? They all agree. No staff member would say it's a nonissue. But they won't enforce the rules."

How do you run a school when everyone around you abdicates responsibility? "I know how to deal with a lot of the problems that everyone says are so intractable. The question is: Is there really support for the solutions?

"Take drinking. Just look at Europe. If we approached alcohol the ways the Europeans do, we wouldn't have this teen drinking problem. But I can't get rid of the rules, the culture that has created the problem. All I can do is to try to clean up the mess that it breeds.

"I know that teachers are frustrated with me over field trips because they're not sure that they justify all the confusion that they cause with all these kids missing other classes. But I believe in experiential education. It's important. I could solve the teachers' problem if we weren't stuck with a school year starting on September 5 and ending on June 9th. But I have no power over that kind of change."

Or consider grade inflation. Olson had just had a conversation with a teacher about his philosophy of grading, "which was that the kid gets an A unless he doesn't do certain things, at which point he starts subtracting," Olson explained. "And I asked, 'Well, if you're going to do it that way, how come you're starting with an A? Shouldn't that be something that they should aspire to attain by doing things above and beyond your minimum expectations?' The honest response was, 'You know, I never thought about it that way before.' And this person isn't a bad or incompetent teacher. It's just that he kind of figured that if you do everything that I tell you to do, then you get an A. That's probably not become the prevalent view, but it's certainly a popular one, that getting something less than an A is the extent to which you fail to do everything expected of you."

Olson understood that grade inflation had created such low expectations that some kids graduated with dangerously overinflated visions of their own abilities, while most were never pushed to discover how far they could go. In their exit interviews with the staff, the seniors had acknowledged that the school needed to be tougher. "They admitted they'd have fought us every step of the way, but they said, 'We don't respect you unless we think you set high expectations for us.' So the kids are basically telling us that it's contemptuous not to expect them to do a lot more.

"But I don't think the grade inflation issue can be addressed until the issue that caused it is addressed, and that's public opinion of education. We give kids higher grades so that we can avoid being criticized for not doing a good job teaching. I have never received, and I will never receive before I retire, a phone call from a parent saying, 'Please explain why my kid is getting straight As and can't do these things.' Or a phone call from a parent who thought that we gave a kid something more than he deserved. If we send every kid home with straight As, our stock goes up in the community because people say, 'Aha, they tell me my kid's doing great.' But, as it is, we give kids good grades if they're basically nice, appear to have decent attitudes, are getting their work done.

"The challenge is—and I've had this discussion with some of our new teachers—that they were raised in an era of grade inflation. It started in the late '70s. I'm looking at college kids' transcripts right now and I've hired some of these people who got 3.8s in their colleges, and they wouldn't have gotten a 3.8 where I went to college because they don't know much. And that doesn't make it easy to raise standards.

"I keep wondering who even wants us to fight this battle. There are a few folks with integrity who don't want to stop fighting it, but I'm not sure how many. If things are going to change, parents need to start communicating to schools that what they expect us to evaluate students for—if that's what we really want—is the quality of their work and how much they learned and not what, in all honesty, we are grading them for now, which is obedience and fulfilling teachers' expectations."

The teacher problem—salaries, shortage and classroom size—were, quite simply, not major issues in Olson's universe. "Yeah, we might get better if we doubled the number of teachers, but the new ones would have to be just as good as the ones we've got or I'm not sure we'd improve."

And teacher pay? "We shouldn't simply pay you more because you've been here longer or because you've taken more courses. We need other reasons for justifying a bigger gap, such as if we paid more to really polished, extraordinary teachers who do a marvelous job of educating kids and getting as much out of them as they possibly can under the circumstances.

There ought to be a financial reward, if that's what would matter to them, although in most cases I don't think it would matter that much. Of the hardest working teachers we've got here, those who put in ungodly amounts of time, not a one of them would do more for more money. And I don't think too many of the people who don't do as much as they do would either."

Mostly, Olson worried more about how much time he spent every day, every year, trying to fit square pegs into round holes, forcing kids who had no interest in learning to sit behind desks for seven hours. "Some kids refuse to be educated," he said. "People don't realize that we're just baby-sitters half the time, but that's what compulsory attendance breeds."

In the evenings, he fantasized about what teachers could do if they didn't have to shoehorn every type of knowledge into a standardized forty-seven minute class period. "The biggest problem with curriculum isn't with what it is, but how we present it. I mean everything that you teach people doesn't logically break up into forty-seven-minute increments for nine months or for twelve weeks." Many teachers and board members agreed, and had become enamored of a new fad, block scheduling, that gave students fewer courses, but longer classes. "We spent two years looking at it but I saw what I was sure I was going to see, which was that every class turns into forty-five minutes of instruction followed by a study hall. Kids will love it because they won't have any homework. But will they learn more? I didn't think so."

Olson harbored few illusions about his ability to reshape American education, although he had some pretty firm ideas on the topic. Even as he and his staff stumbled through, he dedicated more than a passing moment to what the education revolution might look like. He talked like a realist, but the realist was a front for a dreamer. "There are pieces of this that I don't have the slightest idea how to improve in any really meaningful way," Olson said. "But most of the pieces aren't hard. It just takes the will."

Olson's central proposal—a formal, written proposal that he'd sent to every relevant party in the state of Minnesota, to little response—was a revamping of the school calendar to move away from the agrarian model that developed back when families need kids to help plant the fields. "That model makes no sense anymore, we need year-round schooling, period."

In Olson's view, the current school calendar flunks on all counts: It leaves failing students with no time for remediation, which occurs over the summer. It exhausts both teachers and students, turning the final month of school into a sheer waste of energy. Then students have such long breaks that they lose half of what they learned during the year. Finally, it creates no opportunity for study that does not fit into a tidy forty-seven-minute curricular box.

Olson's design for a new calendar would create three sixty-day trimesters separated by three six-week breaks. During the breaks, students in trouble would have time for intensive remediation, staff would attend workshops or develop new curricular materials and students could sign up for special one- or two-week intensive courses in language, field biology or travel abroad— Olson's "experiential education."

Someone else knocked on Olson's door. Especially in the days just before graduation, someone was always knocking on his door. There was no time to think, no time to plan, no time to concentrate. In the end, running a high school was an exercise in crisis management. Boynton, who played mom to Olson's Pop, handled much of the petty disciplinary load—the T-shirt, short-skirt, too-many-tardies and too-much-exuberance problems. But many students preferred Olson's bemused ramblings to Boynton's overt hectoring. The students thought of him as an old hippie, a "'60s kinda guy," although they were puzzled when they ran into him at Nine Inch Nails or Ice-T concerts. They didn't know that he was as likely to go to hear Bruce Springsteen or Patti Smith.

Olson did not deceive himself that year-round schooling would be a panacea for America's educational woes. In Olson's "ideal educational environment," he wouldn't have to waste time monitoring students' clothes, or creating punishments like ISS for latecomers or class cutters. "It wouldn't be an issue that would affect us because kids would be here voluntarily. That's an area where there's probably one of the biggest gaps between the way I would do things if it were completely up to me and the way you have no choice but to do them.

"So, in a perfect world, we wouldn't spend two seconds on what people looked like, what they wore. We wouldn't deal with attendance at all because kids would not have to be here and if they didn't want to be here, that's OK. 'Don't come. I'm not going to tell you whether your attendance is satisfactory as far as I'm concerned because you're the one who's getting something out of being here.'

"In a perfect world, we'd never be baby-sitters, parents wouldn't facilitate their kids cheating and the English department wouldn't run out of supply money and have to run to the student council to bail them out.

"Unfortunately, I'm not a principal in a perfect world."

Chapter Twenty

6:35 P.M., Friday, June 9, 2000

Roger Murphy arrived early, his bemused grin suggesting that even he recognized the minor miracle. For months, he'd never appeared on campus without his signature hooded sweatshirt, but, in recognition of the special occasion, he had uncloaked that afternoon. Roger was still Roger, the backs of both hands painted with fat Xs, a chain around his neck. His green fatigue pants were still folded inside his combat boots, which were held together, as usual, with silver duct tape. But his head had been crisply shorn of his long dreadlocks, and he was wearing the kind of short-sleeved white shirt, blue sweater vest and conservative tie that Mike Carr might have donned.

But no matter the hour or his attire, Roger was adamant about not being excited. "Everyone graduates from high school at some point in time," he said, perched on the edge of one of the blue metal picnic tables embedded in the concrete in front of the cafeteria entrance in a pose meant to convey a blasé demeanor. "It's nothing to be excited about. You have to stop being sheltered sometime. The best part is not having to get up at six A.M. anymore, that that obligation is done. But it's not like this is college graduation."

During the last month of school, Roger had joined Olson, Boynton and the head of the Art department in interviews of candidates for a new faculty position, and had looked almost at home on the search committee, assessing candidates' qualifications, critiquing their art work, discussing their plans for "regulating students." He'd even surprised himself with how frequently he had agreed with the principal. He had begun preparing to take the ACTs and to put together his application portfolio for the Minneapolis College of Art and Design. "A year ago, I thought I'd be dead by now," he said. "The day before I hit eighteen, I thought I'd be dead. Now I just know that I don't want to be another corporate tool."

Only an *F* in Individual Sports had blemished his final months. "We weren't allowed to be individuals and the sports were pointless," Roger said. "We played Ping-Pong, archery, golf, pickle ball, but always as teams, always with collective scores. What's individual about that? And the teacher wanted us to pay $16 to play golf, or to write a report on golf. My family doesn't drive a Lexus. And a report on golf? Tell me how that could possibly be worth my while?" He'd spend part of the summer, then, making up that last credit.

Sauntering up behind Roger, Pete Williams looked around at the growing throng of students that he'd derided for a decade. "I'd rather be in the ninth circle of hell," he announced laconically. "Oh, wait, I already am." Pete's wife, Hillary, was already seated in the bleachers with their newborn, Damon. Finding the stress of pregnancy, work and school too much, she had dropped out of the regional high school for pregnant teens, insisting that she planned to take the GED exams. Pete—Mr. Capitalism-Is-Evil-Conformity-Is-Hell—had finished up at an alternative high school and astounded everyone by enlisting in the Marine Corps. "I have a family now, responsibility," he said shyly.

Jayne Garrison joined her friends, Roger and Pete, Anna Bican and Nick Olson, the usual gang. "Is it bad that I don't know half the people here?" she asked, beaming. She'd been beaming for the month since she and Randy, who had broken up during the first trimester but had remained joined at the hip all year, had decided to get married. Randy still had another year of high school, and her mother despised him. Undeterred, Jayne was making wedding plans.

"So, you passed Phy Ed?" Nick Olson asked. Jayne had suffered through Individual Sports with Roger but had managed to squeak through with a D–. "Well, hell has frozen over," Nick responded to Jayne's good news, then leaned into Anna and squeezed her shoulder. The two had been inseparable for weeks, knowing that in the fall, they'd be thousands of miles apart. Nick had enrolled at Gustavus Adolphus College in St. Peter, Minnesota, while Anna had agreed to travel with the Renaissance Festival to Las Vegas.

Jayne's face relaxed from sassiness into a touch of gravity. In her leopard-print miniskirt and high black boots, she looked positively girlish. No half-gloves, dog collar or multicolored spikes. "I know I've always said that I hate this place, but I'm a little scared to leave. I've always been protected here. I've never had to make a decision on my own. Like, 'Who will I be if I'm not a Prior Lake High School Student?'"

Scott Vig slid off the seat of his enormous pickup truck and strolled slowly toward the swelling mob. He looked like he hadn't slept for days, which was close to the truth. On Tuesday, the seniors' last day of school, he had driven up to northern Minnesota early, hauling fifteen kegs of beer in his trailer, to prepare for the senior party. After the 1998 debacle, the seniors had avoided Wisconsin, and Scott's friend Jon Fox, the perennial class party-planner, had spent weeks looking for the ideal remote site for the Class of 2000 finale and a way to conceal its location from overcurious administrators. If students knew the location in advance, someone would inevitably blab to Boynton or Mary Haugen, or talk in front of a parent, who would then call the school. So Jon had spread the word that interested seniors should meet in the parking lot at Dakotah Sport and Fitness center on the reservation for final instructions.

They'd arrived in droves, in Blazers, old Camaros, pumped-up muscle trucks, dying Ford Escorts and one shiny red Chrysler Sebring convertible. Waiting for Jon, the seniors had looked more nervous than thrilled, as if the prospect of partying with kids they had never considered sharing a beer with had thrown them off balance. When Josh Albright ambled into the mix, consternation lit scores of faces. One boy actually voiced his astonishment, directly in Josh's face. "Class valedictorian, eh?" he remarked, a hint of mockery in his voice. "It's my senior year, too, you got a problem with that?" replied Josh, stepping close to the boy, a challenge hanging in the air.

Their destination was Outing, Minnesota, a small town way up north, 185 miles away. The setup there was far from ideal. Jon had hoped for a lake and a "legal" location. Outing provided neither. But the site was remote, there was no doubt about that, and there was plenty of state land they could flee to. Best of all, not a single member of the Prior Lake High School staff knew where they were going.

That was a good thing, because what the students had contrived in a clearing in the woods was a scene of utter debauchery, an invitation to oblivion: keg after keg of beer, bottle upon bottle of vodka, enough bricks of pot to build a small house and bulging bags of precious Kine bud, the pot-smoker's delicacy. As rap and rock blared from speakers powered by Scott's camper, the students danced and ate and remembered and forgot, finding contraptions and contortions to help them guzzle the alcohol as quickly and as copiously as possible. They passed beer bongs, funnel-rigged hoses that rushed the brew down their throats. At the keg stands, their friends helped hold them upside down so they could wrap their lips around an open tap and suck in the beer until they needed to come up for air. Matt Kelly lasted thirty-eight seconds. Ben Selinske managed only thirty-four.

It was boundless and heedless and Jake Anderson, worried about his friends, checked his own consumption and held a lonely vigil over his pal Luigi, who had passed out after an inverted turn at the tap. Jake watched him until he stirred, then listened hard to make out the first slurred words from Luigi's mouth.

"Give me another beer, man," Luigi said.

Just after noon the next day, the Department of Natural Resources police roused the semicomatose gathering and ordered the kids to move on. By then, almost everyone was so burnt that they were ready to leave. When the sheriff confiscated the beer, without Breathalyzing anyone, the party petered out, and the long trek home began.

The juniors had had less luck. They'd fooled the school about their party plans by leaving an anonymous note on Boynton's desk, ratting out their own location as a campground in southern Minnesota. But they still were nabbed by the police. Their chosen party site was on land in Wisconsin that belonged to the grandmother of the fiancé of the sister of one of their classmates. Since the fiancé had directed the kids to the property, the juniors hadn't considered that they were actually trespassing. But the neighbors, alerted by the noise, and the grandmother, did.

By graduation morning, Boynton and Olson had heard rumors of seventy, eighty, up to ninety-one arrests, including team captains and student council members; two students were still in jail. "God, is next year's class going to be even more trouble?" Boynton sighed as she looked out over the senior party crew and tried to imagine a worse case scenario.

Her head down, her expression almost downtrodden, Ashlee Altenbach trudged into the fray, joining Tina Farrell and Tana Sappington. "I can't believe it, I missed the senior party," she whimpered to a group joking about the keg stand competition. En route to the Dakotah parking lot the day of the party, Ashlee had stopped to check in with her parole officer, a three-times-a-week requirement after her sentencing on the theft charge. She'd been in a festive mood, her car packed and ready for two days of drinking and dancing in the woods.

"You look a little glassy-eyed," the parole officer had commented, probing. Ashlee had squinted her eyes, an expression calculated to convey exhaustion. "I'm just really tired," she said. The truth was that she'd smoked a bowl of pot on her way to his office. The parole officer had dealt with enough stoned teenagers to see through Ashlee's melodrama and ordered a search of her car. When the police found an ounce of pot, she'd been cuffed and kept in a holding cell for twenty-two hours without food or a phone call. Unable to lift any fingerprints from the plastic bag, however, the police had released her. By then, of course, the party was winding down.

"God, isn't this great, isn't this exciting." She suddenly changed gears. Ashlee, whose diagnosis with Attention Deficit Disorder had provided her a bottomless—and guiltless—excuse to indulge her flakiness, could not restrain herself. She never could. "Irrepressible" came to mind. That skirmish with the law, like the last skirmish with the law and a dozen confrontations with her parents, evaporated in her emotion of the moment.

They arrived in twos and threes, their parents posing them against the backdrop of the "Congratulations Class of 2000" marquee above the entrance to the cafeteria. Eric Prchal, Tony Lorenz and Jordan Culver helped adjust each other's hats. Tony's old friend Shannon McGinnis snuck up behind him, a quick shared glance heavy with sadness, as if to say, "We're not going to be able to do this much anymore, huh?" Shannon was off to the University of Minnesota in the fall, while Tony was due to leave for Marine Corps boot camp at the end of August. Unable to imagine life without her boyfriend, Lyndsay had briefly indulged a fantasy about following him, about life as a military wife. But accustomed to a capacious home, a boat and regular vacations, she'd quickly disabused herself of that chimera.

Eric, however, was more chilled by Tony's enlistment, not so much by his departure, but by the prospect of his being sent into a war zone. "I try not to think about it, but am I supposed to feel confident that he won't get sent off to fight a war?" asked Eric. "I don't trust the government that much."

Over by the picnic tables, Justin Jorgenson watched as Jake Anderson draped the gold cord worn by Board Scholars over his gown, a hint of envy fleetingly distorting his face. "I guess they're gonna let me do it," he said, laughing. "I'm gonna walk." His gown was waving in the wind behind him. The sole was still flapping on his heavy boots with the silver hoop.

Justin had taken it down to the wire. The Saturday before graduation, he'd been forced to attend Saturday School, a half-day exercise in boredom and "community service" for students with too many days of ISS to serve. For the first two hours, he and two dozen other kids had sat in a windowless classroom, prohibited from talking or reading anything "enjoyable." For the remainder of the morning, they'd picked up trash outside the school, or cleaned up underneath the bleachers. That awful morning hadn't been the last of his punishments. John Bennett, his advisor, had been blunt: complete your detention or you won't graduate. So Justin had spent the hours before graduation serving his time.

When Travis Reddinger entered the throng of students waving their mortarboards against the late afternoon heat, the waters parted. Changes in the color of Travis' spiked hair were so frequent as to merit zero attention. But, for this special occasion, he'd not only dyed his hair fire-engine red; he'd punched a dozen holes through his mortarboard to make room for the spikes. It wasn't that Travis refused to go spikeless; he frequently combed his hair down around his ears. But Lori Boynton had ticked him off with her instructions about graduation "attire," and he wanted to perform one final act of nose-thumbing.

"Graduates must wear proper attire for the commencement ceremonies in order to participate," she'd written in a letter sent home to all seniors. "[D]ress shoes, dresses or blouses and skirts for girls; sport or dress shirt, slacks, shoes and socks for boys. Shorts and tennis shoes are not acceptable dress for this occasion. Sunglasses may be worn once seated outside but best not to be worn in the processional . . . You will be removed from the ceremony if proper attire is not worn."

Boynton had been trying to avoid the sort of fracas that had erupted at Wayzata High School when all the senior girls decided to wear bikinis under their robes. But Travis didn't give a damn what disaster she was trying to contain. The morning after he received her letter, he'd stormed into her office. "What do you mean by dress shoes?" he demanded. "I always wear boots and I'm not gonna buy special shoes I'll never wear again for graduation." By setting different standards for girls and boys, he continued, the regulations reeked of sexism. "If boys can wear pants, you can't tell girls they can't wear pants, that's ridiculous. And why do you want us to dress up like it's a funeral? It's our graduation." Boynton tried to argue, although, with the sexism comment, Travis had nailed her in a personal weak spot. "It's not just your graduation," she responded. "It's the school's, your parents', even your grandparents' graduation, too."

"No, it's not," Travis fumed. "My grandparents are not graduating from high school."

Boynton had relented, requesting only that students not wear shorts or blue jeans. Travis, however, had gotten the last laugh.

Outside, latecomers, who had to park across the street at the middle school, scurried to join the graduating class, glancing at their watches. Inside, the school was perfectly still. At the end of the year, teachers were instructed to clean out their rooms, as if they were not coming back. So Lynn Lally had stowed Elvis away for the summer and Carr had pulled down his most cherished souvenir, an 8-by-10 flyer that Tony and Eric had plastered all over school after the student-teacher basketball tournament ended with the boys' 4–3 victory. Under a photograph of Carr, the text read: "Male in mid-20s. Has no basketball skills whatsoever. Lost to a couple of high school kids in a pick-up game. Looking for female not afraid to date a loser."

Watching his students gather for the last time, unlike most of his colleagues, Carr wasn't remotely wistful. Other than the basketball tournament with Eric and Tony, his one fond memory of the year was the moment most students considered his greatest humiliation, his dance floor performance at the SnoBall. Working as a chaperone, Carr had endured an hour of "Come on, Mr. Carr, dance with us," "Mr. Carr, you can dance, can't you?" When the DJ began spinning *I'm Too Sexy*, Carr had lost control. Racing into the dimly lit gym from his post in the brightly lit cafeteria, a dark look of concentration furling his brow, he planted himself in front of the speakers to show the kids what the moves really looked like.

I'm a model, you know what I mean/And I do my little turn on the catwalk/Yeah on the catwalk, on the catwalk yeah/I shake shake my little tush on the catwalk. Squatting low to the floor, he moved like a chicken pawing the ground in a barnyard to the chanting of Right Said Fred. Dressed in dark trousers, a white shirt, tie, and jacket, first Carr pulled off his jacket, followed by his tie, which he swung through the air like a stripper. *I'm too sexy for this shirt/Too sexy for this shirt/So sexy it hurts.*

A solid circle of students surrounded him, cheering him on. "Come on, Mr. Carr, take it off," girls screamed, as he opened the top buttons of his dress shirt. "He must be drunk," one boy said. "Nah, I don't think so," another replied. "That's just Mr. Carr." As Carr continued his unwitting imitation of the dance steps immortalized by Elaine Benes of *Seinfeld* fame, the crowd went wild. His roommate, Nate "Boots" LeBoutillier, fled the scene, either in consternation or humiliation. When the music ended, Carr reappeared at his side, a thin sheen of sweat filming his forehead, panting heavily. "Boots, you should've seen me, I was awesome," he said. He'd paid for that performance for six months.

Carr wasn't sure how he felt about returning to Prior Lake in September, to another year of students who wouldn't listen and teachers who didn't teach. "I've been through hell the last month," he said, walking toward the field to join the small klatsch of teachers who showed up at graduation. Roger spotted him in the crush and smiled. "Hey, Slick," he yelled for the final time. Carr still loathed being called Slick, but he had a soft spot for Roger, his one clear triumph of the year.

Two thousand parents and grandparents, brothers and sisters, aunts, uncles, family friends and cousins streamed toward the bleachers above the football field. Tickets, six per graduate, were a hot commodity in a town where graduation was the social affair of the season. The school board had toyed with the idea of remedying the space crunch, and the recurring problems of rain or heat, by moving the ceremony to a different venue, to the Target Center downtown or to a high school with a large auditorium. Move graduation off Laker Field? the community had responded in a single voice. But it's *tradition*.

By 7:30 P.M., the class had turned quiet, their excitement transformed into seriousness overlaid with an ether of sadness and pride. Boynton and Olson herded them along for the final time, ordering them to line up in alphabetical pairs, as they'd been instructed in practice that morning. For most of the school's history, Prior Lake graduates had not marched in alphabetical order; they'd chosen their own companions for the processional. But every year, that custom had disintegrated into a hassle, as couples broke up and demanded new partners, as three close friends insisted on marching as a trio. Boynton had bided her time, waiting for a malleable group of kids. When 1999 came, she had manipulated them into imposing a new order.

That morning, she'd carefully rehearsed the graduates, marching them out onto the field, yelling, "Please maintain equal spacing . . . don't bunch up . . . don't walk past your seats." While she instructed them in how to accept their diplomas—"Take it with your left hand and shake hands with your right"—Eric Prchal was on his cell phone arranging for a 12:30 tee time at the Wilds golf course. "Don't forget to stand through the national anthem," she continued, "and please, please, dress appropriately." By then, Scott Vig had curled up on the grass asleep.

Boynton was reeling. She and the senior secretary had been at school until ten P.M. the night before preparing the programs. And although the sun was low in the sky, the evening was a scorcher, one of those breathless, Midwestern summer nights that feel like the tropics, but without the breeze. Those last days had brought Boynton one concluding moment of ugliness: a particularly raw piece of graffiti was scrawled in the laundry room of an apartment complex in downtown Prior Lake, a crudely drawn caricature of Boynton with enormous breasts and a penis showed her sodomizing Goldy. The message below it read: "Wanted Poster—Dead or In Bed—Ms. Big Boynton."

She'd made it through, but, by the time she'd lined the seniors up, she was staggering. Led by the superintendent, Olson, members of the school board, and their own class officers, the graduates proceeded through the stadium entrance and down the steps onto the field, a long line of odd couples married by the alphabet: Jake Anderson, ever serious, marching with a giggly Ashlee Altenbach, Jayne Garrison with Joey Heinecke, a fun-in-the-sun partier from Cancún. As the seniors began their trek around the long arc of the track, the school band, reduced by the absence of its senior members, struck up Edward Elgar's classical *Pomp and Circumstance*. Despite an injunction in the program against standing, the audience rose as a single body in a long, sustained moment of pride and relief.

Graduations are inherently without drama, except in the eyes of their participants and their families. The ritual has become predictable, and the script is unvarying in an era where neither a streaker nor a potsmoker is likely to surprise the authorities. So Angie Prindle, the president of the class, issued the standard warm welcome. The principal greeted the guests and presented Josh Albright and Jill Sullivan, the valedictorian and salutatorian.

Then, it was my turn. By that time, I'd been a fixture on the Prior Lake landscape for nine months. In September, I'd started out as an object of curiosity, the stranger with the funny accent and quirky clothes who, everyone had been told, was writing a book about Prior Lake High School. A few bridled, put off at the notion of being studied. Most, however, seemed intrigued by the prospect of becoming surrogates for their generation.

I had made myself ubiquitous, my notebook in hand. I'd roamed the hallways, along with the dozens of students who logged mile after mile each day, leaving me wondering when they attended classes. Blessed with the sympathy of intrepid teachers, I'd sat in on classes, provoked discussions in study halls and eavesdropped on faculty gripe sessions. I experienced the smell of a bus filled with sweaty football players who didn't dare shower collectively. Indulged by John Bennett, I'd sat on the bench when Prior Lake played Holy Angels, having promised to excise all "inappropriate language" he might utter from any quotes I might record. I'd attended every band and choir concert, dozens of auditions and plays, dances, Synergy meetings, community nights, soccer games and pep fests. I'd met with school board members individually, and watched them in collective action at their meetings. I'd insinuated myself into the ranks of parents cheering their children at concerts and basketball games, and repeatedly imposed on their hospitality at home.

By the new year, I'd become a fixture on their landscape, my presence taken for granted. I was invited to join Rock-painting forays in front of the school. When a group of senior girls crammed into three cars for their annual ritual of draping the houses of juniors with toilet paper, I risked arrest at their sides. On 4/20, I planted myself in front of a window, hoping to avoid the smoke of pot that was seeping into the pores of the furniture. The only moment I eschewed was the evening Tony Lorenz, Eric Prchal, Jordan Culver and Tom Maust discovered the delights of strip clubs. I sent my husband along instead.

A week earlier, I'd had my first water tour of the lake, on a lazy Sunday afternoon in a boat operated by Lyndsay Schumacher. Four days before, I'd met the seniors in the Dakotah parking lot to receive my map to their party so I, too, could drive the backroads of northern Minnesota in search of their encampment.

The senior class officers had honored me by asking that I speak at their graduation. I said:

Last summer, almost exactly one year ago, I dreamt up a new book designed to answer perhaps the most burning question in America today: What's happening with our teenagers and their educations? The standard approach to this topic would have been to interview so-called experts, pick the brains of politicians and consultants and collect reams of statistics that would have inevitably become the sort of weighty tome no one would read.

As you know by now, I'm not exactly your standard-approach kind of person, so I came up with a different angle. I decided to go right to the source—to find a school that would represent all fourteen thousand of the nation's high schools and spend a year there—hanging out with the kids, interviewing their parents, sitting in on classes and talking with teachers. I envisioned writing a story that would tell the tale more eloquently than any consultant or expert, a year in the life of The All-American High School, complete with a cast of real and, I assumed, vibrant characters, who would show readers, in their words and deeds, what high school is like at the dawn of the new millennium.

Many in publishing circles insisted I would never be able to pull off such a project. No principal in his right mind will let a reporter, especially a—dare I say—somewhat pushy reporter from New York, wander through his or her school for a year. And even if he does, I was told, the kids won't talk to you—not openly and candidly.

One month later, having convinced an intrepid editor that I could perform miracles, I drove down Fish Point Road and walked into the office of a principal who may or may not have been in his right mind—a topic of considerable speculation, especially among Craig Olson's greatest admirers—but who nonetheless believed enough in the value of my project and in the work of his staff and students, to invite me to join this community.

"But what about the kids?" I asked. "Do you think they'll talk to me?" Craig, Lori Boynton and Dan Edwards started laughing. I sat there, confused. Then Lori enlightened me. "Oh, your problem won't be getting our kids to talk," she said. "Your problem will be getting them to shut up." I never imagined how right she would turn out to be.

I prattled on for a few moments, offering the graduates Elli Burkett's Eleven-Step Program for a Good Life. Then, on with it. I was not the attraction. The student speakers deserved full attention.

For years, Reilly Liebhard had dreamed of standing before his class and scores of parents to deliver that speech. In his mind, that meant being valedictorian or salutatorian, an honor he thought he had achieved when the class rankings were announced in April and he'd been tied for second in the class. But Tom Maust, next in line, had questioned the rankings, at which point Olson realized that the guidance office had forgotten to include the winter trimester grades in their calculations. Tom did not rise to second place. But on May 30, Olson had called Reilly into his office and informed him that he had fallen to fifth.

Hardly "my kids have to be first" kind of parents, Joy and Wayne Liebhard were still livid, not just at the guidance office's bungling, but at Prior Lake's approach to number-crunching. Reilly's six As in Math from the University of Minnesota had been weighted no more heavily than the As of students who took Geometry at the high school. "That's the mediocritization of education," said Wayne, whom Reilly affectionately called "the dork."

Reilly might have shared their ire if he hadn't discovered that speaking at graduation had nothing to do with class rank. Rather, seniors were invited to apply for the honor, and Reilly dashed to the office of Jeff Hoeg, who'd been tapped to field and screen the applications—although without much confidence that he'd be chosen. Nothing fired Reilly up hotter than politics than testing the political winds with a moral barometer, and his penchant for indulging that pleasure on Prior Lake High School administrators had not catapulted him to popularity.

In his sophomore year, he'd confronted the principal about the philosophical implications of spending public money on extracurricular sports at a time when the Economics textbooks were so outdated that they still included sections on the command economy in East Germany. In his senior year, he'd demanded that Lori Boynton explain why carrying his friend Hillary around on his back had been deemed inappropriate, even though Jocks were not censured for yelling "Queers R Us" at marginally effeminate students.

"Reilly is always showing off or competing," said Boynton. "He keeps coming in the office to make a big deal out of something that's really not a big deal. I'm sick of it."

Ultimately, Boynton's distaste for Reilly had no impact on the results of the competition. In fact, there really was no competition since Reilly's proposed speech was the single entry written to lend any gravitas to the proceedings. Some of the teachers Hoeg had enlisted to help screen contestants had objected to the "cynicism" of his proposed address, but Hoeg wasn't looking for just another "Hail-Fellows-Well-Met" entry.

That evening, then, Anna Bican took a deep breath before she leaned into the microphone with succinct remarks about roads less traveled. Then the program was handed over to Reilly, who'd threatened to perform all eighteen minutes and thirty-six seconds of "Alice's Restaurant" should Hoeg overedit his draft. The teacher had kept his touch light, so Reilly was free to plead with his classmates to rethink the word "success," to reject measuring accomplishment in dollars or power.

> We are not emotionless machines in a gigantic factory, increasing profits for distant owners without so much as a sidelong glance. We are human beings, and as the French philosopher Jean-Paul Sartre put it, we are "condemned to be free." If we freely choose to go the easy route and just skim the surface, we are indeed choosing a jail sentence. But the opportunities before us are limitless—if and only if we truly experience life, refusing to conform or to "keep up appearances."
>
> Why did we just spend four years of our lives in high school? Was it all about showing that we had learned the exact atomic weight of carbon dioxide, the exact way to solve a math problem, the exact state-mandated specifics of birth control, the exact way to "be a team player"? . . . Or did we attend Prior Lake High

School to learn the importance of really examining what we are told, to view every problem from many different angles, to come up with entirely new views and ideas, to be self-motivated, to learn to work cooperatively without submerging our individuality or "leaning" on our comrades?

You decide. High school was different things for different people, and it's not too late to change roads if the one you're traveling merely has the appearance of being a road. Twenty or thirty years from now, we will know who's chosen the better path. They will be the ones making social and scientific discoveries that chip away at façades and reveal the true nature of reality. They will be the ones getting to know people as *people*, instead of as Murray over in Accounts Receivable. They will be the ones standing up for what they know is right so that they, and their human brothers and sisters, can have a better life. To quote The Dead Kennedys just once more, they won't "fit in like a cog in the faceless machine."

Reilly had poured his heart into his speech, the swan song of an outcast. No one paid much attention, even to be offended by his sarcasm. It wasn't just that French philosophers and the notion of being condemned to freedom soared over the heads of both the graduates and their parents. The ceremony had already been running for more than thirty minutes, the all-night party planned by parents for their children was due to begin at ten P.M., and no one was much interested in anything but the bestowing of diplomas.

Finally, Ron Lachelt, selected by the seniors as one of the evening's presenters, rose to a lectern placed on the field, his back straight, his mien radiating affection, and began calling out the names of the members of the Class of 2000. Matt Brown lumbered up onto the rickety podium, a wide grin on his face. His dream of playing Division I football had not been realized. But he's been recruited by Winona State University, a Division II school, giving the NFL aspirant one last chance to prove himself as a guard.

In dark shades, Nick Busse followed, serious, intent. Most graduates had spent hours planning huge postgraduation open-house parties with their parents. Uncomfortable at the thought of being the center of attention, Nick had told his family that he didn't want a party. He just wanted to be left alone. "I don't know what the future holds," he said. "But I fear I'm just going to exchange one set of problems for another."

As she waited at the bottom of the steps to the stage, Katie Cook tried not to flash back to her brother's graduation, to that awful ceremony in 1998. But she had no more luck than she'd had all year, and remained steeped in bitterness and distrust for the administration. Unwilling to consign herself to stagnant waters, however, she'd ignored John Bennett's advice about choosing to be a big fish in a small pond and had joined the soccer team at Marquette University in Wisconsin, she was the only Laker athlete slated to play in Division I.

A moment later it was Justin Jorgenson's turn. Still intent on receiving some form of recognition, no matter how negative, he'd informed his friends that he planned to pull a dazzling stunt at the ceremony. They waited, then, as his name was called. He walked to the podium and accepted his diploma graciously. That's JJ, just mouthing off again, they concluded, as Isaac Joslin and then Tia Kadelbach followed him onto the stage. They never noticed that Justin didn't sit back down. No one but his parents noticed that he took his diploma and walked off the field, a one-man parade without any spectators.

As he accepted his diploma, Tom Maust radiated pride both in his Board Scholar gold cord and his NHS gold collar. At the Senior Recognition Banquet, Mary Haugen had presented him exaltedly: "Thomas Jennings Maust, doesn't that sound . . . presidential," she'd said, suggesting a grand future for the young man. That morning, he'd brought her a gift to thank her for her support: a Waterford crystal apple.

Olson's face lit up when Kristin Murphy's name was called. He'd broken his own rules for her when she'd moved out of her father's house, the rule he'd refused to break for Scott Vig, and the gamble had paid off. Kristin had stayed clean and earned the chance to shove her diploma in her stepmother's face. "This is my first real accomplishment," she'd said on the last day of school. It was a telling statement from a young woman who'd kicked a serious drug habit. "I have to thank the school for it."

Among the long line of students waiting for their diplomas was a self-effacing girl who'd stopped me one afternoon with a question: "Are you a mandatory reporter?" I was taken aback by her legal savvy. Paula Gaffney and Mara Corey, both magnets for troubled adolescents, had complained about the law that required them to report any sign that a student was living in an abusive environment. But I hadn't understood the full impact of the impossible position the law put teachers in until the young woman explained that she'd been kicked out of her house by her father after she'd blocked him from hitting her pregnant mother. Although he'd changed his mind and tried to induce her to stay, the young woman could no longer face life in a household that reeked of alcohol and abuse. The eldest of several children, she also couldn't bring herself to inform the police or the child welfare authorities, knowing that doing so would destroy her home. She needed to talk to a grown-up. I was, quite literally, the only one available who was not legally obligated to break her confidence.

As he moved toward the podium, Ben Selinske grinned, a full ear-to-ear grin in the style of Howdy Doody. For two years, since the fracas of 1998, he'd waited to tell Mary Haugen what he thought of her, and that pent-up desire had become almost uncontainable in late February, when he'd been expelled from the student council position to which he'd been elected. That morning, at senior breakfast, Ben had appeared in a student council T-shirt, which he'd gleefully defaced. On the front, next to the printed words "Student Council," he'd written "Sucks." On the back, beneath the year's slogan, "The Sky's the Limit," he'd added the Wu Tang verse, "Niggaz be timid." Ten hours later, he still couldn't contain his delight.

Scott Vig's appearance on the stage demanded a serious sigh of relief. At the end of the second trimester, he'd talked to the tribal attorneys about suing Prior Lake High School for racial discrimination. But, in the end, it had been easier to transfer to one of the do-nothing alternative schools in the area, where his total workload for the trimester had been three meager business projects.

The final names were called—Erin Yearneau, Derek Yerxa, LeeAnne Yule. Then, in a flourish of *Sine Nomine*, it was over, not just the ceremony, which was long and monotonous, not just high school, with its familiar routine and familiar faces, but the treadmill of certainty, of twelve years of automatic pilot.

•   •   •

I stood on the podium as the ceremony dissolved into a pointillist sea created by navy-blue mortarboards thrown toward the evening sky, and a stampede of parents and friends galloped onto the field to congratulate the new graduates on their accomplishments, or their endurance, or their willingness to do just enough. I was not sure which.

I still am not.

I had moved to Prior Lake, Minnesota, ten months earlier hoping to resolve a nagging suspicion that what was passing for a "national dialogue" about public education was seriously misdirected. I had long feared that we were mixing the apples of schools deemed "successful" with the rotting oranges that left too many children behind, that our so-called dialogue was a dance of political tango played to momentary hysteria, and that little of what was being preached and written, espoused and proposed, would change the stark reality that, by almost every measure, our teenagers cannot compete with their peers in the industrialized world.

Like most Americans, I could conjure up vivid images of the dismal realities of inner-city schools, thanks to the brilliant work of writers like Jonathan Kozol and Sam Friedman. But my view—our collective view, I believed—of the suburban schools where most children are trained was either a blank slate or some patchwork portrait cobbled together from alarmist reporting, political maneuvering and wishful thinking. When the massacre at Columbine High School focused a spotlight on one of those schools—and, perforce, on the hundreds of Columbines across the country—I concluded that the time had come to move beyond ponderous studies and hand-wringing analyses and to answer a score of troubling questions about suburban high schools by enmeshing myself in the life of a single one for a full school year.

The trick, of course, was finding the ideal high school to serve as the surrogate and an intrepid principal willing to invite me to wander his halls. With the demographics of Littleton in mind, I had looked to the Midwest for my proxy, to high schools in the suburbs ringing Chicago and Cleveland, Minneapolis, Detroit and Kansas City, hoping that in those regions I might find a school readers could identify as familiarly their own, or at least think of as representative. I had only two requirements: Intent on not "stacking the deck," I wanted a *good* school, a school that produced students who, by every objective measure, academically outpaced their peers. And I was looking for a principal who would not only be willing, but enthusiastic about my project.

Chicago, Detroit and Kansas City quickly disappeared from my roster of prospects. The principals I called near those cities all responded to my queries with disbelief, in tones clearly implying "You must be seriously crazy to believe that I would even consider letting you see what goes on in my school." A scattering of administrators in other Midwestern cities proved more amenable. But in the Twin Cities, in the suburbs of Minneapolis and St. Paul, every principal I contacted seemed not only willing to talk with me, but intrigued by my proposal.

After three days driving rings around both cities, speaking with principals and visiting schools, I drove up Fish Point Road and met Craig Olson. On paper, Prior Lake High School was my ideal: It was small enough for me to wrap my mind around, but large enough to approximate the national norm. Serving a third-tier suburb, it drew students from a full range of middle-class families, from the most affluent to the newly comfortable. And its test scores were impressive. Ten minutes after meeting Olson, I discovered yet another Prior Lake virtue: its principal was smart, irreverent and cared deeply about the truth. I knew that I had found a home for my journey through the 1999–2000 school year.

Olson imposed only one condition: No preconceptions. He wasn't about to open his school to a reporter with an axe to grind. And it wasn't difficult for me to assuage his concern because, in all honesty, I had no idea whether I was about to step into a garden of teenage delights or a noncinematic version of *High School High*.

I hadn't been inside a public high school since my own graduation in 1964—which says something about how pleasant I'd found my three years at Harriton High School. One of a handful of Jewish students in a world of the original preppies, I missed every day of school my mother would permit and dreaded most of those I could not circumvent. I joined no clubs. I participated in no afterschool sports or any other extracurricular activity. I resented every hour of gym I was forced to spend on the lacrosse field, dodging sticks swinging wildly at my head, every pep fest, assembly, mandatory "school spirit" activity or other event calculated to make me love school.

Although it has taken me more than three decades to make this admission, I did receive a singular benefit from my time in a public high school: a superior education. Three years of Latin, two more of Spanish, a ferocious English teacher whose idea of a textbook was the *Saturday Review of Literature*. Unlike today's students, I never thought to question the "relevance" of *The Iliad* or Norman Cousins's exegeses on freedom and individual responsibility. Nor did I consider complaining because memorizing irregular Spanish verbs or working on Mrs. Murphy's vocabulary lists was not fun. No one had ever suggested to me that education should be fun. As a consequence, I learned a discipline of mind and a wealth of knowledge no germane divertissement could have afforded me.

An inveterate researcher, I'd read dozens of critiques and countercritiques of American high schools and filed them all away with the appropriate level of skepticism. The stacks of federal reports, think-tank analyses, teachers' union rebuttals, Republican White Papers and Democratic retorts were laced with too much vested interest, too many agendas, to persuade me. And they treated American high schools as if they were a chain of fastfood restaurants offering the same design, menu and service from coast to coast. My interest piqued by the tragedy at Columbine, I had fixed my eyes firmly on suburbia, but I found it impossible to cull the suburban high schools where most American teens spend seven hours a day out of reportage intent on universalizing the nonuniversalizeable.

Captive of the same drumbeat of rhetoric as other news junkies, I knew what I was supposed to discover: This generation of high school students has been branded the most violent, most unruly, most ill-mannered, disrespectful and undereducated generation in the nation's history. That message has been blared so loudly, so regularly, on television, in movies, in books, newspapers and magazines that I could hardly have missed it. And their schools, I'd been told—we've all been told, ad nauseam—are overcrowded, ill-repaired, dangerous places run by underpaid rubes whose classes are too big and standards too low for indolent teenagers so busy tormenting one another that they could not possibly learn anything in any event.

What I discovered at Prior Lake High School bore little resemblance to these stereotypes. The kids had embraced their elders' disparaging view of their generation as a point of pride, precisely the way that the previous generation did before them, precisely as their own children undoubtedly will. But that view had little basis in fact. And, as I had suspected, the politically popular descriptions of American schools as too dangerous, too crowded, too mean-spirited, might characterize some American high schools, especially urban ones. But they had little to do with the suburban reality.

Instead, Prior Lake was another planet orbited by dozens of moons that lit its night sky into brilliance. But those same moons had turned its atmosphere turbulent, its geology unstable, its tides unpredictable. One morning in November, during a student Geography Bee, I listened as teenagers from privileged families identified Jamaica as an island in the Pacific and the mountain range separating India from China as the Indus Mountains—then to their teachers defend that ignorance by arguing "We don't waste time on simple memorization. We'd rather spend it on 'higher orders' of thinking." But the next afternoon, I watched Katie Hallberg's Calculus students perform mathematical feats that were dazzling to even the most educated members of my generation.

One moment, I was awestruck at the sight of varsity football players breaking up fights among sophomores rather than cheering them on, as they had in my day. Five minutes later, I was horrified to read students' papers and realize that even the best hadn't mastered basic grammar, punctuation or spelling—or to hear scores of students blithely inform me, perhaps even boast to me, that they had never read a complete book.

The kids were dizzyingly busy, juggling football and band, theater and tennis, part-time jobs, church volunteer work and full loads of courses. The first day of school they were each handed mini–Franklin planners, and they needed them much more than the adults I knew. For parents and staff, the constant flurry of activity was a point of pride, the modern solution to the old "idle hands are the devil's workshops." Mary Haugen bragged, "They're incredible multitaskers, aren't they?" I, too, was dazzled, but nagged by the sense that kids need down time, that it is dangerous to leave them feeling that something is wrong with them if their day planners have too many blank pages.

They were vulgar in their language, informal in their demeanor and disrespectful to authority in a way that would have earned most members of earlier generations permanent detention. Yet they seemed like teetotalers compared to their parents, who'd smoke dope in school bathrooms, cigarettes in special smoking areas and run to bars for lunchtime scoops of beer. They had no leeway for adolescence. Old adages like "They're just kids" or "Kids will be kids" had become anachronisms, erased, along with so much other innocence, by disasters like Columbine. Everything had become dire, from a single cigarette smoked at a restaurant with friends to the classic tasteless jokes of teenagers. In the 1985 movie *The Breakfast Club*, when a kid says he has a gun in his locker, the teachers panic at the prospect of a suicide. Just fifteen years later, murder was on everyone's mind.

Prior Lake, then, was a shadow planet that threw our world, adult society—a society both more tolerant and more anti-intellectual, more protective of children and more suspicious of its teenagers than any other in our history—into bold relief. Does it make any sense to bemoan the dumbing down of schools when newspapers instruct their writers to keep their articles at a ninth-grade reading level, or when both Al Gore and George Bush organize the vocabulary and syntax of their debate remarks to make them accessible even to middle school students? Should we be impressed with the kids' open-mindedness when even adults raised in a more narrow-minded world have embraced women's equality and gay rights? Should we be appalled by their profanity and insolence when vulgarity has become part of the everyday speech of adults, and irreverence toward authority has become a staple of modern civic life?

Americans, however, have always looked to our public schools to train a next generation that can surpass us, that not only shares our values and understanding, but that builds on them, pushing them where our more calcified imaginations could never take us. At Prior Lake, though, I found a school paralyzed in its ability to educate students to transcend us, deafened by mixed messages, by a cacophony of good intentions, all blaring simultaneously. HIGHER STANDARDS, MORE ELECTIVES, BACK TO BASICS, FUND THE ARTS, POST THE TEN COMMANDMENTS, ZERO TOLERANCE, CRACK DOWN, EASE UP, TOO MUCH HOMEWORK, MUCH MORE RIGOR, I'LL SUE, BUT THE STATE SAYS, GIVE MY KID ANOTHER CHANCE.

It's not just the school that is pulled apart by conflicting exhortations.

The kids are assaulted by the same contradictions. "Act like grown-ups," administrators demand, even as they treat them like children. "America has this terrific constitution with a unique Bill of Rights," Government teachers explain to young people who lack those very rights while on school property. "Get with the school spirit," activities staff encourage, even as they warn against the dangers of caving in to social pressure. "Don't drink or do drugs," say adults, when the kids know grown-ups indulge in both vices.

What must kids think of adults who pen policies that mete out identical punishments for all drug use on school property, whether those drugs are cigarettes, beer or heroin? Or bemoan teen conformism and hierarchy when, in school at least, it is imposed more rigidly by adults than by students? How seriously can they take education when they are pulled out of English class for baseball games or because of the writing on their T-shirts, or they see that their school has ample funds to support a synchronized swimming team but not enough money to buy thirty copies of *Tuesdays with Morrie* for Sociology? What subliminal message do they receive when schools pretend that all students are equal academically, but not athletically? Are they fooled into believing in equality just because every male student is afforded the right to membership on the football team, although not the right to play? What does a gifted kid think when he's trained to have high self-esteem yet simultaneously warned not to express it too loudly lest he make other kids feel inferior?

What lessons do they learn from watching their governors and state legislatures institute mandatory testing in the name of higher standards, and then lower the passing scores when too many students fail? What must they conclude about the national concern for quality education when they hear about teachers and principals who help kids cheat on those exams?

Kids in Prior Lake have to know what the score is. They've watched all the right movies, thumbed through all the magazines, heard all the predictable adult discussions and sat in enough classrooms to have absorbed every contradiction and mixed message. They might not have learned much geography or Shakespeare, but they absorbed from their environment the essential lessons about honesty and integrity, mediocrity and the value of learning by inverting the old principle of "Do as I say, not as I do."

Against this backdrop, current political rhetoric about the challenges plaguing American education—the rhetoric that informed my vision before I moved to Prior Lake, as it informs the fears and anxieties of millions of parents—feels strikingly out of synch with suburban reality. It provides the reassurance of easy answers and the allure of politically viable "solutions" in a world comfortable with sound-bite analysis and "damn the torpedoes, full steam ahead" problem-solving. But detouring around the complex tangle of social changes that undermine our schools is unlikely to lift the malaise dragging down our national system of education.

In debates, press conferences and election crusades, our political leaders make it sound so deceptively simple: If we care enough about our children, spend enough money on their classrooms, send them more teachers, pass heftier bond referenda, provide swifter access to the Internet, our kids will miraculously emerge competitive in this millennium of dizzying change. No doubt, hiring a hundred thousand new teachers will improve the quality of education, if they are the right teachers sent into the classrooms where they are most urgently needed, few of which are in places like Prior Lake. More money will clearly foster improvement, if it is spent on a full set of *Lord of the Flies* for Mike Carr's Sociology classes and test tubes for Ron Lachelt's lab rather than on a new layer of administrators. And higher-speed Internet access will obviously facilitate the uncovering of more information, although such research is meaningless if students lack the tools to cull the kernels of truth from the mass of junk clogging the electronic byways.

But building sparkling-new school buildings will not increase test scores or promote a passion for learning so long as we fail to resolve the cacophony of mixed messages that is our students' daily diet. And bigger budgets for textbooks and equipment can change nothing if we refuse to acknowledge the intellectual ennui that overwhelms our classrooms. In fact, the problems in suburban education are less the result of what we are failing to do than what we are actually doing.

"Think of it this way," explains Ron Lachelt. "You go into the bright, shiny new supermarket, get your shopping cart and start pushing it through the aisles. But every time you move two feet, somebody puts something in your way. The minute you figure out how to maneuver around it, you come up against something else, something new, blocking your path. And you shove and push and detour around the store until you get tired. Then you stop and look at the shopping cart and wonder: Is it really worth it after all?"

Ultimately, it's a miracle that schools like Prior Lake can function at all when we, as a nation, haven't decided what we want them to be or do, but feel free to beat them up for not meeting all our contradictory expectations. Why don't schools raise standards? Well, parents won't let them because they are raising children in a world obsessed with achievement, whether earned or not. Why don't teachers demand more? Some, products of the same system, simply don't know enough to do so. And those who do are worn down by the wrath of parents and their colleagues if they so much as try. Why don't administrators and schools take charge? In a world of local funding and control of education, schools have become a popularity contest, and who wants to provoke two thousand parents who will decide whether you'll have the money for a new building?

Do we want schools to be institutions that will keep all kids off the streets until deemed old enough to behave, or centers of education that expel students immune to, or disruptive of, that core mission? Should they push students to achieve heights they never imagined, or foster egalitarianism? Is their mission to provide all of our young people with shared basic skills and knowledge, or should they teach kids only that which they, as adolescents, deem "relevant"? Are teachers drug counselors, leadership trainers, college advisors, policemen, therapists, guardians of the public health or educators? And who decides? Parents? Politicians? The courts?

If we force schools to be everything to everybody, can we protest when they don't do anything very well?

Craig Olson took an enormous risk when he allowed me into his school, and the biggest part of that risk was that my readers would thumb through these pages and say, "Oh, that's just Prior Lake." Don't even be tempted. Well, go ahead and be tempted. But don't make it that easy on yourself or your schools. By every conceivable measure, from its test scores to its college admission rate, from the quality and dedication of its staff to its graduation rate, Prior Lake High School is a superior American high school.

And if that thought horrifies, you've gotten to the easy part.

Epilogue

Ashlee Altenbach, Tina Farrell and most of Prior Lake's social elite remained in town to "study" at Normandale Community College.

Over the summer after graduation, Jake Anderson was stricken with a series of crippling migraine headaches that delayed his enrollment at Boston University until the fall of 2001.

John Bennett finished the 2000–2001 football season with a 7–4 record. He is attempting to raise $1 million in private donations to cover the new high school's football field with artificial turf and top it with a bubble.

Anna Bican moved to Las Vegas to work with the Renaissance Festival but returned to Prior Lake at Thanksgiving. She is saving money to launch her assault on Broadway by September 2001.

Bill Bond continues to work training new teachers in the district.

Lori Boynton is acting as principal during Craig Olson's leave.

A starting lineman at Winona State, Matt Brown is considering becoming a teacher.

Nick Busse is studying writing at the University of Minnesota, where he is on the staff of the student newspaper. He is at work on a novel about life in a suburban high school.

Mike Carr cracked down on his students from the first day of his second year at Prior Lake High School but found himself discouraged by his Honors students' single-minded focus on grades. He was, however, offered a position coaching basketball at a nearby high school.

Entering her senior year in high school, Marissa Clausen continues to be the best-dressed Goth on campus.

Katie Cook is a sophomore at Marquette University, where she plays on the school's Division I soccer team.

Mara Corey accepted a teaching job in the English department at St. Louis Park High School. While enjoying the new position, she has begun to question how long she can remain in the classroom. "These kids think that learning to cheat is an invaluable tool which will get them further in life than anything I can teach them," she wrote in a recent e-mail. "From Socrates on up, the elders in our society have pointed up the depravity and amorality of youth. I used to quote him to my disheartened teachers. 'We are no worse than you were, than teenagers have ever been!' I would exclaim knowingly. Was I wrong?"

Paul Gaffney's soccer team went to the state championship in the fall of 2000 but was defeated.

Jayne Garrison is living with her mother, working the night shift at Rainbow Foods and engaged to be married to her high school sweetheart, Randy.

Christy Gold is entering her senior year at Prior Lake High School and continues to be active in Friendship Church's youth ministry.

Duane "Goldy" Goldhammer is still patrolling the halls of Prior Lake.

Joe Goracke flunked the majority of his students on the performance packages required for the state's Profiles of Learning. Still active in the union, he continues to be Lori Boynton's nemesis.

Justin Jorgenson did, in the end, enroll at the University of Montana in Missoula, where he turned his Theory of Everything into a paper for an independent study project. After failing all but one class during his first semester, he returned home to Prior Lake.

Katie Hallberg's Class of 2000 AP Calculus students earned a record number of perfect scores on the more rigorous of the two AP Calculus tests.

In the spring of 2001, Tom Hassig took the choir on a trip to Italy.

Mary Haugen banned Prior Lake's most popular cheer, "Shake Your Booty," in the fall of 2000, explaining that it was offensive to many people, and was promptly derided by Reilly Liebhard for her shallow concern for the First Amendment.

Jeff Hoeg continues to teach English and to work to grow the sophomore Honors program.

In late August 2000, Katie Keough enrolled at Edgewood College in Madison, Wisconsin. She attended her first political demonstration, in support of Ralph Nader's presidential bid, one month later.

Ron Lachelt, still God, continues to rule at Prior Lake High School.

Ryan Langhorst remained mired in legal limbo after a judge threw out his confession because the police had ignored his request for an attorney and his plea that he did not understand his rights. Since the alleged "victims" in the case could not identify Ryan, the district attorney appealed that ruling. When the appellate court agreed with the lower court, the district attorney sought relief from the Minnesota Supreme Court, which refused to hear the case. Ryan's trial was scheduled for February. Having located none of the other passengers in the car, and thus lacking any witnesses to identify Ryan, the district attorney sought and was granted a continuance until April. This trial opened and a jury was impaneled, but one of the state's witnesses sustained a serious injury and another continuance was granted.

In the fall of 2000, Reilly Liebhard moved into a fraternity house at Iowa State University, where he promptly ran headlong into a dozen rules and traditions that infuriated him. By the second semester, he was more happily ensconced in a dorm, but still unsure how to chart his educational future. Engineering, he'd decided, was out. "I don't see myself as a widget designer," he said. But he remained caught between his love for the philosophical abstractions of higher mathematics and journalism.

Tony Lorenz enlisted in the United States Marine Corps and finished his basic training in November 2000 with a perfect 100 on his final examination. Why hadn't he followed his Prior Lake formula by shooting for the lowest possible passing grade? "In boot camp, they kick your butt if you don't try your hardest," he said. He is currently stationed in San Diego.

Tom Maust is a sophomore pre-med student at the University of Minnesota.

Shannon McGinnis began her coursework in Chemical Engineering at the University of Minnesota but dropped out of the program when she found it too difficult. She is currently majoring in pharmacy.

Having received his final Physical Education credit, Roger Murphy received his diploma from Craig Olson on Friday, November 3, 2000. He never took the ACT exam or applied to college. He is currently working in a factory that makes air filters.

Craig Olson is on temporary assignment overseeing the design and construction of the new high school due to open in the fall of 2002.

Nick Olson enrolled at Gustavus Adolphus College in St. Peter, Minnesota. By the third week of school, he hated the campus, the professors and the other students and missed Anna Bican desperately. He dropped out of college after his first semester. One month later, Anna broke up with him.

Andy Ottoson is entering his sophomore year at Webster University in St. Louis, Missouri, where he is studying theatrical lighting and scene design. He is also considering adding directing or writing to his plans, moving to New York City or becoming a hermit. Failing that, he is seeking an elite group of nonviolent international terrorists to seize control of Minneapolis's Guthrie Theatre so that he may finally achieve his dream of being its designer.

Eric Prchal is playing Division II basketball at Minnesota State University, Moorhead, where he used Tony's three-month internment at basic training as an opportunity to rack up some points in their competition.

Jenny Reagan returned to New York six weeks after graduation. Reminded of the energy of the city, she found Luther College too tame and Iowa too undiverse. She dropped out after her first semester.

Lyndsay Schumacher broke up with Tony Lorenz six weeks after graduation, having discovered that he had had sex with a somewhat notorious girl from an adjoining town. She is currently studying Interior Design at North Dakota State University, where she pledged Alpha Gamma Delta sorority.

Nate Schweich was elected the 2001 Sno-Ball King and is enrolled in a work-study program in Shakopee, Minnesota.

Dwyne Smith graduated in June and planned to work and go to school part-time.

When new contract provisions threatened his family retirement health insurance, Rick Sohler retired from the Guidance department at the end of the summer of 2000, but he remains on staff in a contractual position.

Les Sonnabend has no immediate plans for a referendum to raise the operating funds for his new high school.

During the fall 2000 Homecoming skit, Sara Strege was lampooned by the students for her ribald sexuality. The faculty joined in the approving laughter.

Scott Vig is still hanging out in Prior Lake, building his home on the reservation, racing his motorcycles and snowmobiles.

Mary Wenner is still nailing students for forged notes and the parents who cover for them.

Pete Williams is a U.S. Marine stationed at Camp Lejeune. His and Hillary's son Damien is 18 months old.

Acknowledgments

In the old Mother Goose rhyme, the kingdom was lost "all for the want of a nail." In the case of this volume, all would have been lost but for an extraordinary educator who believed enough in truth to allow me to hold up a mirror to Prior Lake High School and use it as a surrogate for all suburban high schools. My most heartfelt thanks, and my boundless respect and admiration, then, go to Craig Olson, without whom this book, most assuredly, would have been lost.

Members of his administrative team—Lori Boynton, Dan Edwards, Mary Haugen, Rick Sohler, John Bennett, Pat Jones, Karen Barclay, Nancy Jans, Kathleen Evanson, and, with her special wit, Mary Wenner—guided me through Prior Lake, endured both my ignorance and my teasing, and welcomed me in friendship. To them, I am extremely grateful.

Inviting a stranger into your classroom can be a risky business, yet Mara

Corey and Mike Carr both did so during their first weeks as teachers. To them and to so many other Prior Lake teachers, especially Ron Lachelt, Joe Goracke, Joe Mestnick, Jeff Hoeg, Lynn Lauer, Keith Koehlmoos and Katie Hallberg, my heartfelt thanks.

Members of the community of Prior Lake were extraordinarily generous with both their time and hospitality, and I would be remiss if I did not thank Michelle Lein, Pam Cook, Elaine Pagels, Mark Gold, Lucy Lamp, Dianne Anderson, and Wayne and Joy Liebhard. Superintendent Les Sonnabend and members of the Prior Lake–Savage school board, especially Dick Booth, Sue Bruns and Martha Hoover, were essential to my work, both in permitting it to proceed and in sharing their time and insights. I am most appreciative of their cooperation.

To the students of Prior Lake High School, above all, to the wonderful Class of 2000, what can I say? Scores of you were my finest teachers—and the classes were never boring. Lest my acknowledgments become more lengthy than my text, I cannot possibly thank all of you by name. But I need to mention, as a minimum, the friendship of Nick Busse, Reilly Liebhard, Katie Keough, Justin Jorgenson, Jake Anderson, Jenny Reagan, Christy Gold, Eric Prchal, Tony Lorenz, Lyndsay Schumacher, Tina Farrell, Ashlee Altenbach, Scott Vig, Jayne Garrison, Nick Olson, Anna Bican and Roger Murphy.

In the world of publishing, I would like to acknowledge the encouragement and support of Lisa Bankoff, as always, and Patrick Price. Liz Maguire was there at the beginning. The extraordinary team at HarperCollins— Robert Jones, Susan Weinberg, Cathy Hemming, Alison Callahan—saved me from chaos and despair, turning a promise into a book, and Roberto De Vicq turned that book into a visual work of art.

For special editorial guidance, assistance and hectoring, my thanks to Patrick Wright, Frank Bruni and Dick Blood. None of them, of course, is responsible for this volume's flaws, although Blood, my first mentor in journalism, probably can shoulder some of the blame.

Two years ago I turned to my husband and said: What do you think about boxing up our clothes, most of my office, sheets, towels and some miscellaneous kitchen supplies, closing up the house, loading the dog into the car and moving to suburban Minneapolis for nine months—oh, and, by the way, don't you want to be a substitute teacher so that I can have a second set of eyes? Not only did Dennis neither divorce me nor place an emergency call to a shrink, he actually packed those cars and journeyed with me through this amazing landscape. He is the embodiment of love and true partnership.

Finally, in the beginning, there was Ivan Bernstein—my friend, my encourager, my bottomless font of wisdom about popular culture, my partner in the crime of excess passion and my assistant in this project. By the end, there was an aching hole in my life that Ivan once occupied. I've long understood that Silence=Death. I now understand that Death=Silence. That silence both haunts and inspires.

WHINE

Mary Wenner

Nick Busse

Scott

Girtman

Haugen

Carr

Andy Ottoson

Katie Keough